Add Thou to It

Selected Works
of
Bishop Robert Clarence Lawson

Edited by
Alexander C. Stewart

Seymour Press **SP**
Capitol Heights, MD

Add Thou to It:
Selected Works of Bishop Robert Clarence Lawson

Copyright © 2019 Alexander C. Stewart

All rights reserved. No parts of this book may be reproduced in any form without written permission from Seymour Press.

Unless otherwise noted, Scripture is taken from the Holy Bible, King James Version

Printed in the United States of America

© 2019 Seymour Press
All rights reserved.
ISBN: 13: 978-1938373459
Library of Congress Control Number: 2020937258

Table of Contents

Acknowledgements i

Foreword iii

Preface v

Introduction 3

Part I: From Calvary to The Upper Room: A Glimpse at Bishop R.C. Lawson's Oneness Christology 11

1. How Sin and Why the Cross 19
2. Christ was not Crucified on Friday But on Wednesday 73
3. Seven Reasons Why we Baptize in Jesus' Name 81
4. Pentecostal Power 89
5. The New Testament Church 91

Part II: On Personal Holiness: The Impact of Wesleyan Ideas on The Church of Our Lord Jesus Christ of the Apostolic Faith 107

6. Healing through Christ: Or Divine Healing for the Body 115
7. The Design and Results of Suffering: A Sermon 123

8. Self-Glorification: A Disqualification for God's Work 139
9. Watch your Step! 157

Part III: Lawsonian Doctrine on Marriage and Women Ministers 165

10. A Woman Shall Compass a Man 177
11. What is a Biblical Marriage: or How Men and Women are Joined Together by God as One? 183
12. An Open Letter on the Burning Question on Marriage and Divorce 191

Part IV: Entreating for Justice: The Social Activism of Robert Clarence Lawson 257

13. An Open Letter to a Southern White Minister on Prejudice–The Eating Cancer of the Soul 269
14. The Anthropology of Jesus Christ Our Kinsman ... 297
15. Prejudice 355
16. The Greatest Evil in the World is Race Prejudice .. 359
17. Prayer for Freedom from Race Prejudice 374

Bibliography 377

Index 385

Acknowledgements

For this project, I extend my gratitude to the following for their assistance, Dr. Robert C. Spellman, Mrs. Sherry Sherrod DuPree, Dr. Talmadge French, and Mr. William Aaron Etheridge. I am also grateful for the help of the late Bishop Thomas Richardson, Mother Hattie Banks, Mother Mabel Anderson Thomas, Bishop William, and Mother Ethel Mae Bonner.

To Dr. Estrelda Y. Alexander and the staff at Seymour Press I say thank you for your guidance and support during this project. Also, to Darrin Rodgers and the staff of the Flower Pentecostal Heritage Center, Springfield, Missouri and the staff at the Schomburg Center for Research in Black Culture of the New York Public Library. Many thanks to my friends and colleagues of the Society For Pentecostal Studies.

Special thanks to my wife, Shirlene, for continued support for all my projects and my children, Shechianh, Akilah and Omari, and two grandchildren, Samaj and Symone.

Foreword

"ADD THOU TO IT!" This statement was among the final words uttered by the late Bishop Robert Clarence (R. C.) Lawson as he lay dying in Sydenham Hospital in New York City on Sunday evening, July 21, 1961. This charge inspired the late Apostle William L. Bonner's leadership of the Church of our Lord Jesus Christ (COOLJC) for over forty years as the head of the organization. Moreover, they have motivated the leaders of its missions and churches launched in the latter third of the 20th century, and still, inspire many entering the ministry today.

A debate has surfaced in recent years regarding the meaning of the "it" in this charge. Did this utterance mean that those who would continue Lawson's legacy should add more churches to the 155 churches existing at the time of his transition? Or, perhaps, he intended to inspire leaders, clergy and laity in the tradition to draw from the diverse and powerful activities that characterized his ministry, to determine the areas they might pursue. In this work, Alexander Stewart attempts to unpack Lawson's challenge, to better understand what his charge meant.

For more than six decades, the interpretation of Bishop Lawson's charge was limited, by many, to the building of churches and increasing membership. Recent thinking among a growing number of COOLJC scholars and thinkers, however, sees other areas of ministry through which this challenge can be met, as evidenced in the enthusiasm, of many who hold this charge dear, to develop the denomination's social justice arm.

Stewart's project in bringing these resources to the public eye should be celebrated as key to clarifying the uniqueness of

Bishop Lawson's leadership within the Oneness Pentecostal tradition. This research, however, is not limited to his preaching power within the Apostolic sphere. It also highlights his ecumenical reach and high regard for and among other faith traditions, as well as his work in the political, social, social justice, and international diplomacy spheres. Bishop Lawson was a lifetime learner who pursued opportunities to enrich his knowledge theologically, politically, and socially. The writings contained in this volume reflect the breath of his interest, as well as his courage in, wholeheartedly, pursing these concerns when much of Pentecostalism was considered as entirely otherworldly and many other of its leaders ignored them.

My hope and prayer is that this important addition to the study of the Oneness Pentecostal tradition will inspire others to pursue research in this burgeoning and exciting area of inquiry.

Alexander Stewart should be applauded for his contribution!

Apostle James I. Clark, Jr.
Presiding Apostle
Church of Our Lord Jesus Christ of the Apostolic Faith

Preface

I am maternally a third generation Pentecostal, raised in the Finished Work tradition. As a young teen, I first encountered Oneness Pentecostals through a schoolmate who was a member of Zion Pentecostal Temple a Pentecostal Assemblies of the World (PAW) congregation in the Bronx, New York in 1971. They emphasized that the baptism of the Holy Spirit with the Pentecostal experience of speaking in tongues as a necessity for every believer. And though I did not fully understand all that they espoused; I was drawn to this group because I felt that they had a pneumatological experience I did not have.

On the other side, my father, a former Baptist believer was the impetus for my interest in learning more about my Oneness experience. His questioning how I could join a church about which I knew nothing sent me to the library to find materials on the movement. My searching led me to find works on the Assemblies of God and the Church of God of Christ, but nothing on the Pentecostal Assemblies of the World and the Church of Our Lord Jesus Christ of the Apostolic Faith.

Robert Clarence Lawson, the founder and first presiding bishop of the Church of our Lord Jesus Christ, the parent body of numerous African American churches within the Oneness Pentecostal tradition, was one person who most intrigued me. During the early decades of African American Pentecostalism, Lawson's thinking shaped the development of doctrine throughout the movement, served as a foundational framework for the African American Oneness tradition, while at the same time, identifying the socio-economic disparities within American African communities.

Lawson's theological thinking is enigmatic. It evidences a strong reliance on Scripture, a progressive and nuanced liberative motif and political agenda while holding fast to a rigidly pietistic personal holiness. It was this uniqueness, that motivation my collection of Oneness Pentecostalism documents and artifacts.

In this work, Add Thou To It, we revisit the religious themes that were significant for early African American Pentecostals, as well as broader themes that were—and remain—significant for the struggle for human dignity for the entire African American community. The sixteen works in this collection (which up until now has been in relative obscurity) represent the breadth of Lawson's work while showcasing his intellectual acuity and putting to death, once and for all, the myth that early Pentecostals—especially early black Pentecostals—were semi-literate and almost entirely focused on otherworldly concerns.

Introduction

Bishop Robert Clarence Lawson, an African American Apostolic leader, social thinker, and community activist, was a man ahead of his time in many ways. Yet he held a traditional Pentecostal worldview that colored his thinking on a number of issues including pneumatology and Christian piety.

Lawson was born in 1883 in New Iberia, Louisiana—in the heart of the American South during the height of the era of Jim Crow racial politics. As a young man, he was not particularly religious and had no idea that he would enter Christian ministry or engage in the struggle for justice for his community. Instead, before his conversion in 1913, he was a nightclub and tavern singer who had migrated from the South to Canada and then back to the Midwest.

He began his religious career through the Pentecostal Assemblies of the World (PAW), joining the Apostolic Faith Assembly, a Trinitarian congregation pastored by Elder Garfield Haywood, PAW general secretary. In 1913 at Haywood's church, Lawson received the baptism of the Holy Ghost, learned the "way of Holiness," and was soon called into ministry. Two years later, he accepted the Oneness message concerning rebaptism in Jesus' name and the nature of the Godhead and began promulgating it as the apostolic faith.

In 1914, Lawson became a PAW minister and was assigned to pastor a small congregation, the Apostolic Faith Assembly in Columbus, Ohio. Under his leadership, the biracial congregation grew during a time of rigid Jim Crow and segregationist sentiment throughout much of the country. Within a short time, Lawson had expanded his ministry to Harlem, where he established the Refuge Temple Church of Christ of the Apostolic Faith, organizing two other churches in Columbus and Philadelphia and then organizing these congregations into The Churches of Christ of the Apostolic Faith. While he pastored the churches in Columbus and Harlem, he assigned Sherrod C. Johnson (who would later become presiding bishop of a schismatic denomination) to pastor the Philadelphia congregation. Between 1918 and 1919, Lawson used the Columbus congregation also as his base for evangelizing throughout the Midwest, establishing substantial congregations in San Antonio, Texas and St. Louis, Missouri.

Lawson permanently relocated to Harlem, in 1919, during what became known as Red Summer, in which numerous race riots occurred throughout the United States. Arriving in Harlem Lawson encountered the "New Negro Movement" or "Harlem Renaissance," which was being shaped by Ethiopian ideology, that connected black Americans with their African heritage and shaping the culture, religiosity, and politics for African Americans throughout the United States. But he would almost immediately insert himself into the black Pentecostal religious culture. He began by holding a home prayer group at the home of Brother Glover and preaching on streets. Soon the group grew into a congregation that quickly needed larger facilities. And, with this growth, Lawson moved his headquarters from Columbus to Harlem.

In 1931 he incorporated his Church of Our Lord Jesus Christ of the Apostolic Faith (COOLJC). During the 1920s and 1930s, Lawson used COOLJC as a base to impact the social and religious life of urban African Americans. He created businesses and jobs, including a bookstore, printing company, grocery stores, and funeral parlors in Harlem. But he would also expand his reach beyond the city limits. In Shrub Oak, New York in Putnam County, fifty miles north of Harlem in a predominantly white and affluent community, Lawson established an African American community known as Lawsonville. There, he built Emanuel Cemetery with Attorney Sumner H. Lark, who served as the first African American district attorney in New York. In Southern Pines, North Carolina, he took over a boarding school that became known as the R.C. Lawson Institute and founded an orphanage there. In 1926 he founded the Church of Christ Bible Institute as the theological training center for his denomination.

While Lawson's Oneness Pentecostal views placed him outside Trinitarian Christianity, that did not restrain him from establishing close friendships with other prominent Pentecostal pastors, including Charles H. Mason, founder of the Church of God in Christ or white Oneness leaders such as Andrew David Urshan of the United Pentecostal Church. Lawson was actively involved with the Interdenominational Preachers organization in Harlem.

Neither did it restrain his political involvement in the Civil Rights Movement and other issues. He had an ongoing dialogue with Hulan Jack, the borough president of Manhattan, Congressman, Adam Clayton Powell, Jr., and

Governor Nelson Rockefeller. Lawson also led the prayer at the Prayer Pilgrimage, which was the first civil rights march in Washington, DC, on March 17, 1957. This march was organized by A. Philip Randolph and Rev. Dr. Martin Luther King, Jr, who addressed the crowd with his speech, "Give Us The Ballot."

He served as president of the Ethiopian World Federal, visiting that country in 1950, receiving the Star of Ethiopia from Emperor Haile Selassie in 1954, and sponsoring educational scholarships for two Ethiopians, Befequadu Tadessa and Amaz Tedla and adopted Meatta.

Through his myriad efforts, Lawson became one of the most well-known African American Pentecostal leaders of his day. He began his radio broadcast in 1932, and according to the July 1949, issue of Ebony magazine was among the most widely listened to African American preachers with an audience of 7,000,000. His broadcast and hymns added to his notoriety outside his ethnic-religious community.

He used this following to influence others regarding Oneness doctrine. Including Holiness minister, Thomas Cox, whose Christian Faith Band, which he founded in 1897 was later incorporated as the Church of God (Apostolic), and Baptist pastor, Martin Rawleigh Gregory, who founded the Emanuel Baptist Tabernacle of the Apostolic Faith in 1916. He also influenced the pastor of a Trinitarian Pentecostal congregation, the Pentecostal Church of Leavenworth, Kansas, to accept the Oneness message. That congregation became the mother church for the Pentecostal Assemblies of the World in the state of Kansas, and it would be at this church Lawson would meet his future bride, Carrie Fields

His Apostolic doctrine and anti-racist theology reflected his Christocentric hermeneutic, for Lawson believed and taught that there exists a Oneness of the Godhead and the pneumatological oneness of the church through Christ. Lawson contended that God is one, God expects the Church to be one through the baptism of the Holy Spirit. For him, this spiritual baptism left no room for class or racial distinctions. This spiritual baptism erases boundaries based on ethnic identity; due to the "Fatherhood of God and the brotherhood of man." Because of this posture, Lawson condemned the Euro-Pentecostal denominations who remained silent in the Jim Crow culture in which the American Church of his time existed.

Part I - From Calvary to The Upper Room

A Glimpse at Bishop R.C. Lawson's Oneness Christology

"When we think of Jesus, we must think of Him, the Eternal Spirit, that enveloped Himself in flesh, who was God, the Father."[1]

The discussion over the nature of Godhead has been the source of intense debate within the life of the Church. With the birth of the contemporary Pentecostal Movement, this discussion has been elevated to a central conversation by the dichotomy between Trinitarian and Oneness groups. A vivid depiction of the fracture that exist between the two camps was exhibited in the debates between Bishops Lawson and Charles H. Mason, founder of the largest African American, Trinitarian Pentecostal denomination in the world, The Church of God in Christ that highlighted the issue of the Sonship and the relationship between the Father and the Son.

Early in his ministry Bishop Lawson, then a Pentecostal Assemblies of the World minister, attended the Church of God in Christ convocation in St. Louis, Missouri, and debated the issue with Mason. Mason held the Trinitarian view of the Eternal Sonship; that God exists eternally in three co-equal Persons—God the Father, God the Son and God the Holy Spirit. At the opposing end, Lawson maintained that the Sonship of Christ ended with his death on Calvary and

---

[1] Robert Clarence Lawson, "Unto What Then Were You Baptized?" *For The Defense of The Gospel*, edited by Anderson, Arthur M., (New York, New York: Church of Our Lord Jesus Christ of the Apostolic Faith, 1972), 20.

that the One God manifested Himself as Father in creation, Son in redemption, and Holy Spirit in regeneration. Bishop Sherrod Johnson, former Lawson colleague who founded the schismatic Church of the Lord Jesus Christ of the Apostolic Faith, explained it as,

> There are not three distinct persons in the Godhead as it has been taught for many hundreds of years. There is one, and that one is Jesus. He was the Father in creation for He made all things before He put on a body. He was the Son in redemption when He put on a body. He is now Holy Ghost in the church because His Spirit fills the people. The Bible says there is one God and there is none other but He. (Mk 12:32) We read in John 20:28 that Jesus is Lord and God. So we see according to scriptures that Jesus is Lord and God... There are three manifestations of this One God...[2]

The issue of the nature of the Godhead, which had been hotly debated from approximately 300-500 AD, initially began with a discussion of the relationship between the Father and the Son. The official Trinitarian position was established by the Nicene Creed in 325 and affirmed with anathemas in 381 at the Council of Constantinople by the Niceno–Constantinopolitan Creed. The extra-biblical term, "Trinity," became one of the majority church's yardsticks to

---

[2] Sherrod C. Johnson, *21 Burning Subjects* (Philadelphia: Privately Printed, n.d.), 3.

determine orthodoxy. And with the assumption that most orthodox Christian found it acceptable, for the most part, the discussion was considered settled.

After the Azusa Street Revival that ushered in the contemporary Pentecostal movement, the discussion erupted moved into the center again within Pentecostal circles. This would cause the second major schism within the movement and divide it into Trinitarian and Oneness factions. The Church of God in Christ, founded in 1896, was among the Holiness groups that became Pentecostal in 1907. The then interracial, Pentecostal Assemblies of the World, founded in 1906, accepted the Oneness message in 1915.

Lawson probably accepted the Oneness message through his former pastor, Bishop Garfield Haywood. According to Mason, Lawson stated during their debate that he, "believed in the Sonship of God, and the Fatherhood of God, and the Holy Ghost, in which God was manifested. Yet, after Jesus was put to death in the flesh, he was no longer the Son of God and the scriptures nowhere taught that Jesus was any longer Son, but the Lord, that Spirit as in II Corinthians 3:17:"[3]

> Now the Lord is that Spirit: and where the Spirit of the Lord is, there is liberty" (2 Cor. 3:17).

> Who is the Lord? He is God, "Know therefore this day, and consider it in thine heart, that the

---

[3] Mary Mason, "The Sonship of Jesus," *The History and Life Work of Bishop C.H. Mason* (Memphis: Privately Printed, 1924), 40.

Lord he is God in heaven above, and upon the earth beneath: there is none else" (Deut. 4:39).

In the New Testament, we see included in Saul's conversion experience the revelation of who the Lord is. As Saul asked, "Who art thou Lord? And the Lord said I am Jesus whom thou persecutest…" (Acts 26:15).

For Lawson, Jehovah God is Lord and Jesus Christ is Lord and there is only one Lord. Lawson further contended that the Father and Christ are one and that "Jehovah God of the Old Testament is Jesus Christ of the New Testament."

Haywood echoed this sentiment, stating that, "[t]ouching the doctrine of the Trinity, the Apostles knew of no such thing; they knew nothing about three Spirits; they had no knowledge of three separate Persons in the Godhead."

He further stated that,

> [t]hey had not been informed that the Holy Ghost, the Spirit of God, and the Spirit of Christ were the Spirits of three separate Persons. They knew of but One God, One Spirit, and One Lord. They knew that God was a Spirit (Jn 4:24); and that the Lord was that Spirit (II Cor 3:17) and that Jesus Christ was that Lord.[4]

---

[4] Garfield T. Haywood, n.d., The Victim of the Flaming Sword, Black Fire Reader: A Documentary Resource on African American Pentecostalism (Eugene: Cascade Books, 2013), 101.

For these Oneness leaders, the sole purpose of the Sonship was to provide the plan of salvation for the redemption of humankind. God, through His lovingkindness, provided salvation before Adam ever sinned. He, in His sovereignty, required and provided a blood sacrifice for sin. The blood from a lamb without blemish would be shed for the remission of sins. When the fullness of time came, God sent His Son to be the Lamb that would take away the sins of the world. This was accomplished through the incarnation that is an appearance in human form. God, who is the Word, manifested Himself in the flesh, human flesh, as the Son. This was accomplished when the Holy Spirit overshadowed the Virgin Mary. That was the beginning of the Sonship; He was begotten of the Father.

Sherrod Johnson noted,

> He was sown in the flesh. The flesh was the Son and the Eternal Spirit which was in that flesh was God. Thus the Apostle Paul said, God was manifested in the flesh.[5]

When Jesus died at Calvary, the purpose of the incarnation was fulfilled. That is, the purpose of the Son was accomplished and that was to die for the sins of the world. During the first advent, Jesus was both human and divine, the perfect man and the Almighty God.

---

[5] Sherrod C. Johnson, *Is Jesus Christ the Son of God Now?* (Philadelphia: Privately Printed, n.d.), 4.

Lawson continued the discussion by specifically noting that,

> The Son is the humanity of Jesus Christ made divine and united to the Father-Spirit, or, in other words, the divine humanity answering to the body of man...As Son, the Redeemer in time...The Lord and Saviour Jesus Christ is that God."[6]

Relying heavily on what they insist is the true biblical position on the issues, the Oneness contention agrees with the broader Christian tradition that through the incarnation, God was in Christ reconciling the world unto Himself. That is, "in Christ (through his sacrificial death as Son), God was reconciling the world to himself, not counting their trespasses against them, and entrusting the message of reconciliation to us" (2 Cor. 5:19, NRVS).

And, within this theological framework, the contention that Sonship commenced with the birth of Christ and ended with his sacrificial death is thought to nullify the Trinitarian doctrine of Eternal Sonship. The Oneness assessment is that when Jesus victoriously rose from the dead, He rose not as the Son of God, but as the Mighty God. There is no flesh and blood in Heaven. For according to Lawson's assessment Christ was born as a man with flesh and blood and raised a quickening Spirit (1 Cor. 15:45) There is only one God and

---

[6] Robert C. Lawson, "The Being and Unity of God," *The Discipline Book, The Church of Our Lord Jesus Christ*, (New York: Church of Our Lord Jesus Christ, 1993), 4-5.

Jesus Christ is that Almighty God and "the Lord is that Spirit."

This type of debate is representative of the level of theological discourse that occupied much of Lawson's thought. The issue is among several to which he sought to bring clarity within early African American Oneness doctrine to distinguish it from broader African American Pentecostalism.

How Sin and Why the Cross?

> ... But now once in the end of the world hath he appeared to put away sin by the sacrifice of himself. (Heb 9:26)

These are most profound words. To my mind, this is the perimeter of revelation of the purpose and the love of God. It is so overwhelming to me that for the last ten days I have been inspired to preach this text only.

When we think of God, we may safely consider Him in the light of the prophets as God eternal, God alone or God all by Himself. The prophet says in Isaiah 43:10-11.

> Ye are my witnesses, saith the Lord, and my servant whom I have chosen; that ye may know and believe me, and understand that I am he: before me, there was no God formed, neither shall there be after me. I, even I, am the Lord; and besides me, there is no saviour.

Moreover, we are told:

> I am the Lord, and there is none else, there is no God besides me. I girded thee, though thou hast not known me. (Isa 46:6)

Thus saith the Lord, the labor of Egypt, and merchandise of Ethiopia and of the Sabeans, men of stature shall come over unto thee, and they shall be thine: they shall come after thee; in chains they shall come over, and they shall fall down unto thee, saying, "Surely God is in thee; and there is none else, there is no God. Verily thou are a God that hidest thyself, O God of Israel, the Saviour." (Isa 46:14-15)

For thus saith the Lord that created the heavens; God himself that; formed the earth and made it; he hath established it, he created it not in vain, he formed it to be inhabited: I am the Lord, and there is none else. (Isa 40:18)

God is speaking to Israel. He is dwelling in the midst of the people and declaring that He is God and besides Him, there is none other

Tell ye, and bring them near; yea, let them take counsel together: who hath declared this from ancient time? Who hath told it from that time? Have not I the Lord? And there is no God else beside me; a just God and a Saviour; there is none beside me. Look unto me, and be ye saved, all the ends of the earth: for I am God, and there is none else. (Isa 46:21-22)

So, by the statement of these emphatic fundamental truths of God's being, we may conceive of God as dwelling in the everlastings before the world was, dwelling in the solitude of His incomprehensibility in Spirit-form, and in the blazing light of His nature, for we are told in the 6th chapter of Timothy, verses 13-16:

> I give thee charge in the sight of God, who quickeneth all things, and before Christ Jesus, who before Pontius Pilate witnessed a good confession; that thou kept this commandment without spot, unrebukable, until the appearing of our Lord Jesus Christ; which in his times he shall show who is the blessed and only Potentate, the King of kings, and Lord of lords; Who only hath immortality, dwelling in the light which no man hath seen, nor can see: to whom be honor and power everlasting. Amen.

Moreover, we are told in Hebrew 12:29; "For our God is a consuming fire." Hence we learn that the nature of God and the dwelling place of God is in light, and that in some sense is a shekinah glory, a blazing light, an effulgence. His being is incomprehensible, that is, He cannot be approached. He is by Himself God, and God alone. We may conceive of Him, therefore, back in eternity, before time was born. He made the world by the behest and action of His own being. He expressed or activated Himself in "world-making." He made space, yea. wrapped Himself in space and made room for the universes, the planets, blazing suns, smiling moons, a galaxy of worlds, solar systems unnumbered out in infinity, by the word of His power. We understand that there is no law germane in nature that can tell us how God made nature. We are told:

> Through faith, we understand that the worlds were framed by the word of God, so that things which are seen were not made of things which do appear. (Heb 11:3)

So, there is no one that can find out the secret process through which God made the world. David, possibly by revelation, said. "For he spake, and it was done; he commanded, and it stood fast." ... (Ps 33:9)

In as much as He is omnipotent, omnipresent and omniscient, that is the way God ought to work. He spake worlds into existence. There is in God, therefore, that element of incomprehensibility that we will probably never understand. But, He has revealed Himself in the measure of our consciousness and our comprehension. He has come and revealed. Himself to us in and through a plan of redemption. He made the world; He made angels, cherubims, archangels and all manner of creative intelligences in the heavens above. They were created to glorify His name, to praise Him, to honor Him, to shout His praises.

No doubt upon an occasion after their Creation, He assembled the host of Heaven and declared unto them that He was their creator. He was God the all-wise; He was God the all-merciful, the Almighty. He was life and love and all that made up His nature as far as they Were able to comprehend. They accepted it on the declarative basis that God was as He declared, But as to know Him, they did not know Him. The glory of God was so potent, so heavy and weighty that angels, with uncertain proximity of His presence, covered their faces and feet with their wings. They cried, "Holy, Holy, Holy Lord. God Almighty," as they flew away in ecstatic, hilarious, and joyous worship of their Eternal Creator. The fascination, the glory, the attraction and the thrill of His presence gave them such joy as they drew near, that they ceased not to praise Him, crying, "Holy, Holy, Lord God Almighty"—for, "In His presence is fullness of joy; at His right hand there are pleasures for evermore. (Ps 16:11)

I believe and reverently adjudge that God was not satisfied with the worship of those who had no knowledge and love, of His nature and being, but worship Him mechanically without love and affection which is based upon experience and knowledge. For his nature is love. The Scriptures declare that God is love.

> Hereby perceive we the love of God because he laid down his life for us: and we ought to lay down our life for the brethren. (I Jn 3:16)

> For God so loved the world, that he gave his only begotten Son, that whosoever believeth in him should not perish, but have everlasting life. (Jn 3:16)

If God is love, He not only desires to love and to bestow love, but desires, too, to be loved. In order for Him to be loved, it was needful and necessary that man should know him. Angels by nature worshipped Him because it was their nature and constitution to glorify His name. Yet, this was not based upon experience or upon reciprocity. It was not based upon knowledge, upon the empiricism that love through contact, admiration, and attraction of two people to each other.

There was a lack in the worship of angels that did not satisfy the heart of God. So, the Lord, in His infinite wisdom spoken of in Ephesians 1:3-12, purposed in Himself a process of revelation according to His will and to the praise of His glory:

> Blessed be the God and Father of our Lord Jesus Christ, who hath blessed us with all spiritual blessings in heavenly places in Christ: according as he hath chosen us in him before the foundation of the world, that we should be holy and without blame before Him in love: having predestinated us unto the adoption of children by Jesus Christ to himself, according to the good pleasure of his will, to the praise of the glory of his grace, wherein he hath made us accepted in the beloved: in whom we have redemption through his blood, the forgiveness of sins, according to the riches of his grace: wherein he hath abounded toward us in all wisdom and prudence; having made known unto us the mystery of his will, according to his good

pleasure which he hath purposed in himself: that in the dispensation of the fullness of times he might gather together in one all things in Christ, both which are in heaven, and which are on earth; even in him: in whom also we have obtained an inheritance, being predestinated according to the purpose of him who worketh all things after the counsel of his own will: that we should be to the praise of his glory, who first trusted in Christ. (Eph 1:3-12)

So, in my mind, I conceive of Him, therefore, planning the whole order of things to reveal Himself, to show His love, and in turn to be loved, that He might satisfy His own nature and His own being to the glory and praise of his grace. To this end, He predestinated all things.

After making all the angels and archangels God made a great creature called Lucifer, the son of the morning, the covering cherub, the guardian of the thrones of God, chorister of Heaven, perfect in wisdom and beauty from the day that he was created.

He was a powerful creature. God's masterpiece. As Lucifer roamed the expands of the worlds and creations that God had made, he was given due obeisance by all other angels of different orders. He was given respect as the most powerful, the most beautiful and the wisest physical creature that they had seen.

Because of his beauty and wisdom and the honor that was given him, Lucifer became lifted up with pride. The Bible refers to it in Timothy as "the condemnation of the Devil." (I Tim 5:6)

God was unknown to Lucifer as He was unknown to other angels and intelligences. God was dwelling in the fiery nature of His being, in the ineffable light of His nature—that light that no man could approach unto, yea, not even Lucifer:

> Which in his times he shall show, who is the blessed and only Potentate, the King of kings, and Lord of lords; who only hath immortality, dwelling in the light which no man can approach unto; whom no man hath seen. Nor can see; to whom be honor and power everlasting. Amen. (I Tim 6:15-18)

To Lucifer, the Lord was known only in a declarative sense. He declared Himself to the angels and to Lucifer that He was the Almighty. But they did not know Him as Almighty. So, the ambition of Lucifer was to be a god because of the fact that there was no creature that he met in his traveling in the universe of God that was as beautiful and powerful as he. He presumed, therefore, that although he was not the Almighty, he was at least a god.

The Bible says in Jude 6:

> And the angels which kept not their first estate, but left their own habitation, he hath reserved in everlasting chains under darkness unto the judgement of the great day.

To me, this is an intimation that there was a rebellion and that there was an insurrection in the Heavens. The angels kept not their first estate, the place that they were given in which to abide. It seems that there were principalities and powers, that there were certain angels according to Daniel 10:10-21 that had rulership over certain nations and certain principalities. There was an angel, we are told in the Book of Daniel, chapter 10, verses 10-21, that was over the nation of Persia. There was also a great arch angel, an evil spirit, over Grecia.

And so, we judge that Lucifer was given rulership over this world. He was also guardian of the thrones of principalities and rulers of the universe of God: that is, he saw to it that these angelical orders remained loyal and obedient and discharged their duties to God.

Under him were millions of angels. I believe that Lucifer, in his ambition to be a god according to Isaiah 14:12-26 and Ezekiel 28:11-20 spoke what was in his heart to the angels that he was over:

> ... I will ascend into heaven, I will exalt my throne above the stars of God: I will sit also upon the mount of the congregation, in the sides of the north: I will ascend above the heights of the clouds; I will be like the Most High. (Isa 14:13-14)

The angels were so inspired by Lucifer's brilliancy and fascinated by his wisdom that they entered with him into his ambition to be a god and participated in the insurrection. In my mind's eye, I can see Lucifer and his angels ascending up against God, transgressing that order to abide in their habitation... up, up, higher, above stars and planets into interstellar space, to set his throne and proclaim himself as god, for had he not said, "I will sit also upon the mount of the congregation?" To sit upon the "mount" of the congregation, meant to fix his throne there as one who had triumphed over the God of Eternity.

Now the hour had come—the psychological moment when the Devil had his announcer to declare his godhead when he would take his seat upon his throne. And when he did that, the Eternal One who declared "I am God and besides me, there is none other," countermanded, discounted that order and Lucifer was cast down from the high places above the stars where he had attempted to set up his throne. Jesus witnessed this when He said in Luke 10:18 "I beheld Satan as lightning fall from heaven." Jesus must have existed as God before He was on the Earth, for Satan fell from Heaven long before Jesus Christ came into the world.

I believe that God Almighty allowed or permitted this event in order that He might prove and verify the declaration that He was Almighty God. He let the most powerful creature that He had made, together with billions of angels under him enter into this rebellion to test whether or not He was Almighty and to substantiate His claim. Jesus Christ, God Almighty, who was in this ineffable light and consuming fire and glory spoke out, "I am God besides me there is none other."

God cast Satan out of the Heavens and down through fathomless space he was hurled. Disembodied from his angelic form, dispossessed of his office, he came hurdling down through tractless space with angels following him. The impact of the destructive casting out of Satan on this earth was with such terrific force that it extinguished the luminaries of Heaven and plunged the world that then was, into darkness. The very earth was plunged into chaos and torrential floods of God's power and lightning flashes of His anger unstopped the bottles of the earth's water, and the floods from beneath and above inundated the world until the earth was without form and void, and darkness moved upon the face of the deep.

This is the period of time spoken of in Genesis 1:1-2. No one knows how many billions, or trillions, of years elapsed between verses 1 and 2 in the first chapter of Genesis.

All of God's works are perfect, and I believe that the world, in the beginning, was perfect. The Bible says in Isaiah 45:19: "For thus saith the Lord that created the heavens; God himself that formed the earth and made it; he hath established it, he created it not in vain, he formed it to be inhabited: I am the Lord and there is none else." He created it not a waste. The Hebrew words "tohu va habu" mean without form and void. God did not create the earth without form and void as recorded in Genesis 1:2.

I believe the earth was inhabited by angels, and when the judgement of God fell upon the angels, they were thrown back to this world. The earth was dissolved into chaos and the vegetation was turned inside out. During that period of time. the oil deposits were formed, the coal, copper, diamond mines, etc., were formed.

God foresaw the corning of man and knowing his body and constitution he made these provisions. What wisdom God has? Looking down the line of time, He declared the end from the beginning and declared His counsel shall stand and He would do all of His good pleasure. Even in His judgement, we find God making provisions for us for heat and for food. Surely God is wisdom! Surely God is Almighty! So, we thank the Lord for His foreknowledge and forethought. Thank God for His providence, Thus, He showed to unfallen worlds and angels His power and wisdom. I am reminded of the song:

His Mercy Flows An Endless Stream
He lives and loves, our Saviour King,
With joyful lips your tribute bring;
Repeat His praise, exalt His name,
Whose grace and truth are aye the same.

Whose wisdom gave the heavens their birth,
And on the waters spread the earth;
Who taught yon glorious lights their way,
The radiant sun to rule by day.

The moon and stars to rule the night,
With radiance of a milder light;
Who smote the Egyptians stubborn pride,
When in His wrath their first born died.

Each day reveals His constant love,
With "mercies new" from Heaven above;

Thro' ages past His word has stood;
Oh, taste and see that He is good![7]

Surely, as we contemplate his foreknowledge and determined counsel, we are amazed and transported out of ourselves. And like the Apostle Paul we exclaim:

O the depth of the riches both of the wisdom and knowledge of God! How unsearchable are his judgments and his ways past finding out! For who hath known the mind of the Lord? Or who hath been' his counselor? Or who hath first given to him, and it shall be recompensed unto him again! For of Him, and through him, and to him, are all things: to whom be glory for every. Amen.

What a wonderful revelation passes before our mind's eye. We see God, as it were, following up His victory after casting Satan out of the heavens. He pursues the rebellious angels to their estate. With his Judgment, their habitat is demoralized, resolved into chaos, inundated with water, and shrouded in darkness, He lays hold upon Satan and his angels and binds them in everlasting chains of darkness. That is, he limits them to a certain area beyond which they cannot pass. Thus was fulfilled Jude 6:

---

[7] James McGranahan. "His Mercy Flows An Endless Stream" n.p., Chas. M. Alexander, Owner. 1890,

And the angels which kept not their first estate, but left their own habitation, he hath reserved in everlasting chains under darkness unto the judgement of the great day.

The unfallen angels that did not take part in this insurrection, but were spectators of this tremendous spectacle, no doubt, shuddered in fear as they saw the mighty power of God manifested and demonstrated in the overthrow of Satan. Then, they knew beyond a doubt that the Lord was God alone, omnipotent, omnipresent and omniscient. They saw the most powerful creature that they had ever. Seen utterly defeated and imprisoned. They resolved, no doubt, that the red flag of insurrection against God would never again be raised on the plains of heaven. If Lucifer came to such a fate, they knew what would happen if any other angels rebelled against God.

Thus far the angels knew God as Almighty, but they did not know Him by experience as Creator. They knew Him only as Creator of the world in a declarative sense. In the beginning, when God made the world, the angels were not created. He created the world first arid then the angels. So, they could not have known His as the One who made the world. For at that time they were non-existent. As to God's destruction of the world that then was, it did not imply that He was the creator of the world because He could and had destroyed the world. One can destroy and yet not build. A child, for instance, can set a match to a building and bum it up, but cannot build one.

After it's destruction, the world remained for some time in the chaotic form. How long before God made a move or acted, no one knows, for He counts not time by years. When people presume to tell how old the earth is, do not believe them, because the earth was created before man. The earth is from the beginning. (Gen 1:1) Mankind began about six thousand years ago. How long the world stayed in chaotic condition, no one knows. It may have been a billion years that God allowed the earth to stay under that condition in order that the coal beds be formed, and the oil deposits made for these things are the result of heat and fire in the heart of the earth, the judgment of God upon the earth and the water covering the earth. God during this period, developed the various minerals and chemicals to be used by man in his day. What catastrophic drama and display of power in a destructive way, did God show. But, also, He proved His power to create when the Spirit of God moved upon the waters. God said, "Be Light!" not "Let there be light," but "Be Light!" He did not have to ask anyone to turn light on, but light sprang out of His creative word and darkness ran over the rim of things and hid itself. Then God looked upon the vast expands or ruination. Angels looked down upon Him in His creative roll of operation and creation, no doubt, wondering what He would do next. He next spoke to the depths of a chaotic world and said: "Let the dry land appear." Out from the depth of chaos, out of muck, ruck, mire, gravel and ell manner of chaotic matters there arose mountains that lifted their adamantine heads above the waters and shook them down their rock-ribbed shoulders and kept on rising until they challenged the clouds for the highways of the sky.

They lined up side by side, in mountain ranges. Methinks, in the language of the Rock of Ages, they said. "Good Morning, God!" Then followed hemispheres, peninsulas, islands, rivers, lakes, and oceans, etc., shining like shields of mighty men in creation's light over the vast expands of this mighty world. God called forth the stars in the order of their being. They marched forth in the blue azure as fire-tinted blossoms upon fields of immeasurable space. The sun was created also the moon, and the sun came forth in a roll as a bridegroom that rejoices to run a race, the moon his consort, as it were, is seen as a bride with stars in attendance trailing her in her majestic ways across the sky. The angels that beheld this melodrama could not restrain themselves any longer, but broke forth in a mighty chorus of praise and glory unto God, the "world maker." The record states: "When the morning stars sang together and the sons of God shouted for joy. (Job 38:7) When the angels saw God in operation making a world, they shouted… who wouldn't shout, seeing a world being made. The Lord with satisfaction beheld his work. He saw that it was good and reckoned it perfect. He commanded morning and the day spring to know their places. He bound the sweet influences of Pleiades and the bands of Orion. He brought forth Mazzaroth in his season and gave being to the Zodiac's monthly signs, gave definite guidance to Arcturus and his sons. He inaugurated the statues of Heaven gave the circuits and schedules of Heaven to the planetary world. He sendeth for the lightning that they may go; they returned and said, "Behold us here we are." (Job 38:31-35) The whole order of things was created by the word of His command when He spoke things came to pass; or as the record says:

"And it was so"—no strain, just commanded and it was so, for we understand that the world was framed by the Word of God. "Through faith, we understand that the worlds were framed by the word of God, so that the things which are seen were not made by the things which do appear." (Heb 11:3 The Psalmist said, "He spake and it was so, He commanded and it stood fast." (Ps 33:9)

All these are the manifestation of the wisdom and power of God, but the supreme thing God desired was to reveal Himself as LOVE. Yea, for God is love, and so to win man that man would love Him of his own volition. He made man different from angels. He made him from the dust of the earth and breathed in his nostrils and he became a living soul. He endowed him with the power of autonomy the power to do what he wanted, independent of God.

When the Lord made angels, he did not make them autonomous. He did not give them the power of choice, the power of sovereignty, the power to do or choose what they wanted independent of God… because these are dangerous powers. However, the Lord wanted a creature that would know Him and love Him, and, therefore He saw it needful to give man the power of choice, autonomy, etc. No doubt, it came to God's mind if He gave man those powers, he would do something contrary to His will and man would not choose what God wanted him to choose and do. Then what? In the wisdom of God to have love that would respond to His love, it was necessary that these powers be given. In the mind of God, the contingency that man might make the wrong choice was foreseen by God. Hence, if man disobeyed God, disorder could come into this world. That is what sin is. Some would confine it to the Greek verb "Harmartano"—meaning to miss the mark or aim. But, it is more properly understood in noun "harmartena" which means, evil principle in action, [a] sinful act, disobedience, [an] act done in defiance of authority, hence disorder.

Whosoever committeth sin transgresseth also the law; for sin is the transgression of the law." (I Jn 3:4) Thus, sin would be born. God taking this into consideration assumed the responsibility to destroy this evil power and remove it out of His world. If man would go contrary to My will and sin, I will redeem Him by the precious blood of Christ as a lamb without blemish and without spot whom I hereby foreordain before I lay the foundation of the world, but will manifest it in the last times. All this was in the mind of God and in His purpose that in the fullness of time He would gather in Christ through whom He will adopt man in His family as children of God according to the good pleasure of His will, to the praise and the glory of His grace. (Eph 1) To this end God inaugurated after man was created and fell, the system of Levitical sacrifices; but these could never take away sin. They could only answer the good conscience towards God in the purification of the flesh, these all pointing to Christ. "Now once in the end of the world hath He appeared to put away sin by the sacrifice of himself." (Heb 9:26)

The Lord by His permissive will gave man the power of choice. He also gave Him the law of His life.

> And the Lord God commanded the man, saying, of every tree of the garden thou mayest freely eat; but of the tree of the knowledge of good and

evil, thou shalt not eat of it: for in the day that thou, eatest thereof thou shalt surely die! (Gen 2:17-18)

In the original Hebrew, the latter part of the above passage reads, "Dying thou shalt surely die," This was the test of man's obedience to the known will of God and, His punishment followed the disobedience.

"Dying, thou shalt surely die," means that Adam would lose the morel image as well as the favor of God and become mortal, exposed to sickness and eventually would succumb to death. The story goes that Eve was approached by one, a fascinator, a beautiful creature, who asked her:

> ... Yea, hath God said, Ye shall not eat of every tree of the garden? And the woman said unto the serpent, We may eat of the fruit of the trees of the garden: But of the fruit of the tree which is in the midst of the garden,' God hath said, Ye shall not eat of it, neither shall ye touch it, lest ye die. And the serpent said unto the woman, Ye shall not surely die: For God knows that in the day ye eat thereof, then your eyes shall be opened, and ye shall be as gods, knowing good and evil. And when the woman saw that the tree was good for food and that it was pleasant to the eyes, and a tree to be desired to make one wise; she took of the fruit thereof, and did eat, and gave also unto her husband with her, and he did

eat. And the eyes of them both were opened, and they knew that they were naked, and they sewed fig leaves together and made themselves aprons. (Gen 3:1-7)

Satan was a shining one, not a snake or a serpent as so many people think. It is not plausible that a snake would tempt a woman. He is loathsome, repulsive and highly dangerous. A woman would be frightened rather than tempted and fascinated by a snake. The reaction of Eve to a serpent would be the same as women of today. She would run or would seek to kill it. And as to a serpent speaking in a man's voice this is preposterous. A snake has never talked as a man. To identify the Tempter, one has but to read the statement of Jesus in John 8:44:

> Ye are of your father the devil, and the lusts of your father ye will do. He was a murderer from the beginning, and abode not in the truth, because there is no truth in him. When he speaketh a lie, he speaketh of his own: for he is a liar, and the father of it.

In Genesis 3:4-5 Satan answered Eve and said unto the woman, "Ye shall not surely die; for God doth know, that in the day ye eat thereof, then your eyes shall be opened, and ye shall be as gods, knowing good and evil." This is the first lie recorded in the Bible. Satan was its author, and he is justly called the father of lies. Thus, the identity of the Tempter is clearly seen to be Satan and not a snake, for Lucifer was the most subtle (wise) creature that God had made. More accurately translated— "But the nachas was more wise than any living being of the field which Jehovah Elohim had made and knowing evil and not ashamed to question the truth of God's word." Opposition to God's word is Satan's sphere of activity.

The word "serpent" is taken from the Hebrew word "nachas" meaning to hiss, to mutter as do enchanters. Satan visualized himself and approached Eve, questioned her to cast doubt upon the Word of God, thus bringing in unbelief. He divined, as it were, through mental telepathy the mind of Eve. The old serpent of II Corinthians 11:3 transformed as an angel of light (II Cor 11:14, Ezek 28:14:17) fascinated Eve. Various passages of Scripture tell us that Satan possessed a glorious appearance (Ezek 28:13-17, II Cor 11:14) as recorded in verse 13 of Ezekiel 28: "Thou hast been in Eden, the garden of God; every precious stone was thy covering..."

Here is no evidence of a legend, but a reality. Satan, the "nachas" or shining one is placed by the finger of prophesy in the garden, see Genesis 3:1. Eve was smitten with his beauty as an angel of light and deferred to him as one possessing superior wisdom, and she believed in his power to make good his promises. Yea, this element of fascination in Satan was the influence that he used in persuading Eve.

To further confirm the above we note in Isaiah 6:2 that the Hebrew words "seraph" (sing.) and "seraphim" (pl.) designate glorious celestial beings. It is used also of fiery serpents and the word "nachas" is similarly used to designate a serpent and a glorious being, proving in meaning synonymous. The word "zoon" is the Greek word used to mean "living creatures" or living ones" as in Hebrew 13:11 where it first occurred, and is translated "beasts," showing that it is used interchangeably to mean 'living ones,' 'creatures' or 'beasts' as in the Hebrew relative to the words 'nachas' and 'seraphim'; This 'nachas,' the shining one was none other than Satan, whom the Lord had cast out of Heaven and bound in the limitations of the chains of darkness. (Jude 6)

Being a superior being, Satan materialized himself and asked the woman a very technical question intimating psychologically that God was not stating the whole picture or truth and aspect of her state. In other words. God was keeping back from her privileges and knowledge that would bring her into complete freedom and privileges. (Gen 3:4-8):

> And the serpent said unto the woman, Ye shall not surely die; for God doth know that in the day ye eat thereof, then your eyes shall be opened, and ye shall be as gods, knowing good and evil. And when the woman saw that the tree was good for food, and that it was pleasant to the eyes, and a tree to be desired to make one wise, she took of the fruit thereof, and did eat, and gave also unto her husband with her and he did eat.

The three-fold temptation of man today comes through the lust of the flesh, pride of life and lust of the eye. Just as Eve was tempted, Jesus also was tempted. Jesus met each temptation with the written word of God. To the lust of the flesh, He answered. "... It is written, Man shall not live by bread alone, but by every word that proceedeth out of the mouth of God." (Matt 4:4) To the pride of life temptation, Jesus answered, "... It is written again, Thou shalt not tempt the Lord thy God." (Matt 4:7) To the lust of the eye temptation, (Matt 4:10): "Then saith Jesus unto him, Get thee hence Satan; for it is written, Thou shalt worship the Lord thy God, and him only shalt thou serve."

Eve and the first man, Adam, failed, but the second man, Adam, the Lord Jesus, triumphed.

Nothing lives under suspicion, and the suspicion that one's rights or privileges have been invaded or that one has been treated unfairly constitutes a pressure most demoralizing to the human mind. A woman's love for her husband dies when suspicion enters her heart. When the love of man fell under the bane of suspicion, it died. Jealousy is as cruel as the grave. The seed of suspicion was born in Eve's mind by Satan. She suspected that God had not told her all of the facts, thus depriving her of her rights and privileges. Satan directly contradicted God. Moreover, Satan deliberately changed a certainty into a contingency. God said: "...Ye shall not eat of it, neither shall ye touch it, lest ye die. And the serpent said unto the woman, Ye shall not surely die." (Gen 3:3-4)

When Eve partook of the fruit of the tree of knowledge and in accordance to God's pronouncements, "dying, thou shall surely die" she began to deteriorate physically; she began to die, that is, in accordance with the above translation. She began to age and fade. The earmarks of her deterioration or dying could be seen in her body. Adam saw her dying before she became a corpse. Rather than lose her, he took of the fruit she gave him. The eyes of both of them were opened, and they knew that they were naked and were dying. Thus, records the first suicide. When Adam saw Eve dying, he knew that he would eventually lose her. He partook of the fruit rather than be parted from her. This I hold to be deliberate suicide.

Then, the Lord, the world's first missionary came walking in the cool of the day, seeking Adam and Eve. God's broken heart can be heard in His call for Adam— "Where art thou?" Probably God had been visiting man from time to time in the evening of the day, holding communion with man. But this time He found him not in the customary trysting place. Man and wife, having sewed fig leaves together, made themselves aprons and hid themselves from the presence of the Lord God, among the trees of the garden. Finally, God located man, not that He did not know where man was all the time; but He wanted man to know where he was after he had disobeyed God," He was lost until found of God, like all mankind today."

> And the Lord God called unto Adam, and said unto him, Where art thou? And he said, I heard thy voice in the garden, and I was afraid because I was naked; and I bid myself. And he said, Who told thee that thou was naked. Hast thou eaten of the tree, whereof I commanded thee that thou shouldest not eat And the man said, The woman whom thou gavest to be with me, she gave me of the tree, and I

did eat. And, the Lord God said unto the woman, What is this that thou hast done" And the woman said, the serpent beguiled me, and I did eat. And the. Lord God said unto the serpent, Because thou hast done this, thou art cursed above all cattle, and above every beast of the field; upon thy belly shalt thou go, and dust shall thou eat all the days of thy life and I will put enmity between thee and the Woman, and between thy seed and her seed; it shall bruise thy head, and thou shalt bruise his heel. Unto the woman he said, I will greatly multiply thy sorrow and thy concept; and in Sorrow thou shalt bring forth children, and thy desire shall be to the husband, and he shall rule over thee. (Gen 8:9-16)

Adam, instead of acknowledging his sins, said, "The woman whom thou gavest to be with me she gave me of the tree, and I did eat." Thus, in a sense, Adam blames God for his downfall. The woman when questioned confessed, "... The serpent beguiled me, and I did eat." The Lord addressed the serpent, in verse 13 and 14 of Genesis 3 in figurative language. "Because thou hast done this, thou art cursed above all cattle... and upon thy belly shalt thou go, and dust shalt thou eat all the days of thy life." The idea that dust shall be the serpent's meat, and he shall crawl upon his belly denotes defeat. The serpent does not eat dust now, neither did he then. He eats insects, etc. There is also a figure of speech denoting the dele¢ of Satan. In verse 15 of the same chapter. "And I will put enmity between thee and the woman, and between thy seed and her seed; it shall bruise thy head, and thou shalt bruise his heel." The Lord Jesus was the seed of the Woman, whose heel was bruised on the Cross of Calvary. Jesus is the humanity of God; it was His heel spoken of that was bruised on the Cross. There Satan through wicked men put Jesus to death. Jesus did not bruise the natural head of Satan, neither did Satan bruise the heel of Jesus. This is all figurative. We know it was the Cross of Calvary referred to in Genesis 3:15—the death of the seed of the woman. To this agrees Galatians 3:16. It was not the literal serpent's "head spoken of. It was the humiliating defeat of Satan as picturesquely delineated in the phrase "Upon thy belly shall thou go, and dust shall thou eat." This is commonly understood in the phrase, "licking the dust" It denotes utter defeat and the making of the vanquished to prostrate himself in the dust before the victor.

Now we find that Satan, by subterfuge and beguilement has wrested from Adam the sovereignty of this world. He has become the god of this world, the prince of the powers of the air and the ruling power over death. Death was born when the word of God was transgressed by Adam—"dying ye shall surely die," was confirmed, and man has been dying ever since; Thus, Satan became the ruling power over death, also the prince of the powers of the air that covers the earth, Moreover, Satan became the spirit of disobedience that now worketh in the children of disobedience (Eph 2:2) Many have entered into a world and an order of terrible dimensions—lying and murder brought sorrow, tears, pain, and death. Through the years, man has gone from one degree of degradation to another—anger, shame, morose and anguish until the "whole creation groaneth and travaileth in pain together until now." (Rom 8:22)

Man became so corrupt upon earth that God destroyed him with a flood. He preserved Noah and his family to replenish the earth. However, man was still under the power of Satan who corrupted the earth through men, The Lord ordained the Levitical priesthood from the tribe of Levi and the nation of Israel as a depository of truth and a theater of revelation of His will and purpose The Law was given through Moses that sin might appear exceedingly sinful.

> Now we know that what things soever the law saith, it saith to them who are under the law: that every mouth may be stopped, and all the world may become guilty before God. Therefore, by the deeds of the law there shall no flesh be justified in his sight: for by the law is the knowledge of sin. But now the righteousness of God without the law is manifested, being witnessed by the law and the prophets; even the righteousness of God which is by faith of Jesus Christ unto all and upon all them that believe; for there is no difference; for all have sinned and come short of the glory of God; being justified freely by his grace through the redemption that is in Christ Jesus: whom God hath set forth to be a propitiation through faith in his· blood, to declare his righteousness for the remission of sins that are past, through the forbearance of God; to declare, I say, at this time his righteousness: that he might be just, and the

justifier of him which believeth in Jesus. (Rom 8:19-26)

Now, we find a law in Israel that if a man has lost his property through mortgage and died, that the next of kin should redeem the lost inheritance and take unto himself the widow of his kinsmen and. raise up a family unto his name. In the Book of Ruth, this is beautifully illustrated in the case of Boaz, Naomi, and Ruth. Remember how Boaz came into the right to redeem Naomi's lost inheritance. Naomi was a widow who had journeyed with her husband to the country of Moab because there was a famine in Israel. And there with her husband and two sons, who married daughters of the Moabites, they lived and prospered. But, alas, her husband died and eventually her two sons; she fell upon evil days and decided to go back to her homeland She tried to persuade her daughters-in-law to return each to their mother's house. She kissed them and bade them good-bye. They lifted up their voices and wept. One returned, but Ruth clave unto her and would not leave her. They returned to Israel, having heard that the Lord had visited His people and given them bread. Naomi had the right to redeem her lost farm, but did not have the money so it devolved on the next of kin to redeem her lost inheritance and raise up a family unto Elimelech's name. Now, it so happened that one Booz was of the family of Elimelech and a near kinsman; howbeit that there was a kinsman closer than he. Boaz was willing to do all that was required on the part of a kinsman, but he had to consult the one that was a nearer kinsman than he to see whether he would do the part of a kinsman. Hence, he resorted to the gate of the City,

> And sat him down there: and behold, the kinsman of whom Boaz spake came by; unto whom he said, Ho, such a one! Turn aside, sit down here. And he turned aside and sat down. And he took ten men of the elders of the city and said. Sit ye down here. And they sat down. And he said unto the kinsman, Naomi, that is come again out of the country of Moab, selleth a parcel of land, which was our brother Elimelech's; and I thought to advert.se thee, saying, Buy it before the inhabitants, and before the elders of my people. If thou wilt redeem it: but if thou wilt not redeem it, then tell me, that I may know; for there is none to redeem it besides thee: and I am after thee. And he said, I will redeem it. Then said Boaz, What day thou buyest the field of the hand of Naomi, thou must buy it also of Ruth the Moabites, the wife of the dead, to raise up the name of the dead upon his inheritance. And the kinsman said, I cannot redeem it for myself, lest I mar mine own inheritance: redeem thou my right to thyself: for I cannot redeem it. Now, this was the manner in former times in Israel concerning redeeming and concerning changing, for to confirm all things; a man plucked off his shoe and gave it to his neighbor: and this was a testimony of Israel. Therefore, the kinsman said unto Boaz, Buy it for thee. So, he drew off his shoe. (Ru 4:1-8)

So, Boaz took Ruth, and she was his wife ... the Lord gave her conception, and she bare a son and they called his name Obed." (Ru 4:13, 17)

Thus, Ruth became one of the ancestors of our Lord in the Tribe of Judah. The foregoing was an intimation of how our Lord would become a kinsman to the human family and redeem the lost inheritance of Adam, our forefather.

The prophets that spoke of Jesus from Moses to Malachi pictured Him as the Coming One. Isaiah 7:14 says:

Therefore, the Lord himself shall give you a sign; Behold, a virgin shall conceive, and bear a son, and shall call his name Immanuel.

Also, in Isaiah 9:6, Jesus is pictured as already come in the following words:

For unto us a child is born, unto us a son is given; and the government shall be upon his shoulder; and his name shall be called Wonderful, Counsellor, The mighty God, The everlasting Father, The Prince of Peace

Isaiah 40 speaks of the messenger going before His face as:

> The voice of him that crieth in the wilderness, Prepare ye the way of the Lord, make straight in the desert a highway for our God. Every valley shall be exalted, and every mountain and hill shall be made low and the crooked shall be made straight, and the rough places plain: and the glory of the Lord shall be revealed, and all flesh shall see it together: for the mouth of the Lord hath spoken it. (Isa 40:3-5)

This Coming One was heralded from time to time throughout prophecy, Isaiah spoke of a Messenger going before Him and also pictured Him as the Shepherd of His flock. Jacob pictured Him as Shiloh. Jeremiah spoke of Him as the Branch. Micah spoke of where He would be born; Daniel when He would be born. Other prophets spoke of what He would do and what He would suffer. The Psalmist spoke of Him and how He would be crucified and would be resurrected for the redemption of the world because man, under complete domination of Satan was unable to redeem the lost inheritance of Adam. Moreover, man's moral degradation described in Romans 3 sets forth that he had no desire to serve God or even to seek Him.

> And it is written, There is none righteous, no, not one: there is none that understandeth, there is none that seeketh after God. They are all gone out of the way, they are together become unprofitable; there is none that doeth good, no, not one. Their throat is an open sepulchre; with their tongues

they have used deceit; the poison of asps is under their lips: whose mouth is full of cursing and bitterness; their feet are swift to shed blood, destruction and misery are in their ways: and the way of peace have they not known; there is no fear of God before their eyes. Now we know that what things soever the law saith, it saith to them who are under the law: that every mouth may be stopped, and all the world become guilty before God. (Rom 8:10-19)

In the following verses of the 64th chapter of Isaiah, Isaiah indicates mankind as an apostate from God, having lost faith, and as being wholly indifferent and insensible to his own needs,

And there is none that calleth upon thy name that stirreth up himself to take hold of thee: for thou hast hid thy face from us, and hast consumed us, because of our iniquities. (Isa 64:7)

Isaiah further states:

For our transgressions are multiplied before thee, and our sins testify against us: for our transgressions are with us; and as tor our iniquities, we know them; in transgressing and lying against the Lord, and departing away from our God, speaking oppression and revolt, conceiving and uttering from the heart words of falsehood. And judgement is turned away backward, and justice standeth afar off: for truth is fallen in the street, and equity cannot enter. Yea, truth faileth; and he that departeth from evil maketh himself a prey; and the Lord saw it, and it displeased him that there was no judgement. And he saw that there was no man, and wondered that there was no intercessor: therefore, his arm brought salvation unto him; and his righteousness, it sustained him. For he put on righteousness as a breast plate, and an helmet of salvation upon his head (Isaiah 59:12-17)

God marveled at all this—that there was none to help (redeem) and wondered that there was none to uphold. Therefore, said He, "... Mine own arm brought salvation unto me." (Isaiah 63:5) This is an intimation of His Incarnation whereby He became a kinsman (redeemer). The Hebrew word for "redeemer" is "ga'al" which means to purchase, by assertion of the kinship right. (Hosea 13:15) Of this Isaiah sings in Isaiah 63:7-8;

> I will mention the lovingkindness of the Lord, and the praises of the Lord, according to all that the Lord hath bestowed on us, and the great goodness toward the house of Israel, which he hath bestowed on them according to his mercies, and according to the multitude of his lovingkindness. For he said, Surely they are my people, so he was their Saviour.

A Virgin was overshadowed by the Holy Ghost. In her body by the process of his own creative genius, a God-child was formed; and from her body was born into the human family, the Saviour who thus became One with us according to Matthew 1:18-20. All this was done that it might be fulfilled which was spoken of the Lord by the prophet, saying, Behold a virgin shall be with child, and shall bring forth a son, and they shall call his name Jesus for he shall save his people from their sins." (Matt 1:22-23)

Some say that the Lord came down through forty and two generations, but this is not true. Our Lord came into our human from the outside. It is truly said,

> And Jesus himself began to be about thirty years of age, being (as was supposed) the son of Joseph, which being the son of Heli. (Lk 3:23)

The above statement of "coming down through forty and two generations" is a supposition. Luke 3:23 states in the above-mentioned verse the real truth. Jesus cannot be accounted for on purely human grounds. He was born in and of his own generation. He is the beginning and the end. He is not the Son of David, per se. He is more. He is the root and offspring of David. He is called the Lion of the Tribe of Judah because the Virgin Mary was of the Tribe of Judah.

> Forasmuch then as the children are partakers of flesh and blood. He also himself likewise took part of the same; that through death he might destroy

him that had the power of death, that is, the devil; and deliver them who through fear of death were all their lifetime subject to bondage. For verily he took not on him the nature of angels; but he took on him the seed of Abraham. Wherefore in all things it behooved him to be made like unto his brethren, that he might be a merciful and faithful high priest in things pertaining to God, to make reconciliation for the sins of the people. (Heb 2:14-17)

In order to be made "like unto His brethren," Jesus entered the human race by being born of a woman, which in itself was "like unto his brethren." The seed of the woman was the Word. The Word became flesh and dwelt among us. The flesh of Jesus was therefore the Word of God; and the blood of Jesus was not the blood of Adam, but the blood of God. For the blood of Adam had been contaminated with sin, as had that of David and of all men. Hence, human blood could not cleanse sin, for who can bring a clean thing out of an unclean thing? Man could not cleanse himself in his own blood.

Who can bring a clean thing out of an unclean? not one." (Job 14:4)

What is man, that he should be clean? and he which is born of a woman, that he should be righteous? Behold, he putteth no trust in his saints; yea, the heavens are not clean in his sight. (Job 15:14-15)

> It took blood that was clean and pure to cleanse us. Take heed therefore unto yourselves, and all the flock, over which the Holy Ghost hath made you overseers, to feed the church of God, which he hath purchased with his own blood. (Acts 20:28)

What a wonderful story—God becoming man, God becoming one with us in the family of mankind, O, kinsman, redeemer of the lost inheritance of Adam, who sold himself to Satan for naught, but who was redeemed not by silver and gold, "but with the precious blood of Christ, the lamb without blemish and without spot; who verily was foreordained before the foundation of the world, but was manifest in these last times for you, who by him do believe in God that raised him up from the dead, and gave him glory; that your faith and hope might be in God." (I Pet 1:19-21)

> God so loved the world that he gave his only begotten son that whosoever believeth in him, should not perish but have everlasting life. (Jn 3:16)

There are two opinions of the Atonement that are erroneous:

One is the opinion of those who state that the sacrifice of the cross was necessary to make God willing to forgive man. The second is that the sacrifice was necessary in order to make man fit to be forgiven. Both of them miss the central point. The atonement has no regard to the production of love, but simply is a mode of expression, not the cause, but the effect of love not its origin, but its manifestation. To picture God as mercenary in His gifts of salvation, unwilling to forgive or bless, except for value received, in terms of suffering of His son, who is represented as inducing God to be propitious, merciful and forgiving is libelous. The Greek word for "love" is "agapao" which means to regard with favor the thing or person on principle. So it was the nature of God to love. The plan of salvation originated in the love of God and was consummated in the life and death of Jesus. The Atonement does not purchase Grace, but Grace provides the Atonement.

Love by its very nature is vicarious. We may define the Cross as God's method of putting away sin by a love that shareth, that breaks down and overcomes the partition between Jew and Gentile, between God and man. Through incarnation, God became, in a very real sense, one with us.

> Hereby perceive we the love of God, because he laid down his life for us and we ought to lay down our lives for the brethren. (I Jn 3:16)

> ...But now once in the end of the world hath he appeared to put away sin by the sacrifice of himself. (Heb 9:26)

Praise be to God for coming into the human race as a kinsman, a relative in the person of Jesus Christ, the Son of God in flesh and the Mighty God in Spirit.

To wit, that God was in Christ, reconciling the world unto himself, not imputing their trespasses unto them. (II Cor 5:19)

The humanity of Jesus Christ was the only flesh that was begotten by the Spirit of God. Adam was created out of the dust of the earth. All other men were begotten by man through procreation, but the body of Jesus Christ was begotten by the Holy Spirit, which overshadowed the Virgin Mary. That body was the body of God (the Tabernacle) not like man pitched in the wilderness in Moses' day, but that which God pitched, the same as recorded in John 1: 14, "... the word became flesh and 'Skennay' (Greek, meaning, dwelt, tabernacled, pitched his tent) among us." This was a new mode of His being, limiting Himself to the capacity of man, known as the Son of Man, limited in knowledge, subject to the Father's (Spirit's) will, doing only that which was revealed, saying that which was dictated by the Spirit. Apostle Paul expresses it in these words:

> Who, being in the form of God, thought it not robbery to be equal with God: but made himself of no reputation, and took upon him the form of a servant, and was made in the likeness of men: and being found in fashion as a man, he humbled himself, and became obedient unto death, even the death of the cross. (Phil 2:6-8)

In other words, according to Professor Lightfoot, "He emptied, stripped Himself of the insignia of Majesty." Dr. Moffett translates:

> Though He was by nature, He did not set store upon equality with God, but emptied Himself by taking the nature of a servant; born in human guise and appealing in human form, he humbly stooped in his obedience even to die and to die upon a cross.

The Lord Jesus Christ is and always was God and did not cease to be God when He clothed Himself with a human body. His virgin birth was not the origin of His person, but of His humanity. He did not cease to be God when He came down from Heaven, neither did He cease to be man when He returned to Heaven. He was always God, but He was not always man. He will continue to be both God and man throughout all eternity. He voluntarily emptied Himself, that is, He made himself dependent during His earthly career, not on His fleshly wisdom or Godhead but on the Holy Spirit (Father) for all things. He, being, God, did not, while in the flesh, always exercise His divine attributes, but voluntarily depended on the Holy Spirit (Father) for all things.

Redemption
Before the pendulum of time
Swung out to mark the span
Of years and ages yet to be

> God wrought redemption's plan.
> in the bosom of the Father
> Heaven's well-beloved Son
> Laid by His robes of majesty
> Man's ruin to atone.
> Down the vista of the ages
> Through earth's darkness, pain and dross
> Glows a light with love resplendent
> Shining forth from Calvary's Cross.
>
> - Elizabeth Edmonds [8]

To wit, that God was in Christ, reconciling the world unto himself, not imputing their trespasses unto them..." (II Cor 5:19)

Moreover, for this purpose was the Son of God manifested that He might destroy the works of the Devil. When the Levitical Priesthood and the Laws of Sacrifice were inaugurated, they were to typify the sacrifice supreme that was to be made by God in Christ Jesus. Although Levitical sacrifices were offered yearly, it was impossible for them to take away sin. Through faith in them, man felt an ephemeral justification, but the guilt would return again because of sins committed and the sacrifices had to be repeated all over again.

---

[8] Elizabeth Edmonds "Redemption" s.l , s.p., s.d.

"For the law being a shadow of good things to come, and not the very image of the things, can never with those sacrifices, which they offered year by year continually, make the comers thereunto perfect for then would they not have ceased to be offered because that the worshippers once purged should have had no more conscience of sins. But in those sacrifices, there is a remembrance again made of sins every year. For it is not possible that the blood of bulls and of goats should take away sins. Wherefore, when he cometh into the world, he saith, Sacrifice and offering thou wouldest not, but a body hast thou prepared me: in burnt offerings and sacrifices for sin thou hast had no pleasure. Then said I, 'Lo, I come (in the volume of the book it is written of me) to do thy will, O God.' Above when he said, Sacrifice and offering for sin thou wouldest not, neither hadst pleasure therein; which are offered by the law; then said he, Lot I come to do thy will, O God. He taketh away the first, that he may establish the second. By the will which we are sanctified through the offering of the body of Jesus Christ once for all. And every priest standeth dally ministering and offering oftentimes the same sacrifices, which can never take away sins." (Heb 10:1-11)

But Christ being come a high priest of good things to come, by a greater and more perfect tabernacle, not made With hands, that is to say, not of this building; neither by the blood of goats and calves but by his own blood, he entered in once into the holy place, having obtained eternal redemption for us. (Heb 9:11-12)

Nor yet that he should offer himself often, as the high priest entereth into the holy place every year with blood of others; for then must be often have suffered since the foundation of the world: but now once in the end of the world hath he appeared to put away sin by the sacrifice of himself. And as it is appointed unto men once to die, but after this the judgment: so Christ was once offered to bear the sins of many, and unto them that look for him shall he appear the second time without sin unto salvation. (Heb 9:25-28)

When no kindred of Adam (mankind) was able to redeem the lost inheritance, God became a kinsman born into the human race, through the Virgin Birth. He became Son of God and Son of Man as well as Mighty God in Spirt He became Our "ga'al" (Hebrew meaning to redeem through purchase and assertion of the kinship right). The price of the redemption of this lost inheritance was death. The hour came for the price to be paid Satan, no doubt, judged, that if Christ would die to redeem man, then Christ's spirit would be under the power of death, consequently under his power, for Satan through man's unbelief and disobedience had become the god of this world, the prince of the power of the air and of death. (Eph 2:2; Heb 2:14) Christ would be bound in the heart of the earth, e. g. in Tartarus where the spirits of men who once lived are incarcerated. One can all but hear Satan thinking on this wise. "Once Christ is imprisoned and in the coils and pangs of Death, He shall beholden by me (Acts 2:24). I can then go up into the Heavens and be God as I desired before I was defeated and cast down to the earth. There will now be no opponent able to defeat me and prevent my coronation. I will be God of Heaven and earth."

Jesus said, on one occasion, "No man can enter into a strong man's house, and spoil his goods, except be will first bind the strong man; and then he will spoil his house." (Mk 3:27) Moreover, Jesus said, "I lay down my life, that I might take it again. No man taketh it from me, but I lay it down myself. I have power to lay it down, and I have power to take it again..." (Jn 10:17-18) In the consciousness of this omnipotence, our Lord Jesus Christ went to the Cross. He had come into our world of life through the channel of human birth. Now, through the channel of death, He is invading the world of the dead, where the spirits of men who have died are incarcerated.

> For Christ also hath once suffered for sins, the just for the unjust, that he might bring us to God, being up to death in the flesh, but quickened by the Spirit: by which also he went and preached unto the spirits in prison; which sometime were disobedient when once the long-suffering of God waited in the days of Noah while the ark was a preparing, wherein few that is, eight souls were saved by water. (I Pet 3:18-20)

All this, of course, was unknown to Satan, but unto God this was known before the foundation of the world, for "He declares the end from the beginning, and from ancient times the things that are not yet done, saying. My counsel shall stand and I will do all my pleasure." (Isa 46:19)

God writes History before it happens. He has already seen future events because He is the omnipotent, omnipresent God, dwelling in the everlasting now. An of God's prophetic statements were present observations to Him, even though· they were future to us. But, Satan did not know what was the purpose of God in Grace to abolish death and bring life and immortality to light through the gospel. To this end; the Son of God was manifest that He might destroy the works of the Devil. (I Jn 3:8)

Satan, no doubt, was exultantly jubilant that his hour of triumph had come. Probably, he gave Death a vacation for a day, and gave orders to the underworld to anticipate the hour of his triumph by declaring holiday throughout its dark domains.

Hell was decorated in all of its dismal glory and Death was commanded to dress in the garments of State and to take his seat upon the throne of doom to await the bringing in of this most august and regal prisoner by Satan himself. To this end, Satan had given Death a day off, saying, as it were, "I will bring in this prisoner myself." Death had never had a vacation until then and the only other time will be in Revelation the 9th chapter, when he shall have five-months' vacation. The locusts shall take over as a judgement from God and torment men for five months. The torment will be like the torment of a man bitten by a scorpion.

So, one can picture Satan standing ready at the cross to take into captivity the spirit of Jesus and carry it down into the region of the dead to the prison house of the spirits of men In the meanwhile, I fancy Death arrayed in gorgeous apparel, taking his seat upon the throne in the Room of Damnation and Doom, waiting for the prisoner to be brought in by Satan. But. Christ, foreseeing this, commended His spirit to God, His Father, and as it is above stated, He was put to death in the flesh, but quickened by the Spirit. He had power to lay down His life; which he did, and immediately picked it up again. In the hour of death, He grappled with the strong man. Satan, and quick and terrific was the struggle, but it was decisive and now the next task was to spoil His goods. Instead of being carried a captive by Satan, Christ took the keys of the underworld, having bound Satan; and carried Him down a prisoner.

The Crucifixion scene is the most dramatic and poignant event of all times and places. When it occurred, the sun veiled itself in sackcloth, the stars left their sapphired thrones and buried themselves in oblivion. The moon convulsed and, as it were, had a hemorrhage and ran down in blood. The heavens and earth quaked in sympathetic agitation. All creation and the celestial world looked on in bewilderment, not understanding why God the Son was lifted upon a Cross, hands, feet and side, pierced with nail and spike. When He was lifted towards the sun, nature, as it were, was affrighted with pains of alarm and gave birth to a premature resurrection.

> And the earth did quake, and the rocks rent, and the graves were opened; and many bodies of the saints which slept arose, and came out of the grave after his resurrection, and went into the holy city, and appeared unto many. (Matt 27:51-58)

Operation Calvary took from nine until three o'clock. It was the paying of our redemption's price. Towards its end, a despairing cry of appeal was uttered by one of the thieves upon a cross to Christ with these words, "Lord, remember me when thou comest into thy kingdom." Jesus answered and said, "... Verily I say unto thee, Today shalt thou be with me in paradise." (Lk 23:42-43)

During the further process of Operation Calvary, our Lord was taunted.

> And they that passed by railed on him, wagging their heads, and saying, Ah, thou that destroyest the temple, and buildest it in three days, save thyself and come down from the cross. Likewise, also the chief priests mocking said among themselves with the scribes, He saved. others; himself he cannot sate. Let Christ the King of Israel descend now from the cross that we may see and believe. And they that were crucified with him reviled him. (Mk 16:29-82)

If He had saved Himself, He would have lost us, but He came to seek and to save those that were lost. Jesus could have took His hands from the nails and reached into invisibility grabbed a thunderbolt of power and hurled the mockers, tormentors and the world into oblivion, but love held His hands there. Because He loved, He was willing to drink the last dregs of the cup and pay the last infinitesimal cost of your redemption and mine. In this process of dying, the just for the unjust, we perceive the love of God in its superlative degree.

> For scarcely for a righteous man will one die; yet peradventure for a good man some would even dare to die. But God commendeth his love toward us, in that, while we were yet sinners, Christ died for us. (Rom 5:7-8)

Yea, John explains it in the Golden Text of the Bible:

> For God so loved the world, that he gave his only begotten Son, that whosoever believeth in him should not perish, but have everlasting life. (Jn 3:16)

As the end approached, "... Jesus knowing that all things were now accomplished, that the Scripture might be fulfilled, saith, I thirst. Now there was set a vessel full of vinegar, and they filled a sponge with vinegar, and put it upon hyssop, and put it to his mouth." (Jn 19:28. 29; see also 19:20-21) When Jesus, therefore, had received the vinegar and the final tidal wave and billows of death struck his bosom and overflowed him, as they broke, He lifted His face, swollen from tears, beatings. and suffering. He cried, "It is finished!" He then bowed His head and gave up the ghost.

Here God revealed not only His wisdom in the full sense, but His great love wherewith He loved us, (Eph, 2:4) through which he absorbs our sins by the sacrifice of Himself. (Hebrew 9:26) His wisdom in devising such a plan and through it putting away this disorder, God, our kinsman and redeemer ransomed us (Hebrew for "ransom" is "padah," meaning to redeem by power in virtue of a legal right). The legal right meant as a kinsman God did not take advantage of the mortgagor, Satan, but through the Incarnation became one with us, having the right, thereby, to redeem the lost inheritance of mankind. Moreover, His love is shown in that He humbled Himself and paid the price—death—demanded by Satan.

> Forasmuch then as the children are partakers of flesh and blood, he also himself likewise took part of the same; that through death he might destroy him that had the power of death, that is, the devil; and deliver them who through fear of death were all their lifetime subject to bondage. For verily betook not on him the nature of angels; but he took on him the seed of Abraham. (Heb 2:14-16)

Through this price and the payment therefore, the above text shows· that the works of Satan were destroyed.

He that committeth sin is of the devil, for the devil sinneth from the beginning. For this purpose, the Son of God was manifested, that he might destroy the works of the devil! (I Jn 3:8)

This is the final thing that Jesus cried on the cross was finished. The love of God is spelled out in terms of the wounds in His hands, head, feet, and side.

I am reminded of the touching experience of Harold and Mildred in Houston, Texas, some years ago. They were engaged to be married. She was the daughter of a rich planter and lived on a farm some distance from the city. On a certain day, she drove into the city in a surrey with a very spirited. horse, harnessed to it. Her object was to finish purchasing her trousseau. While driving through the city, Mildred carelessly let one of the reins of the horse drop while looking in the windows of the shops. The horse being semi-wild and very spirited and excited by the city traffic, was alarmed by the fall of the rein upon his back. Sensing the occupant's lack of control of the surrey began to run away, increasing his speed until he was all but impossible to stop though many tried to grasp the reins.

Harold, her fiancé, worked in a bank on the same street. Coming out of the bank, he saw the runaway and recognized his fiancée, Mildred. He ran into the street to intercept the horse. He succeeded, but at the cost of his life, for in stopping the horse, he fell beneath its body as it, too, fell and overturned the surrey. Mildred was thrown out but only suffered a few abrasions. Harold's body was crushed under the weight of the horse. When the wreck of the runaway was straightened, Harold's body was moved to the curb. Mildred, during all this, recognized Harold, and saw what had happened to him.

She pushed her way through the crowd and had gathered and put his head in her lap and began to call his name, saying. "Harold, Harold, speak to me." First-aid restoratives had failed to bring him back to consciousness, but the call of love through the voice of Mildred penetrated his deep unconsciousness and he answered it by opening his eyes and lifting his face. His lips moved and she heard him say as she bowed closely over him. "I loved you, Mildred, didn't I? I loved you, Mildred, didn't I?" Then he died.

Harold gave his life for the one that he loved and who loved him, but God, when we were enemies, died for us in order to reconcile us unto Himself; and through His suffering and wounds, Be says to us and to every man, "I loved you, didn't I?"

Such is the message of the Cross. The poet looks upon Him and says:

When I survey the wondrous cross
 On which the Prince of glory died,
My richest gain I count but loss,
 And poor contempt on all my prude.

Forbid it, Lord, that I should boast,
Save in the death of Christ, my God;

All the vain things that charm me most,
I sacrifice them to His blood.

See, from· His head, His hands, His feet,
Sorrow and love flow mingled down:
Did e'er such love and sorrow meet,
Or thorns compose so rich a crown?

Were the whole realm of nature mine,
That were a present far too small;
Love so amazing, so divine,
Demands my soul, my life, my all.[9]

"But God forbid that I should glory, save in the cross of our Lord Jesus Christ, by whom the world is crucified unto me, and I unto the world." (Gal 6:15)

This is the boast of the Apostle Paul. It was not in the Tribe of Benjamin or in that he was of the stock of Israel, a Hebrew of Hebrews, but in the love of God for him as shown upon the Cross of Calvary through which God intends to win and conquer the world.

Alas! And did my Saviour bleed,
And did my Sovereign die,
Would he devote that sacred head?
For such a worm as I?

---

[9] Isaac Watts, "When I Survey the Wondrous Cross", Isaac Watts, in Hymns and Spiritual Songs, 1707.

Was it for crimes that I have done,
He groaned upon the tree?
Amazing pity! Grace unknown
And love beyond degree.

Well might the sun in darkness hide,
And shut his glories in,
When Christ, the mighty Maker, died,
For man, the creature's sin.

Thus might I hide my blushing face
 Where his dear cross appears,
Dissolve my heart in thankfulness,
And melt mine eyes to tears.

But drops of grief can n'er repay
The debt of love I owe:
Here; Lord, I give myself away,
'Tis all that I can do. [10]

The implications of the Cross, to us, is as the Apostle Paul succinctly puts it in 2 Corinthians 5: 14-20:

---

[10] Isaac Watts, "Alas! And did my Saviour Bleed," in Hymns and Spiritual Songs 1707–09, Book II, number 9;.

"For the love of Christ constraineth us; because we thus judge, that if one died for all, then were all dead: and that he died for all, that they which live should not henceforth live unto themselves, but unto him which died for them, and rose again~ Wherefore, henceforth know we no man after the flesh, yet now henceforth know we him no more. Therefore, if any man be in Christ, he is a new creature: old things are passed away; behold, all things are become new. And all things are of God, who hath reconciled us to himself by Jesus Christ, and hath given to us the ministry of reconciliation; to wit, that God was in Christ, reconciling the world unto himself, not imputing their trespasses unto them and hath committed unto us the word of reconciliation. Now then we are ambassadors for Christ, as though God did beseech you by us: we pray you in Christ's stead, be ye reconciled to God!

"Beloved, if God so loved us, we ought also to love one another. No man hath seen God at any time. If we love one another, God dwelleth in us, and his love is perfected in us. Hereby know we that we dwell in him, and he in us, because he hath given us of his Spirit. Herein is our love made perfect, that we may have boldness in the day of judgement: because as he is, so are we in this world. There is no fear in love; hut perfect love casteth out fear! Because fear hath torment. He that feareth is not made perfect in love. We love him because he first loved us." (I Jn 4:11-18; 17-19)

Hence, we give our lives our bodies to His Spirit to live through us, to preach through us, to save through us and to continue the work of redemption based upon the love of God on Calvary.

"O Love that wilt not let me go,
I rest my weary soul in Thee;
I give Thee back the life l owe,
That in thine ocean depths its flow
May richer, fuller be. [11]

---

[11] George Matheson, O Love that Wilt not Let me Go", Life and Work, s.l., Church of Scotland, January 1882.

Christ was not Crucified on Friday But on Wednesday

It is generally believed that Wednesday of Holy Week was a day of retirement and silence. No event or saying can be definitely assigned to this day. The two symbolic pageants of Palm Sunday and the cleansing of the Temple were over. The day of criticism and controversy had ended. The record of Jesus' life and teaching, his protests and his proposals, were all in. He had done all that He could with the outer world. He now retired to the inner world of silence, meditation, and spiritual renewal. Recognizing that the outer world, the controlling, dominant, organized forces of His day, had rejected Him, he now turned to the ordering of his own inner life and that of his disciples to withstand the inevitable storm about to break upon them.[12]

What is generally believed to be a day of silence and meditation, as stated by the above quoted paragraph: taken from a monthly publication of the devotion called, "Today," by Walter R Clyde, PhD, was indeed and truth the actual day of crucifixion. The need for careful and scrupulous study of the Bible is seen in the general ignorance manifested concerning Wednesday of the Holy week: which is termed a day of retirement, of which the

---

[12] Walter R Clyde "Today," s.l., s.n., s.d.

Scriptures are silent and have nothing to say about Christ during the most momentous week of His life in the flesh. When the truth of the matter is, the scripture is most voluble to the minutest detail about every hour of that day.

This is a remarkable fact rediscovered that Christ was not crucified on Friday but on Wednesday. The following information had been culled and Sent forth as a matter of enlightenment also as a plea for scriptural exactitude as to date and time relative to our Lord's crucifixion and resurrection according to the Scripture. From time immemorial, we have been observing Friday as the day of the Lord's crucifixion and preaching all the time that Jesus Christ was crucified and buried and rose again on the 3rd day, not realizing that by saying so, we were inconsistent with ourselves and with the scriptures. Christ could not have possibly risen on the 3rd day, if he was crucified ·on Friday and resurrected on Sunday. The following quotation is offered as proof that our Lord was not crucified on Friday but rather on Wednesday, thus fulfilling the words of our Lord Jesus Christ that, "as Jonah was three days and three nights in the belly of the fish, so shall the Son of Man be three days and three nights in the heart of the earth."

We are furnished by Scripture with certain facts and fixed points which, taken together, enable us (1) to determine the events which filled up the days of "the last week" of our Lord's life on earth, (2) to fix the day of His crucifixion and (3) to ascertain the duration of the time. He remained in the tomb.

The difficulties connected with these three have arisen (1) from not having noted these fixed points; (2) from the fact of Gentiles not having been conversant with the law concerning the three great feasts of the Lord; and (3) from not having reckoned the days as commencing (some six hours before our own) and running from sunset to sunset, instead of from midnight to midnight.

To remove these difficulties, we must note:

1. That the first day of each of the three feasts, Passover, Pentecost and. Tabernacle, was "a holy convocation" a "sabbath" on which no servile work was to be done. (See Lev 23:7, 24,35; Ex 12, 16)

   That sabbath" and the "high day" of John 19:31, was the "holy convocation" the first day of the fast was quite overshadowed by ordinary weekly sabbath. It was called by the Jews Yom tov (Good day), and this is the greeting on that day throughout Jewry down to the present time. This great sabbath, having been mistaken from the earliest times for the weekly sabbath, has led to all the confusion.

2. This has naturally caused the further difficulty as to the Lord's statement that "even as Jonah was in the belly of the fish three days and three nights, so shall the Son of man be in the heart of the earth three days and three nights. (Matt 12:40). Now, while it is quite correct to speak according to Hebrew idiom of "three days" or "three years," while they are only parts of three days or three years, yet that idiom does not apply in a case like

this, where "three nights are mentioned" in addition to "three days." It will be noted that the Lord not only definitely states this, but repeats the full phraseology, so that we may not mistake it.

3. We have therefore the following facts furnished for our sure guidance:

   1. The "high day" of John 19:31 was the first day of the feast.

   2. The "first day of the feast" was on the 15th day of Nisan.

   3. The 15th of Nisan, commenced at sunset on what we should call the 14th.

   4. Six days before the Passover (Jn 12:1) takes us back to the 9th day of Nisan.

   5. After two days is the Passover (Matt 26:2 Mk 14:1) takes us back to the 13th day of Nisan.

   6. The first day of the week, the "day of the resurrection" (Matt 28:1, etc.) was from Saturday sunset to our Sunday sunset. This fixes the day of the week, just as the above fixes the day of the month for:

7. Reckoning back from this, "three days and three nights" (Matt 12.40), we arrive at the day of the burial, which must have been before sunset, on the 14th of Nisan, i.e. before our Wednesday sunset.

8. This makes the sixth day before the Passover (the 9th day of Nisan) to be our Thursday sunset to Friday sunset.

Therefore Wednesday, Nisan 14th (commencing on the Tuesday at sunset) was "the preparation day", on which the Crucifixion took place; for all four Gospels definitely say that this was the day on which the Lord was buried (before our Wednesday sunset), "because it was the preparation (day)" the bodies should not remain upon the cross on the sabbath day, "for that sabbath day was a high day," and, therefore, not the ordinary seventh day, or weekly sabbath See John. 19:31.

4. It follows, therefore, that the Lord being crucified on "the preparation day" could not have eaten of the Passover lamb, which was not slain until the evening of the 14th of Nisan (i.e. afternoon). On that day, the daily sacrifice was killed at the 5th hour (1 p.m.) The killing of the Passover lambs began directly afterwards. Thus, it is clear, that if the killing of the Passover lambs did not commence until about four hours after our Lord had been hanging upon the Cross, and would not have been concluded at the ninth hour (3 p.m.) when "He gave up the ghost" no "Passover lamb" could have been eaten at the "last supper" on the previous evening.

5. With these facts before us, we are now in a position to fill in the several days of the Lord's last week with the events recorded in the Gospel. By noting that the Lord returned to Bethany (or to the Mount of Olives) each night of that week, we are able to determine both the several days and the events that took place in them.

The fact that "three days" is used by Hebrew idiom for any part of three days and three nights is not disputed; because that was the common way of reckoning, just as it was when used of years. Three or any number of years, as may be seen in the reckoning of the reigns of any of the Kings of Israel and Judah.

But, when the number of "nights" is stated as well as the number of "days," then the expression ceases to be an idiom and becomes a literal statement of fact. Moreover, as the Hebrew day began at sunset the day was reckoned from one sunset to another, the "twelve hours in the day" (Jn 11:9) being reckoned from sunrise and the twelve hours of the night from sunset. An evening morning was thus used for a whole day of twenty-four hours, as in the first chapter of Genesis. Hence the expression "a night and a day" in II Corinthians 11:25 denotes a complete day.

When Esther says (Esth 4:16) "fast ye for me, and neither eat or drink three days," she defines her meaning as being three complete. days, because she adds (being Jewish) "night or day." And when it was written that the fast ended on, "the third day" (5:1), "the third day must have succeeded and included the third night.

In like manner, the sacred record states that the young man (in Sam 30:12) "had eaten no bread, nor drunk any water, three days and three nights." Hence, when the young man explains the reason, he says, "because three days ago I fell sick." He means, therefore. three complete days and nights, because, being an Egyptian (vv. 11,13) he naturally reckoned his day as [the] beginning of his sickness, and includes the whole period, given the reason for his having gone without food during the whole period stated.

Hence; when it says that "Jonah was in the belly of the fish three days and three nights" (Jn 1:17) it means exactly what it says, and that this can be the only meaning of the expression in Matthew 12:40; 16:4. Luke 11:30, is shown in Ap, 156.

In the expression, the heart of the earth:" (Matt 12:40), the meaning is the same as "the heart of the· sea" "heart" being put by the Metonymy [of the subject] (Ap.6), for "the midsts" (Matt 12:40; 16:4; Lk 11:30), is shown in Ap, 156 and is frequently so translated. (See Ps 46:2, Jer 51:1, and Ezek 27:24-28) It is used of ships when sailing "in the heart of the seas," (i.e., in, or on the sea); also, of the people dwelling in the heart of the "sea," (i.e., on islands (Ezek 28:2). Jonah uses the Hebrew [term], beten (womb) in the same way. (Jn 2:2)

May the foregoing enlighten our eyes and show us the need for a more careful scrutiny of the; Word of God and a wholehearted consecration to God and to the Bible. May we take this as our slogan, "Back to the Bible, Back to Pentecost, Back to God," Churchanity and tradition to the contrary notwithstanding, "Let God be true: and let every man be a liar.

Seven Reasons
Why We Baptize In Jesus' Name

There has been much controversy about baptizing in Jesus' name. People talk and dispute for and against baptizing in the name. Being honest, they say and do many things contrary to that name, not having had an explanation given them why we baptize in the name of Jesus Christ only, and not in the formula Father, Son and Holy Ghost, as is commonly done by other ministers of the Gospel throughout Christendom. We purpose by this article to show, by seven reasons, why we baptize in the name of Jesus only.

First, because it is apostolic in origin and practice. (Acts 2:38; 4:12; 14-18; 19:1-6) It is agreed by Bible students that the apostles are the founders and the foundation of the Church; Jesus Christ being the chief corner stone. That is to say, their teachings and doctrines are the fundamental principles upon which the church is built. Jesus in the days of His flesh taught His disciples the plan of salvation, opening their understanding and making them to know the mysteries of the Kingdom. He said, "Thus it behooved Christ to suffer and to rise from the dead the third day, and that repentance and remission of sins should be preached in HIS NAME."

Thus, the apostles obeyed the command of Jesus in Luke 21:46-47, where He said that repentance and remission at sins should be preached in His name, among all nations, beginning at Jerusalem. Thus, the apostles, in obedience to the command of Jesus, became the originators of baptizing in the name of Jesus Christ. Baptizing in the name of Jesus Christ is apostolic, not in origin only, but in practice, for no other mode of baptism is to be found in the New Testament. Upwards of one hundred years after Pentecost, believers were baptized only in the name of Jesus Christ, for the remission of sins. All other modes and methods of baptism have arisen since and not in the days of the apostles.

Second reason—Because we are exhorted to believe, to obey and follow the teachings of the apostles. (Heb 2:1-5; Acts 2:38-43; Col 2:3-9) Jesus told the Apostles that he that rejecteth thee, rejecteth me. Moreover, he prayed that we should believe in Him through their [the Apostles] words, John 17:20. Paul said in the Second chapter of Hebrews, verses 1,5, that we should give the more earnest heed to the things which we have heard lest at any time we should let them slip. The gospel that was preached by the apostles was according to the will of God, for God confirmed it with signs and wonders as if to say to us, Amen, follow as they have taught.

The saints on the day of Pentecost set us an example that we should follow in their steps. In Acts, 2:38-43, we read that they that gladly received his word, were baptized and they continued in the apostles' doctrine and fellowship; great fear came upon all the people and many wonders were done by the apostles. Jesus said unto Peter: "Upon this rock, I will build My church and the very gates of hell shall not prevail against it."

Third reason—WE DO NOT BELIEVE THAT THE THREE COMMISSIONS CONTRADICT EACH

OTHER, (Matt 28:19; Lk 24:45-48; Mk 16:15-19) We hold that there is no discrepancy in God's word, therefore we believe that the three commissions all mean the same thing, and all meet their fulfillment in Acts 2:38, where Peter said, "Repent and be baptized in the name of Jesus Christ for the remission of sins." All three commissions are given by the same person and all three mean the same thing. Matthew 28:19 says, "Go ye therefore and teach all nations, baptizing them in the name of the Father and of the Son and of the Holy Ghost." Notice, He said not baptize them in the Father and Son and Holy Ghost, but in the name of the Father and of the Son and of the Holy Ghost. What is the name? And again, He said not names as if more than one (plural), but NAME (singular). We believe that the NAME of the Father and of the Son and of the. Holy Ghost in Matthew 28:19 and the MY NAME in Mark 16:15-18, and HIS NAME in Luke 24:47 all mean the same name—JESUS CHRIST. For neither is there salvation in any other, for there is no other name under heaven given among men whereby we must be saved. (Acts 4:12)

Fourth reason—BECAUSE TO PUT on CHRIST we MUST be BAPTIZED IN HIS DEATH AND BURIAL, (Rom 6:3-6; Jn 3:5; Acts 2:38) We are all children of God by faith in Christ Jesus, for as many of you as have been baptized into Christ have put on Christ. (Gal 3:26-27) If the above Scripture is true, then the only way we can put on Christ is to be baptized into Him. Now the above has reference to the baptism of the Spirit which puts you into the spiritual Body of Christ, but pray, how shall we receive the baptism of the Spirit? Peter beautifully answered that question on the day of Pentecost (Acts 2:38), Repent and be baptized every one of you in the name of JESUS for the remission of sins and ye shall receive the gift of the Holy Ghost. We identified ourselves with Christ in His death (Conversion), burial (Baptism of water), resurrection (Baptism of the Holy Ghost), Hallelujah! Know ye not that so many of us as were baptized into Jesus Christ were baptized into His death? Therefore, we are buried by Baptism into death. For if we have been planted together in the likeness of His death we shall also be in the likeness of His resurrection. (Rom 6:3, 6) The mode of sprinkling people for baptism was never the practice of the apostles and has no foundation in Holy Writ. Jesus said, "Except a man be born of water and the Spirit, he cannot enter the Kingdom." Now to be born of things you must first be conceived, and that which is conceived is covered or hid. Then to be born of water one must be, conceived of water which cannot be unless one is immersed and then born from [it]-Amen.

Fifth reason—BECAUSE WE ARE SAVED BY BELIEVING IN AND ON HIS NAME, (I Jn 2:12; Prov 18: 10; Acts 4: 12) The name of the Lord is a strong tower; the righteous runneth into it and are safe. I write unto you, little children, because your sins are forgiven you for His name's sake. We are saved not because of our righteousness nor praying or faith or works; these are conducive to salvation, but not because of these things we are saved, but for its Name's sake. From time immemorial God proposed to make for Himself a mighty name. (Isa 64:1-2), and in our time He has made the Name Jesus high over all the earth and sea and sky, yea it is above every name. Today God wants us to exalt the mighty name of Jesus. Whatever we do in word or deed, do it in Jesus' name.

Sixth reason—FATHER IS NOT A PROPER NAME, NOR SON, NOR HOLY GHOST. Father expresses a relationship, also Son; and the Holy Ghost means the Holy Spirit, but does not mean His name but His nature. "Holy" is an adjective, meaning "more excellence," "pure in heart," and Spirit is a noun but not a proper name. So that they who baptize in the formula by saying the following words: "I baptize you in the Name of the Father and of the Son and of the Holy Ghost," do not baptize in any name at all. There are many fathers and sons, but what father and son's name do they baptize in, seeing they do not designate? For this very reason, the Lord Jesus told the apostles not to depart out at Jerusalem, but to wait for the Spirit of Truth who would lead them into all truth and bring all things to their remembrance whatsoever He had spoken unto them. When the Holy Ghost came on the day of Pentecost He brought to the minds and hearts of the apostles what the name of the Father and of the Son and of the Holy Ghost was; and when the people asked, what shall we do? Peter answered, "Repent and be baptized every one of you in THE NAME OF JESUS CHRIST." Amen. The Name Jesus Christ is the name of the Father and of the Son and of the Holy Ghost. If not, then all the apostles disobeyed the command of Jesus and baptized the people wrong; but who will dare say that the apostles were wrong. Some say Peter said that, and I'm not following Peter, but Jesus. Well, the same Spirit that gave the command through Jesus, spoke through Peter on the day of Pentecost.

The word (gospel) of reconciliation was committed to the apostles. (II Cor 5:17–21) Jesus said, "Go ye therefore and teach all nations, baptizing them in the Name"—not names but Name (one) of the Father and of the Son and of the Holy Ghost, and if there is none other Name under heaven given among men whereby we must be saved cut Jesus Christ, then if we have not been baptized in the NAME of Jesus Christ, then we have not been baptized in the NAME of the Father and of the Son and of the Holy Ghost.

Seventh reason— "BECAUSE JESUS IS ALL AND IN ALL, (Col 2:9, 3:11; I Tim 3:16; Isa 9:6; Matt 1:21-24; Jn 1:1, 10; Gen 1:1). "Beware lest any man spoil you with philosophy and vain deceit, after the traditions of men, after rudiments of the world and not after Christ, FOR IN HIM DWELLETH ALL OF THE GODHEAD BODILY. Christ is all and in all, Praise His name forever. He is indeed "the mighty God, the Everlasting father, the Prince of Peace." If the God-head bodily dwells in Jesus, then the name of the Godhead must be Jesus. "And without controversy, great is the mystery of Godliness; God was manifested in the flesh, justified in the Spirit, seen of angels, preached unto the Gentiles believed on in the world and the world was made by Him, and the world knew Him not. Jesus Christ is the Lily of the Valley, the Bright and Morning Star, the Rose of Sharon, the Lion of the tribe of Judah Praise God, He is all and in all.

Pentecostal Power

The Lord Jesus Christ told Peter that He was going to build a church and would give him the keys so that he could open the door and let everybody that wanted to escape damnation and destruction come in (Matt 16:18-19). The keys that Jesus gave Peter are the gospel or doctrine or plan of salvation making plain to the people how to be born again as spoken of in (Jn 3:5), see (Acts 2:38) The Lord Jesus laid the foundation of the church by fulfilling all prophecy (Lk 24:44) and confirming every word by signs and wonders through the apostles (Mk 16:20), also (Eph 2:20) (see I Cor 3:11)

Jesus said He was the door (Jn 10:9) and Peter has the key and is giving it to you so you can come in (Acts 2:38); about 3,000 souls went in on the day of Pentecost. (Acts 2:41) All who do not come in with Peter's key which is repent and be baptized in Jesus' name, and get the Holy Spirit, are thieves and robbers (Jn 10:1) and no thief nor robber is going in God's Kingdom. See (I Cor 6:9, 10).

When Peter took the keys and opened the door so the people could come in the church, he preached the Gospel and made them to know that Jesus was God, so they could believe in every word spoken by the prophets and see that all the prophets spoke about Jesus. (see Isa 9:6; Ps 100:3; Matt 1:21-23; and Lk 2:11).

May. God help you to understand that the invisible God which is a. Spirit and has all the power to create and destroy the universe, was born of a virgin; He made—and came into the world as a man having two lives. One life was the eternal life of God the other, a natural human life as we have. The human life was the Son of the eternal life which is God, and both lives were in one body making the Father and Son one Person named Jesus Christ (Jn 10:30); see Col 2:8-9), and He gave the natural human life on the cross for the human family: that whosoever believeth in Him would inherit eternal life (Rom 6:23)

So all who believe the truth will repent and he baptized in the name of Jesus Christ for the remission of sins, (Acts 2:38), and shall receive the gift of the Holy Ghost (Acts 2:4) and continue in the Apostles' doctrine and fellowship and prayer (Acts 2:42), living holy and following peace with all men. (Heb 12:14) Consider what I say and the Lord give thee understanding in all things, and thine ears shall hear a word behind thee saying, "this is the way, walk ye in it." (Isa 30:21)

Do not guess about your salvation. The Bible says, "prove all things and, holdfast to that which is good. Beware of false prophets: (Matt 7:15) Many false prophets shall arise and shall deceive many. (Matt 24:11)

Unto our God whose name is Jesus Christ, be blessing, and glory, and wisdom, and thanksgiving, and honor and power, and might, forever and ever.

Amen

The New Testament Church

The business of the Church is God. To know God, to honor Him, to promote His interests, to extend the knowledge of Him to all parts of the world that is our primary work, and there is no secondary.

When other objectives are adopted, we cease to be a church and become a religious organization merely, doing some good, no doubt, but failing miserably to be what we call ourselves, a true Christian church. And Worst of all, we may then do real injury to the cause of Christ by misrepresenting Him among men and by giving to the world an inadequate or false conception of God.

The church established by Jesus Christ and His apostles was a unit and was designed to remain so throughout all time. It had one sure foundation and one divine rule for building thereon. The Gospel was preached for the people. They heard it, believed it; obeyed it. Those obedient ones that were baptized and filled with the Holy Spirit, were instructed to keep the unity of the Spirit in the bonds of peace and to continue steadfast in the Apostles' doctrine and fellowship and breaking of bread and in prayers. Now it is evident that there have been many innovations upon and departures from the teachings and practice of the primitive church, as laid down in the Scriptures.

Divisions and strifes and speculations exist, and while they exist the world cannot get a clear comprehension of the way of salvation, without the light of understanding being flashed upon the whole complex situation. Amid the multiplicity of religions and variety of churches, the intelligent observer and careful seeker ponders over in his mind such questions as these:

What is the true church?
What is its Name?
What is not the True Church?

An organization correlated by men, perpetuated by their posterity, upheld by the laws of the land, named after its founder or originator, whose members are joined through the system of probation, voting, handshaking, card- signing, etc.

The various churches and their names are not all the true church of Christ, but if any of them is right, the rest must needs be wrong, for there is but one church. One striking thing that is to be noted about various churches is that their names are not found in the Bible, moreover, their origin or organization is of recent date, for instance, there is not one of the popular known churches, whose origin is above a thousand years old, from the standpoint of organization, save the Roman Catholic Church, which was begun around the year 315 A.D., three hundred years too late to be church of Christ, which was founded on the day of Pentecost, A.D. 33. The Lutheran Church, founded in 1530; the Methodist, founded in 1729 by Mr. Morgan and Mr. John Wesley, 1686 and 1487, respectively, are too late. The Baptist, founded by Calvin in 1538, 1505 years too late. I could multiply the number, but the above is sufficient to exemplify the point I desire to set forth. But over against the above the Church of Our Lord Jesus Christ was founded by Jesus Christ very nearly 2000 years ago on that memorial day called Pentecost, when the Holy Spirit descended upon the waiting disciples, and they spoke in tongues and glorified God.

The True Church is not an organization formulated by man and perpetuated by his posterity and upheld by the laws of the land, but it is an organism, born by and in the Spirit of God, perpetuated by His ever-living presence, and upheld by His omnipotence.

All Bible students will agree that the Church of Christ was founded on the day of Pentecost, and not as some mistaken, zealous and even wise, honest and intellectual men have supposed that when Jesus was baptized in the river of Jordan by John and the Holy Ghost descended in the bodily shape of the dove, and the voice of God was heard saying, "This is my beloved Son in whom I am well pleased," then was the Church of Christ founded. Nor as yet as some have set forth that when Jesus said to Peter, "Upon this rock I will build my church and the gates of hell "will not prevail against it."

John the Baptist had nothing whatever to do in the building of the Church of Jesus Christ. His work was the introduction of the Messiah, Christ, and when said work was finished, John sealed his testimony by his blood on the chopping block of Herod and went the way of all flesh, with the approbation of the Son of God as his epitaph, saying, "Of men born of women, there is none greater than John the Baptist." When Christ said unto Peter, "Upon this rock I will build my church," it is evident that He did not build His church at that time, for He said, I will, signifying that at a future time He would build His church upon the revealed word of God, through which the revelation of Jesus as Son of God and redeemer, and not upon Peter nor his confession, as the Roman Catholic church interprets it. But upon this rock (the word of God yet to be revealed in like manner) as the identity of Jesus was revealed to Peter by the Spirit of God.

The church is the mystical body of Jesus Christ, born of His Spirit, through the process of regeneration and the renewing of the Holy Ghost. (Tit 1:5) Christ is the only head, administrator and teacher. Its members are built upon the foundation of the apostles and prophets, Jesus Christ, Himself, the chief cornerstone: in whom all the building fitly framed together groweth into a Holy Temple in the Lord, in whom ye also are builded together for the habitation of God through the Spirit. (Eph 2:19-22)

The Beginning of the New Testament Church

On the day of Pentecost, the hundred and twenty waiting disciples, in obedience to the command of Jesus, had tarried in prayer and supplication ten days waiting for the Holy Spirit. They were all in one accord and in one place, when suddenly there came from heaven the sound of a rushing, mighty wind, the Holy Ghost descended, and filled all the place wherein they were sitting. There appeared unto them cloven tongues as of fire and they all were filled with the Holy Ghost and began to speak with other tongues as the Spirit gave them utterance. Jerusalem was stirred by the wonderful phenomenon and came together as one man to the place where the disciples were praising and blessing God and staggering around as though they were drunk, speaking in other languages as the Spirit of God gave them utterance. When some were in doubt as to the nature and meaning of that which they had seen and heard, some said, "Are not all these men Galileans?" "We do hear them speaking in our tongue of the wonderful works of God." Others, mocking said, "These men are full of new wine." Peter, standing up with the eleven preached unto them Jesus Christ, buried, resurrected, and ascended, and the shedder forth of that which they had seen and heard. The multitude, stung, with conviction, cried out, "Men and brethren, what shall we do?"

And Peter said unto them: "Repent and be baptized every one of you in the name of Jesus Christ, for the remission of sins and you shall receive the gift of the Holy Ghost. The thousand gladly received his word and were baptized and continued in the Apostles' doctrine and breaking of bread and in prayers."

The contrast can be readily seen in the beginning and origin of the true church and the above-mentioned churches of recent origin. None claim the mighty baptism of the Spirit accompanied with speaking in other tongues, as the Church of Christ did on the day of Pentecost.

The Nature of the True Church

We mentioned above in this article at the church as touching its nature, being an organism and not an organization. Its nature is not composed of by-laws, rituals, ceremonies, covenants and other ecclesiastical millinery. All these things may have some use, but they are not the nature of the church and never were instituted by Jesus Christ. Moreover, expensive cathedrals and buildings are not the church. The church is the mystical body of Jesus Christ, whose nature is spirit. Therefore, it is invisible, and it cannot be gotten into by joining, handshaking, etc., as is commonly thought. It is the invisible presence of Jesus Christ, who is above all and in all that are born of His spirit. (Jn 3:5; Acts 2:38)

The church is visible only in the person of spirit-filled believers, who according to Ephesians 2:19-22 "Now therefore we are no more strangers and foreigners, but fellow-citizens with the saints, and of the household of God; And are built upon the foundation of the apostles and prophets, Jesus Christ himself being the chief corner stone. In whom all the buildings fitly framed to get her, groweth unto an holy temple of the Lord; In whom ye also are builded together for an habitation of God through the Spirit.

Peter elucidates on this profound point by saying, "Unto you who believes, He is precious if so be, ye have tasted that the Lord is gracious, to whom coming, at; unto a living stone, disallowed in deed of men, but chosen of God and precious. Ye also as lively stones, have built up a spiritual house, an holy priesthood to offer spiritual sacrifice, acceptable to God by Jesus Christ."

We judge therefore by the above that this is far in a way different from a chartered organized position, this is none other than the body of Christ at; spoken of in the 4th Chapter of Ephesians 4-6th verse. There is one body and one spirit. Every true believer is a cell in the body of Christ and is joined by the spirit and the bounds of peace to other believers, who together, form the Church of God! Lord Jesus Christ. Wherever there is a group composed as a local church, they should be a Christian microcosm, representing within itself all the life, purity and power of the church universal.

The Character of the Church

If the nature of the church is Spirit, that is to say, Jesus Christ in the person of the Holy Ghost, then the character of the church must be holy, "And ye know that He was manifested to take away our sin; and in Him is no sin. Whosoever abideth in Him sinneth not; whosoever sinneth hath not seen Him or known Him." (I Jn 3:5-6)

For to this end Christ shed His blood outside the gates of Jerusalem, that He might sanctify the people with His own blood. (Heb 13) Yea; He gave himself unto death and rose again that He might sanctify and cleanse the church with the washing of the water by the word that He might present it to himself a glorious church, not having spot, or wrinkle, or any such thing; but that it should be holy and without blemish. (Eph 5:25-28)

God has no other church, nor will have, save a sanctified and holy church. Follow peace with all men and holiness, without which no man shalt see the Lord. Heb 12:14 is the divine admonition setting forth the requirement of God, not only upon the church in the collective sense, but each member individually must perfect holiness in the fear of God. The church being the mystical body of Jesus Christ, that is, His Spirit, no one that habitually lives in sin can be in it, not one that practices sin, for as many as are led by the Spirit of God, they are the sons of God and will not fulfill the lust of the flesh. For their lives are hid with Christ in God, You cannot live in sin and be in the church or in His Spirit, for in Him is no sin. (I Jn 3:5) You may be in the congregation of spirit-filled believers, but to be in the real church (that is Christ's Spirit) we cannot remain in and be unclean, for sin breaks fellowship with God. There is no one congregation or organization called the church that has not some hypocrite or pretender, but the Church of Christ (i.e., those in the Spirit of Christ) are without spot or blemish, but it is wholly without blame. Wherever there are children of God, born of water and Spirit, according to Acts 2:38, regardless of what church they attend, if they live in the Spirit, they are in the church, triumphant, yea, in the Saviour's bride.

How to Become a Member of the True Church

It is evident that there are true disciples of our Lord in all of the various churches, but the scriptures emphatically declare that there is but one body or church, one Lord, one Faith, and one fold and one Shepherd. What shall be the sequence of this complex condition of the Christian world? I must perforce take you back to the words of our God Oil the true church, its Founder, origin, nature, etc.

The church started on the day of Pentecost, fresh from the heart of God, born with a rushing, mighty wind, gave to the world the institution called church, an organism, the medium of salvation through which man can be saved. It opened up business for God on that very day the people who, under the preaching of Peter, were convicted of sin, asked for remission of sin and for admittance into the church, Peter said, "Repent and be baptized every one of you in the name of Jesus Christ for the remission of sins and you shall receive the gift of the Holy Ghost." (Act 2:38)

Three thousand gladly received His word and were baptized and were filled with the Holy Ghost, thereby being added to the church. Peter thus established a precedent, or rather the way to get into the Church of Christ. You will notice he did not use any of the modern methods of the latter-day evangelist: "join the church," "shake my hand," "hit the sawdust trail" "sign card" or voting, ·but repentance was the keynote and the baptism of the Holy Ghost was the entrance into the church.

The apostle, Paul said in I Corinthians 12:1-3, by the one Spirit we are baptized in one body (church), whether we be Jew or Greek, bond or free, we have all been made to drink in one Spirit. And the body being the church, according to Ephesians 1:22-23, and Colossians 1:24. Therefore there is but one way into the church and that is by the baptism of the Holy Spirit. Water baptism does not put one into the church as some suppose. The place in the plan of salvation given water baptism is that it makes you eligible through faith in the atoning blood of Jesus to receive baptism of the Holy Ghost, which puts you into the church.

The Lord said, "Other sheep I have that are not of this fold, them I must bring. There shall be one fold and one Shepherd." Therefore, the sequence is that the pure in heart, the honest seeker of whatever church, will eventually receive the baptism of the Holy Ghost, thereby becoming the member of the Church of Jesus Christ, wherein there is no denominational or racial distinction.

The Name of the True Church

As above noted, a striking thing is manifest when one peruses the Holy Writ, and that one thing is, that the names of the majority of churches are not in it. The churches mostly have taken their names from their founders or organizers or the polity of their organization. For instance, the Congregational and Presbyterian churches each derived their names from their peculiar church policy; Baptist and Methodist likewise. The Lutheran and Swedenburgh churches derive their name from their founders. Other churches are known because of their peculiarities and modes of worship and thereby derive their names. But none of the following reasons are excuses for the unscripturality of the names of these churches. Many of the more recent churches have names that are so unscriptural that one has no reason that comes to mind why they chose such names. The Church of Divine Ascension, for instance; also, the Church of Divine Paternity, etc. The Pentecostal Assemblies of the World; the Apostolic Faith Mission or Assembly. If we are of Christ Jesus, then we are not of the world even though we are in the world. If we take upon us the name of Jesus Christ individually why should not the church be named by that name that is above every name and at that name every knee shall bow, namely Jesus Christ. Ephesians 1:22 says that He is the head of the body, the church; Colossians 1:24 says the church which is His body. If the church is the body of Christ and He is the head, then the body should be named after the head, therefore the proper name of the church should be the Church of Our Lord Jesus Christ and not the many unscriptural names we now have. For example, if a man dies, people recognize his body by his head and straightway say that the body of John Brown was interred at such and such a time. Therefore, the body of Jesus Christ should be named after its head. To the honest seeker, I commend the above truth set forth to answer the question that may perplex your mind. Moreover, since the church is the body of Christ and His body is mystical or spiritual the true church is the Church of Our Lord Jesus of the Apostolic Faith, the Faith is that of the Apostles for it was unto them that the faith was delivered. Therefore, earnestly contend for the faith that was once delivered unto the saints.

To merely name the Church of Jesus is not giving the full title and respect to our Lord for the Jehovah God of the Old Testament is Jesus Christ of the New Testament. Hence the word Lord, which in the Greek means "Jurios" acknowledged and recognizes his deity, The word Jesus is like to that of the name of his humanity, however, the word Jesus is equivalent to Jehu-Shuha, which means Jehovah, the Saviour; and the word Christ is equivalent to the Hebrew word Messiah, which denotes his work of redemption, and in itself is taken from the Greek word Christos, which means anointed—so the full regal name of Our Saviour, is the Lord Jesus Christ.

Another reason that this name should he used in reference to naming the church is because there are many people in foreign lands, such as Mexico, Greece, and Spain, where the name Jesus is commonly used by the people in naming of their children, hence, to make an emphatic distinction, one should always refer or prefix the name of Jesus, with the word, Lord. Hence the true name of the church should be the Church of Our Lord Jesus Christ.

Part II: On Personal Holiness

The Impact of Wesleyan Ideas on The Church of Our Lord Jesus Christ of The Apostolic Faith

Entire Sanctification —John Wesley's doctrine of Christian Perfection was a hallmark of his theology and shaped the theology of his followers who would ultimately come to be known as Methodist. Wesley desired within himself holiness of heart, and his devotion to God caused others to criticize him as being too strict. In his journal, he would write,

> I had much talk with one who is called a Quaker, but he could not receive my saying. I was too strict for him, and talked of such perfection as he could not think necessary...[13]

Wesley believed that one could obtain Christian Perfection; that sanctification was the mark of God's Holy Spirit in the life of the believer, and that a Christian's life beginning with justification should move on to sanctification.

For Wesley only after one has experienced justification by faith can he or she have the experience of sanctification. And, it is only through the process of sanctification that one can become the "perfect man" in

---

[13] John Wesley, *The Works of John Wesley, Volume I: Journal from October 24, 1725 to November 29, 1745*. Grand Rapids, MI: Zondervan Publishing House, n.d. 203

Christ Jesus who has a pure heart and a pure love towards God. Wesley viewed sanctification both as an initial experience and a progressive work. For him, the work begins with justification and continues until one has reached perfection. Yet, though he felt that perfection can be reached in this life, he believed it was reached right before death. Yet, he contended it was a goal to which Christians should strive. This is the perfect love of God which is exhibited through ethical, moral behavior that exemplifies the fruit of the Spirit. It is this perfect love that prepares one for heaven and is the consummation of glorification.

> The bond between the state of perfection and the state of glorification in Wesley's theology is strong. No one can enter fully into the presence of God without having been freed from sin and perfected in love. Only a perfectly holy person could truly enjoy the life of heaven.[14]

For Wesley, holiness involved one's conduct and lifestyle, which reflected one's love for God and in a practical lifestyle that eschewed worldly pleasures. Early Methodists were encouraged to refrain from theater-going, dancing, wearing useless jewelry and imbibing alcoholic beverages. In England, during the 1700s it was the Wesleyans who were vocal against societal ills caused by alcoholism, dueling, and gambling.

---

[14] Egardo A. Colon-Emeric, *Wesley, Aquinas & Christian Perfection* (Waco: Baylor University Press, 2009), 53.

Lawson's Interpretation of Wesleyan Sanctification

In spite of the "strictness" of his teaching, many African Americans who were attracted to Methodism and, later, to the African American Pentecostal church would be shaped by it. Many leaders within the African American Holiness and Pentecostal movements, including Lawson, were strongly influenced by it, as clearly evidenced by the personal holiness stance of many Classical Pentecostal churches. The major theological stance of COOLJC as a Pentecostal Church revolves around the "initial evidence" ideology for the baptism of the Holy Spirit with the physical evidence of speaking in tongues. Yet in the African American community, it is more known for its stance on personal issues, it is known as a "Holiness" or "Sanctified Church."

> Eschewing the world's pleasures was the first step to proving that one allowed the Holy Spirit to work in one's life. Drinking, smoking, snuff dipping, promiscuity, and revealing clothing were the hallmarks of the unsanctified life.[15]

For Lawson, as a Holiness preacher, perfection was twofold—instantaneous and progressive. However, he did not see it apart from grace as a second experience. He agreed with Wesley that,

---

[15] The Discipline Book of The Church of Our Lord Jesus Christ of the Apostolic Faith, Inc. (New York: Church of Our Lord Jesus Christ, 1975), 33.

> Perfection is not an experience to be attained in a moment. It must be attained round by round, from glory to glory, and from faith to faith...In this regard, our completion or perfection is accredited to us through the merits of our Lord Jesus Christ and based upon his death, burial, and resurrection. [16]

Most Pentecostals defined Wesley's sanctification through the three works of grace, each building on the other. with the first being justification, followed by sanctification and finally, baptism of the Holy Spirit. The major departure from this position was introduced by William Durham who in 1910 formulated the theology of "Finished Work." Durham emphasized sanctification as a benefit of justification, followed by the baptism of the Holy Spirit. His teachings challenged entire sanctification as a second work of grace. He held that the death of Christ on the cross provided both justification and sanctification. Sanctification then became seen as instantaneous work beginning at conversion and continuing throughout the life of the believer because of Calvary.

Pentecostal churches— whether they are Trinitarian or Oneness, whether Wesleyan or Finished Work—hold a common commitment to fundamental views of sanctification. Therefore, with the Holy Spirit baptism, they see a wholly sanctified life is the only true standard of a Christian life. They all promoted personal holiness among

---

[16] Thomas A. Langford, *Wesleyan Theology A Sourcebook* (Durham, UK: The Labyrinth Press, 1984), 101-102.

their members congregates that included no gambling, dancing, smoking, and fornication. Members were to refrain from going to the movies and dances. Only functional jewelry was to be worn and they were to abstain from intoxicating beverages. The sanctified life changed one's life and their reaction to the outside world and their appearance, They are to "come out," and this coming out, causes a difference. COOLJC members, like most other Pentecostals, were told to "cleanse themselves from all "filthiness of the flesh and Spirit" including use, growth, sale or handling of tobacco in any form, or of morphine or intoxicants, filthiness of speech, foolish talking or jesting, or the use of slang language; to abstain from all appearance of evil.[17]

Cheryl Sanders description of Pentecostal aptly describes the personal holiness code of COOLJC when she states,

> ... the Sanctified church is an African America Christian reform movement that seeks to bring its standards of worship, personal morality, and social concern into conformity with a biblical hermeneutic of holiness and spiritual empowerment.[18]

---

[17] The Discipline Book of The Church of Our Lord Jesus Christ of the Apostolic Faith, Inc. (New York: Church of Our Lord Jesus Christ, 1975), 33.

[18] Cheryl J. Sanders, *Saints in Exile The Holiness-Pentecostal Experience in African American Religion and Culture* (New York, NY: Oxford University Press, 1966).

Lawson used a holiness lens to interpret all of Scripture and applied it to the members of his denomination. For him, a sanctified lifestyle was a mandate for heaven. Yet, he viewed acceptance of this mandate through an Arminian lens. He offered the invitation to holiness to all who would accept the call of God's grace. Lawson did not view outward standards as requirements for heaven but as a reflection on the inner man. For him, the outward adorning should be the direct reflection of the inner adornment of the heart. This is also a reflection of the love of God abiding in the heart of the believer. However, Lawson did realize that people can look "sanctified" and act sanctified and not be sanctified in their heart.

Lawson, as well as early Methodism, viewed holiness in the same light. Christians were to come out from the world and to live a life above sin. They were to strive to have a perfect love for God. Lawson's "wholly sanctified life" paralleled Wesley's "entire sanctification." Both sought to bring the believer into a closer relationship to God as they progressed in their sanctification.

Healing Through Christ
or
Divine Healing for the Body

The Bible offers Christ Jesus the Lord to the world, as the Saviour from sin, and Healer for the body. SALVATION for both soul and body if we will believe it.

Prophecy concerning our High Priest and Redeemer, seven hundred years before He came reads on this wise, in Isaiah 53:4,5, "Surely He hath borne our griefs, and carried our sorrows; yet we did esteem Him stricken, smitten of God, and afflicted. But He was wounded for our transgressions. He was bruised for our iniquities; the chastisement of our peace was upon Him; and with His stripes, we ARE healed." This prophecy was fulfilled in Christ and His life's work, and atonement on Calvary, after seven hundred years as we read in Matthew 8:6, 17. "When the evening was come, they brought unto Him many that were possessed with devils and He cast out the spirits with His word, and healed all that were sick; that it might be fulfilled which was spoken by Isaiah the prophet, saying Himself took our infirmities, and bare our sickness."

Again, in I Peter 2:21-25, "Who His own self bares our sins in His own body on the tree, that we, being dead to sins, should live unto righteousness; by whose stripes ye ARE healed." When we really see that Jesus bore our diseases and infirmities on the Cross, and that we do not have to bear them, it should give us boldness of faith to claim the provisions of redemption for our souls and bodies.

Christ marked His ministry from the beginning conspicuously by healing all who came to Him. (Matt 4:23, Mk 3:9-11; Lk 9:11) Twenty and two special cases are given for special teachings; (Matt 8:5-13, 9:32-34, 12:10, 12:22-30, 15:22-28, 17:14-21; Mk 1:23-28, 40-45, 5:2-20, 8:22,10:7, 32-37; Lk 4:38, 8:43, 13:11-17; 14:2-6, 18:35; Jn 4:46-53; 5:5-16, 9) Fulfilling the prophecies of the Old Testament. Christ's farewell words at the close of His ministry, returning back to His glory, should give world-convincing proofs of the continuance of this ministry through His disciples. (Jn 14:12) The Holy Ghost carries on the work which Jesus began. (Acts 1:1) Physical healing is as much a part of the Gospel as salvation of the soul. Many cases of healing are recorded in the Acts of the work of the Holy Ghost through the apostles.

Though Himself invisible, the power of the risen Lord and Savior is present to heal now, as when He healed the lame man at the Beautiful Gate. (Acts 3:1-10) Aeneas at Lydda, Acts 14:8. Paul's experience of healing, Acts 14:19; Publius' father; and others. (Acts 28:8-9) The gift of healing is a part of the ministry (I Cor 12:9-30), the which is to be continued on, as long as the Gospel is preached by the ministers and Elders.

The Gentiles come into the same blessings of health of Israel, and also of an eternal salvation, through the Gospel of Christ. (Gal 3:8-29) Therefore, we are full heirs to these blessed promises; both on salvation and healing. The twain are counted in one, in the suffering, death, and resurrection of Christ. Our risen Lord and Savior being the head of the Body—His Church—His life is imparted to the members through the Holy Ghost. (Rom 8:11) "His words are spirit and are life." We should be steadfast to hold fast His blessed word of promise that shall never fail. Healing for the body is a fruit of His suffering. (Isa 53:4-11)

How To Appropriate Healing Of Our Bodies

The scripture sayeth, "Is any sick among you? let him call for the Elders of the church; and let them pray over him, anointing him with oil in the name of the Lord. And the prayer of faith shall save the sick, and the Lord shall raise him up; and if he have committed sins, they shall be forgiven him. Confess your faults one to another, and pray one for another, that ye may be healed. The effectual fervent prayer of a righteous man availeth much." (Jas 5:14-16) After obeying the word of God, the next step, then, is to take our healing by faith. The truth of the matter is, God gave us this part of our inheritance nineteen hundred years ago and is waiting for us to BELIEVE IT and take our healing by faith, which is the only scriptural way. The promises were given to teach us just how to do this. (Mk 11:24) "Therefore, I say unto you, what things soever ye desire when ye pray, believe that ye receive them, and ye shall have them." The condition of receiving what we ask for is to believe that we have it when we ask, and this without waiting to see or feel that we are healed. We are to count it done on the authority of God's word.

Many have tried to go this far, and yet have not received a perfect healing; but there is still ANOTHER VERY IMPORTANT STEP of faith to take, besides asking and saying we believe; and that is, we should immediately begin to act out our faith, as if we believe it answered, and God is faithful. The apostle says, "What doth it profit, my brethren, if a man say he hath faith, but have not works? Can that faith save him?" (Jas 2: 14) Action must follow, both in words and deed.

With the heart man believeth unto healing; and with the mouth confession is made unto deliverance, healing e.g. Abraham believed the promise of God relative to his son Isaac, and though he was aged; and Sarah was dead in her body, he staggered not at the promise of God; but was strong in faith, giving glory to God; being fully persuaded that what He had promised, He was able also to perform. (Rom 4:20)

We gather from the above that the principle of obtaining promises, is to believe with the heart, and confess with the mouth; then to hold on in faith, praising God for His faithfulness in doing, and power to do, what we believe Him for, and what He has promised. Many fail to grow stronger in faith for their healing, because they don't praise God for His faithfulness in healing their bodies, even though symptoms remain.

"With joy, we draw water out of the wells of salvation." And again, "the joy of the Lord is our strength," sayeth the prophet. "Faith is the substance of things hoped for, the evidence of things not seen... But without faith it is impossible to please God; for he that cometh to God must believe that He is, and that He is a rewarder of them that diligently seek Him." The Psalmist says, "Let them that seek the Lord rejoice, and let them say continually, the Lord He is our God."

Rejoicing is an evidence of our faith in the accomplished work of Christ on Calvary for our healing; and even though we may not feel it, yet faith being a conviction of unseen facts, we rejoice with joy unspeakable and full of glory. "Faithful is He that calleth you, who also will do it. (I Thess 5:24) Again "Let us hold fast the profession of our faith without wavering; for He is faithful that promised." (Heb. 10:23)

In other words, we are to act like a well person on the authority of God's promise, before we see or feel our healing starting to work. It is just here where the real battleground lies. When we start out in naked faith, the adversary usually makes our symptoms worse, and tries to persuade us to resort to other means or take the case out of God's hand. But it must be CLEARLY UNDERSTOOD that CHRIST is HEALER, and that Drugs and Medicine, however simple, being unscriptural, are to be laid aside.

In the very nature of the case, we could not expect God to heal us, unless we sought it from him alone. The Lord knows just how much we can bear, and will only permit the adversary to go so far, for as soon as He sees that we mean to be steadfast, and die trusting Him, He will rebuke the adversary and our healing will come instantly. Many start to act out their faith but when the enemy makes their symptoms worse, or they do not see great results at once, they give up the battle, and so often when right at the threshold of victory.

Testing That Goes with Our Testimony

One feature of the life of real Christians, or saints, which seems so hard for many to understand, is that our testimony involves testing. Those who take Christ Jesus as their complete Salvation for both soul and body, will be tested by the world, the flesh, and the devil. In all these testings, the enemy will put forth his best efforts. It is easy to testify, preach, and tell others of these things; and say that Jesus is all and in all, but many, oh so many fail rather than stand the testing of their testimony.

It is not because there are not hundreds who believe our testimony, that our ranks are not full of witnesses, but because so few are willing to stand the testing that goes with the testimony. It is a great thing to say that you believe that He is, but the testing comes when He is taken as a Healer, and the case left absolutely in His hands, though facing death. Amen. It is necessary to see the important bearing that divine healing has on our spiritual life. Many seem to think that it only concerns the body, and is a side issue, and has no bearing upon our relation with God spiritually.

Trusting For Healing Of Our Bodies Has Bearing On Our Spiritual Life

These few scriptures might help you to see that it has much to do with our spiritual condition. (Rom 4:19-22; Matt 8:5-13; II Chron 16) In fact, sickness entered through sin. "Dying thou shalt die." (Gen 2:17). Mortification began in the flesh, or it became subject to disease and death, but, "in Christ death is abolished, and life and immortality brought back to life," through the Gospel.

When Israel's deliverance began, God separated them from Egypt and promised exemptions from disease, on certain conditions. (Ex 15:25, 26) In case of transgression and disease, God provided, not medical treatment, but healing through confession and priestly functions (Lev 13:14). Medical science, introduced by Egyptians, and first referred to in Genesis 50:2, was in preservation of the bodies of the dead. When Israel left Egypt, no mention is made of accompanying physicians. At the outset of their pilgrimage, the Lord proclaimed Himself Jehovah-Rapha is The Lord Thy Healer. (Ex 15:25, 26)

Disease appeared four times in the wilderness, and each time healing came by supernatural means: First Miriam, leprosy, caused by jealousy. (Num 12) Second, The plague, result of Rebellion. (Num 16:36-40) Third, Fiery serpents, result of discontent and murmuring. (Num 21:4-9) Fourth, Another plague [was the] result of uncleanliness and idolatry. (Num 25:1-9) Those who confessed and obeyed the Lord, crying unto Him for healing, they were healed. (Ps 105:37, 107:20) The book of Job, one of the oldest records extant, 1520 B.C., gives the source of sickness, divinely permitted for self-knowledge, (Job 2:3-7) He was healed when he humbled himself at the feet of Jehovah. (Job 40:4-5, 42:2-6)

Time would fail me to make mention of Jehoram, (II Chron 21:12); Naaman, (II Kgs 5:1-14); Gehazi, (II Kgs 5:20); Hezekiah, (II Kgs 20:1-11), etc. Seeing the connection of sickness with sin and disobedience, the remedy coming through confession and obedience; and through intercessory prayer, and the functions of the ministers or Elders, we can readily see that it has a great bearing upon the entire life.

May God bless every reader to receive faith to trust the word of God; and thereby receive results, as God hath promised. **Take our blessed Lord Jehovah as healer as well as savior**, for He accomplished both in His suffering and death on the Cross.

The Design and Results of Suffering

For we would not, brethren, have you ignorant of our trouble which came to us in Asia, that we were, pressed out of measure, above strength, insomuch that we despaired oven of life: But we had the sentence of death in ourselves, that we should not trust in ourselves, but in God which raiseth the dead, who delivered us from so great a death, and doth deliver: in whom we trust that he will yet deliver us. (II Cor 1:8-10)

Dr. Moffet translated this passage of Scripture very clearly and very emphatically: "Now, I would like you to know about the distress which befell me in Asia. I was crushed and crushed, far more than I could stand. So much so that I despaired even of life. In fact, I told myself, it was a sentence of death, but that was to make me rely not only on myself, but on God who raises the dead. He rescued me from so terrible a death. He rescues still, and I rely upon Him for the hope that He will continue to rescue me." A. B. Simpson in one of his writings, says that the pressure of hard places makes us value life.

Every time our life is given back to us from such a trial, it is like a new beginning, and we learn better how much it is worth, and make sure of it for God and man. The pressure helps us to understand the trials of others and fits us to help and sympathize with them. There are shallow, superficial people that consider the promises of God lightly, and who talk very flatly about the distress of those who shrink from sore trials, but the man or woman who has suffered much never does this but is very tender and gentle and knows what suffering really means. This is what Paul meant when he said, "Death worketh in us, but life in you."

Trials and hard places are needed to press us forward, even as a ship's furnace fires are needed to hold that mighty ship to its course, moves the piston and drives those mighty engines, propelling the great vessel across the sea of this world in the face of wind and rain. So out of our trials and temptations and experiences, God teaches us how to sympathize with others, and in the crucible of experience, God develops that which Paul speaks of, "All things work together for good..."

That "good" to me is character, an inestimable value that comes only by continuous choosing that which is right and good; a continual willingness to suffer to maintain that choice, and a spirit of obedience to follow God's Word.

Out of experience of my own life, this text was given to me when I lamented my own failure to triumph more decisively over life's problems and fears, and it came to me as assurance and comfort not withstanding all, I had been delivered by God, who hath delivered, who doth deliver, and Who, we trust, will yet deliver.

And so, I pass on to you this text to encourage you along life's highway. God is endeavoring to guide you and to perfect you in the most inestimable value that the world knows, and that is character, imperishable and indestructible. Life is designed to that end.

> Behold, what manner of love the Father hath bestowed upon us, that we should be called the sons of God: therefore the world knoweth us not,

because it knew him not. Beloved, now are we the sons of God, and it doth not yet appear what we shall be; but we know that, when he shall appear, we shall be like him, for we shall See him as he is. And every man that hath this hope in him purifieth himself, even as he is pure. Whosoever committeth sin transgresseth also the law: for sin is the transgression of the law. And ye know that he was manifested to take away our sins, and in him is no sin. (I John 3:1-5)

In order to develop the Christ life, the old self-life must be crushed, must be beaten, must be defeated—yes, put to death. "Knowing this, that our old man is crucified with Him, that the body of sin might he destroyed, that henceforth we should not serve sin. (Romans 6:16)

Our old natural life must be beaten to the dust and defeated, and Christ must become the master of sur own person, and through Him, we also achieve the kinship of self-control. We don't achieve that mastery by an experience of blessing.

You must achieve it by Constant reaffirmation of your faith and choice of what is right. You must be willing to stand by your ideals and principles of truth, yes, even by the Word of God, and in order to do that, you have to get the "old self" out of the way.

So, we find that as Paul said, he would not have us ignorant about the distress that came upon him in Asia, and he said how he was crushed far more than he could stand. That's when God comes in—man's extremity, God's opportunity. And we find further that Paul said that he despaired, even of life, and he told himself it was a sentence of death.

God brings us to the end of ourselves to let us know that without Him (He said... "without me ye can do nothing") we can do nothing. He brings us to the end of ourselves in order that we might reach out for a power higher than ourselves, That is when we know that life is too hard for us by ourselves, and we can't win out against the various vicissitudes and trials and experiences of life without a higher power than ourselves.

For instance, God came to Elijah when he was discouraged by his experience with the Prophets of Baal on Mt, Carmel, and with Jezebel, the wicked Queen, and the Prophets of the Grove after he had defeated them, and the fire of God from heaven descended upon the sacrifice at the behest of the Man of God, and the people were turned back to God, saying, "The Lord, He is God. It was that fearsome woman who sent that terrible message... "But let the gods do to me, and more also, if I make not thy life as the life of one of them by tomorrow about this time." (I Kgs 19:2) Through fear and intimidation, scared and frightened by this formidable opponent and terrible threat, Elijah ran for his life until his physical strength gave out, and he was exhausted under a juniper tree and he requested that he might die and said... "It is enough; now, O Lord, take away my life for I am not better than my fathers." And as he lay and slept under a juniper tree, behold, an angel touched him, and said unto him, "Arise and eat." And he looked, and behold, there was a cake baken on the coals, and a cruse of water at his head. And he did eat and drink and laid him down again. And the angel of the Lord came again the second time, and touched him, and said, "Arise and eat," because the journey is too great for thee. And he arose, and did eat and drink, and went in the strength of that meat forty days and forty nights unto Horeb the mount of God." (I Kgs 19:8)

So every man is going to come to the end of himself, God is going to bring to you the end of yourself, regardless of your education, your money, your position—somewhere, sometime, down the highway of time in your life, God is going to bring you to the end of yourself, and that is when you will realize that you will have to have food and strength from on high, power beyond and above, outside of you to come to your rescue; for the journey of life is too great for you. The purpose of all that— our trials that come upon us— is to bring us to the end of ourselves, to the end that we should rely not upon ourselves but upon God. Temptation is designed for that purpose also. So, don't be discouraged, your trial or your temptation, whatever it may be, God will not suffer you to be tempted above that which you are able to bear, but will, with the temptation, when you acknowledge that you are not able to withstand, make a way of escape that ye may be able to bear it. (I Cor 10:13)

Yea, whatever may be your trials, especially you that desire to be a worker for God, remember always that God sends you through the crucible of suffering to refine and teach you so that you might help others who are in similar or the self-same trials. He allows you to be tempted in order that you might come across some other tempted, harassed, storm-tossed and driven soul, and give him the comfort wherewith you were comforted of God. (II Cor 1:6) So, Paul says in verses 3-5: "... God of all comforts who comforteth us in all our tribulation, that we may able to comfort them that are in any trouble, by the comfort wherewith we ourselves are comforted of God. For as the sufferings of Christ abound in us, so our consolation also aboundeth by Christ. And whether we be afflicted, it is for your consolation and salvation, which is effectual in the enduring of the same sufferings which we also suffer; or whether we be comforted, it is for your consolation and salvation."

If you want consolation, if you want the great blessing and nearness of God, remember it comes in immensible measure, according to your need and inadequacy—your need and lack is supplied to carry on.

I remember being blessed of God to write a well-beloved song, "Praise Thy Name." I was inspired to write it after a man had threatened me with arrest and got the policeman to put me out of the Church for preaching the Deity of Jesus, the mighty God. When the policemen came and saw my credentials, and listened to what I told them I was doing, they refused to take any actions. One of them said to the man, "Why don't you make up with this man—you are all brethren? The man replied, "The only way we can settle is to fight out. I answered, "Brother, peace has been declared long ago in my soul, and I study war no more."

I was so humiliated. I had never had an experience like that, and being a young preacher, I stayed up most of the night after that until around three o'clock, crying to God because of this disgraceful experience, so mortifying, so humiliating. But in the darkest hour of my great spiritual depression, the Lord revealed the fact to me in the words of that song:

>Take the cross, thou need not fear
> I have tried the cross before you
>And the glory lingers near

Then I visualized the cross and the suffering of my Lord, I then saw myself, and I felt ashamed because He had suffered so much, and I was murmuring over the little I had to suffer for Him. I know I wasn't guilty, that I wasn't doing anything wrong, and that's where the pungent, intense feeling of mortification came in. I felt and knew I was right and had done no harm to the man. Why should he have such a reaction and attitude towards me? But the lord then revealed Himself in glory and sweetness as I confessed my weakness before Him. It seems as though He came into my room where I was praying, as a cloud of Shekina glory. I felt like a troubadour, as I imagined a young Spanish man would feel, serenading his fiancé on a balcony, And my heart was lifted as I thought of His goodness to me, and I wrote the song, "Praise Thy Name."

>Blessed Jesus, thou hast saved me,
>Thou has filled my heart with joy;
>In thy name I have salvation,
>Through Thy precious, cleansing blood.

Chorus:
Praise Thy name, praise Thy name,
The Rock of my salvation, Hallelujah
Praise Thy name.

Thou art God, my Holy Father,
Bread of life thou art to me;
Living water from the fountain,
Thou hast giv'n me liberty.
Thou hast borne my sins and sickness,
Thou from death hast set me free,
Thou hast gone and prepared a mansion
Where I may dwell eternally.

I have called thee, "Abba Father."
I have stayed my heart on thee,
Son of God, Thou Holy Spirit,
Thou art all in all to me.

The presence of God was so pronounced and so real that I sang that song as a love song to God. I wrote that song feeling an emotion of such great gratitude and love to God that I had to say to Him in that third verse:

Thou hast borne my sins and sickness,
Thou from death hast set me free.

For His presence was so great. I want you to note, however, that this came only after my humiliating experience with that man. So, when you want consolation, and hear others talk about how God consoles them and comforts then, don't forget that the complement of consolation is pain. Yea, if you want the glory and consolation of the Lord remember it comes when you need Him most." It is not so much to shout it out, but for the comfort of your heart and to strengthen you. "Just when I need Him most," says another poet, "Jesus is here, to comfort and cheer, just when I need Him most."

Someone said, "Out of the press of pain comes the soul's best wine—the eyes that shed no rain, can shed but a very little sunshine." So, through suffering, you will learn to know that God is near you. When I was coming from Kingston, Jamaica, during a terrible Caribbean storm, the plane struck an air pocket, and it shuddered and took a nosedive, I threw my chair back and buckled my belt around me, and I thought, surely the end had come. It looked like every second it would split asunder and the waters would drown us all. And at that time of danger, I said, "Well this is it" and that is all that I said, and then the arms of an invisible one seemed just to encircle and entwine around about me, and I felt the presence of God as I had never felt it in my life before. Then, I understood what it meant for martyrs to go to the stake singing.

In the greatest danger, the presence of God is felt more pronouncedly. He comes near to comfort and sheer; even in death, to take away the sting. His presence Gives the victory over everything.

We have the advantage when we trust in God. When I thought of the experience of my past, this message was given to me to preach. Then I understand, that whatever God Almighty sends me through, as Paul said, that whether you are afflicted, it is for your consolation and salvation, which is effectual in the enduring of the same suffering which we also suffered, or whether we, be comforted, it is for your consolation.

Now the idea is that when you want God to use you and make [you] a blessing, you must be willing to go through the trials and sufferings and receive instruction and comfort, and the consolation and salvation which is the deliverance of God.

Then you can tell somebody else about it, because you have gone through it yourself, Then you know what you are talking about So, don't ask God to make you a leader unless you are willing to be, as it were, God's guinea pig—willing for Him to lead you through the trials and fires of affliction, so that you will know how to comfort and instruct and sympathize with others who are afflicted, with others who are tempted; just as Our Lord Jesus was tempted, "For we have not a high priest which cannot be touched, with the feeling of our infirmities; but was in all points tempted like as we are, yet without sin..." Hebrews 4:15. And so to be able to sympathize with others, we must learn through bitter experience—a husbandman must be a partaker of the fruit. When I look back now, I remember when I was praying the

Lord said, "who doth deliver, who hath delivered." I look back over the highway of the past and my soul rejoiceth, and I can take comfort out of the fact that I know Him whom I believe. And I am persuaded that He is able to keep that which I have committed unto Him against that day. Why? Because as I look, I remember that He hath delivered me. Like the poet, I can say:

> Through many dangers, toils and snares,
> I have already come
> 'Tis grace hath brought me safe thus far
> and grace will lead me home.
>
> The Lord has promised good to me;
> His word my hope secures;
> And he my shield and portion be
> As long as life endures,
>
> Yea, when this heart and flesh shall fail,
> And mortal life shall cease,
> I shall possess, within the veil
> A life of joy and peace.[19]

---

[19] John Newton, "Amazing Grace" in John Newton and William Culper, Olney Hymns, s.l., authors, 1779.

My wife used to sing years ago a song, "Is not this the Land of Beulah," one verse of which goes like this:

I can see far down the mountain,
Where I wandered weary years,
Often hindered in my journey
By the ghosts of doubts and fears;

Broken vows and disappointments
Thickly sprinkled all the way,
But the Spirit led, unerring,
To the land I hold today.[20]

Yea, over the past, all of us can look back, We can count the times when we have given up and God has come in and rescued our souls. Many a time we have been sick, and the doctors have given us up and have not held out any hope for us. Neither the doctors nor ourselves had any hope, but somehow, we don't understand, God met us one morning or one night. We do not know whether he smiled or touched our hands, but he touched us, and one touch of His hand healed our body. And we got up, to the surprise of the doctors, came on out of the hospital and moved all around. Yea, God is able. He that delivereth back there is the one that delivereth us now from dangers seen and unseen, from death that rages at noonday, that flies upon the wings of the wind, in germs that

---

[20] William Hunter, "Is Not This the Land of Beulah?", s.l. s.n, 1882?

destroy us, in things we eat, and in the water we drink... Germs that can take you away in a moment, but for the mercy of the Lord, that doth deliver us continuously. We can say like Paul, "having obtained help from God, we continue until this day."

Jeremiah said, "It is of the Lord's mercy that we are not consumed, because His compassion faileth not—they are new every morning. And great is His faithfulness." Surely the Lord is good, and His mercy endureth forever. For, I am alive, and you are alive today, and then when you think of so many of your friends and relatives that are dead, and read in the papers of so many killed by car, by plane, by train and on the streets, So many dying with diseases, but you somehow live until this day. God hath delivered you constantly, continuously every day. Right now, He delivers you. But when you look to the future, wondering what shall befall you, and then you look back and think of Him who did deliver you, and then, you look around and you think of Him who is keeping you and delivering you, why you can snap your fingers in the face of the future with its varying vicissitudes, and say like David, "though the earth be removed, and though the mountains be carried into the midst of the sea, and the waves roar with the swelling thereof, the Lord is our refuge and our strength and the very present help in the time of trouble."

He who did deliver me, He who doth deliver me, will surely see me through the future. Yea, through many dangerous trials, you can say, I have already come. Tis grace that brought me safe thus far, and grace will lead me on. The

Lord has promised good to me, His word my faith secures. He will my shield and portion be, as long as life endures.

Yea, though he slays me, yet will I trust Him all the days of my appointed time. I will wait until my change comes, though after my skin worms destroy this body, yet in flesh, I shall see God. Mine eyes shall behold Him for myself and not another. For I know that my Redeemer lives, and He shall stand on earth in the latter day. Like Paul you can say "For we would not, brethren, have you ignorant of our trouble, which came to us in Asia, that we were despaired even of life: But we had the sentence of death in ourselves, that we should not trust in ourselves, but in God which raiseth the dead: Who delivereth us from so great a death, and doth deliver: in whom we trust that he will yet deliver us:

O God, our help in ages past,
Our hope for years to come –
Our shelter from the stormy blast
And our eternal home

Under the shadow of thy throne
Thy saints have dwelt secure;
Sufficient is Thine arm alone
And our defense is sure.[21]

---

[21] Isaac Watts, "O God, our Help in Ages Past" in The Psalms of David Imitated in the Language of the New Testament. N.l. Isaac Watts, 1719.

Therefore, I will trust in the Lord, I will trust in the Lord, I will trust in the Lord till I die.

                                          Amen.

Self-Glorification:
A Disqualification for God's Work
Is it a Sin to Straighten the Hair or Wear Sandals?

Dare any of us say with the French King, "The State is myself—I am the most important person in the Church?" If so, the Holy Spirit is not likely to use such unsuitable instruments; but if we know our places and desire to keep them with all humility, He will help us, and the Church will flourish beneath our care.[22]

Spurgeon.

The above statement is true. The spiritual poverty of both Ministers and Churches today, to my mind, is caused by pride and self-glorification of the Ministers and of the Churches in their particular faith or denomination, for God resisted the proud, but giveth grace unto the humble.

Pride is like the beautiful acacia, that lifts its head proudly above its neighbor plants forgetting that it too, like them, has its roots in the dirt.

For that reason, I would like to puncture the inflated bump of egotism and self-glorification that seems to be the make-up of a certain preacher who emphatically declares his

---

[22] Charles Haddon, "The Holy Spirit in Connection with ou Ministry" in The Complete Works of C. H. Spurgeon, s.l., s.n., s.d.

gospel is the only true gospel being preached, and moreover that he is the only one with the whole truth. [He] declares himself Bishop of all the Bishops in the world and like the French King dares to say, "I am the most important person in the Church." He speaks contemptuously concerning people who are saved or Christian people who have self-respect enough to go decent in their apparel condemning them as backslidden or unsaved because of the fact that they dress decently. This preacher doesn't even want them to straighten their hair or wear silk stockings. He claims that if they do, they are proud and are not saved. I want to answer him and all those who might be impressed by such ignorance. There is but one reason one would preach against wearing fine clothes, silk stockings and the straightening of hair, and that is, they that do such things are proud, and therefore guilty of the fatal sin of pride.

Let us study what the Scriptures say about pride. (Ps 10:2-4; Prov 8:13; 11:2; 13:10; 29:23: Dan 4:37; 5:20; I Tim 3:6; and I Jn 2:6, I would call your attention to Proverbs 13:10, for this particular passage says, "Only by pride cometh contention; but with the well advised is wisdom."

We find some preachers cannot preach unless they are contending and laying out some one, I have tried to discover wrong in the world and preach against that wrong, but I haven't tried to persecute people and call them names because they didn't agree with me. I have warily kept away from denominationalism, for there are good people in every Church and every denomination and every race, and the name of the denomination doesn't make any difference, for it is the truth and life they live that is important.

When it comes down to rebuking people because their faith is different, this I have scrupulously avoided I have simply tried to preach the Word and let the Word take care of itself.

As a certain philosopher has said, "Give the people light, and they will find their own way." In the Psalms, it is recorded, "Thy Word is a lamp unto my feet, and a light unto my pathway."

Let us continue our study together of the following Scriptures: Proverbs 1:6-18; 29:2-3; Daniel 4:37; 5:20: I Timothy 3:6; and I John 2:15-17. This last-mentioned Scripture says: "Love not the world, neither the things that are in the world. If any man love the world, the love of the Father is not in him. For all that is in the world, the lust of the flesh, and the lust of the eyes, and the pride of life is not of the Father, but is of the world. And the world passeth away, and the lust thereof but he that doeth the will of God abideth forever.

Let us first consider the etymology of the word "**Pride**." It means to envelope with smoke, (i.e., to inflate with self-conceit), to be proud means virtually the same thing. Taken from the word, "Hoop-er-ay-fan-os," meaning, appearing above other—loving to be conspicuous, that is. Haughty. Now pride is manifested in more ways than one. (Prov 6:17) It can be manifested in a proud look—whether you are well-groomed or raggedy. It can be unmanifested and be a matter of the heart. (Proverbs 16:5)

Everyone that is proud in heart is an abomination to the Lord. Though hand joined in hand, he shall not be unpunished. Proverbs 21:5 confirms this also. Pride can be manifested in stirring up strife, Prov 28:2:5. He that is of a proud heart, stirs up strife. The desire for preeminence was a cause of strife among the Apostles. Luke 22:24-27. "And there was also strife among them; which of them should be accounted the greatest. And he said unto them,

> The kings of the Gentiles exercise lordship over them, and they that exercise authority upon them are called benefactors, But ye shall not be so; but he that is greatest among you, let him be as the younger; and he that is chief. as he that doth serve. For whether is greater, he that sitteth at meat, or he that serveth? Is not he that sitteth at meat? But I am among you as he that serveth.

In this instance, pride evinces itself in dispute, strife over position. Now then, our Lord Jesus rebuked the disciples for the pride that evinced itself in contention and strife as to who would be the greatest. Now, it certainly must be conceded that when one thinks they are the only Samuel (prophet) that God has on the earth—the only one that has the truth, and the only one that is preaching the Gospel that is pride—such a one is proud, when he Bets himself up above everybody else and makes himself conspicuous, and then contends with everybody else they are inferior to him and is not saved unless they agree with him—that person shows beyond a doubt that he is proud.

You know there is a certain philosophy that tells us that when you find people excessively condemning a thing, it is because they are most guilty of it themselves. Now, if it is pride to lift oneself up and appear before others in a conspicuous sense, and as above everybody else, that's evidence of pride, for the Lord tells us that he that is greatest among you, let him be servant of all, and that type of servant never pretends he is bigger than his fellow workers or the one he works for, but he esteems his brothers better than himself.

The origin of pride seems to have been in the devil, Satan, as recorded in Ezekiel 28:12-18. Satan was lifted up because of his beauty. Not because he was beautiful, for God created him so, but his worship of his beauty, self-love, above his love of God, a narcissus complex, which was the reason for Satan being cast out of heaven.

Ezekiel 28:12-18 will tell you the origin of Satan, and the source and means whereby he became Satan, which was through pride.

> Son of man, take up a lamentation upon the King of Tyrus, and say unto him, Thus saith the Lord God. Thou sealest up the sum, full of wisdom and perfect in beauty. Thou hast been in Eden. the garden of God, every precious stone was thy covering, the sardis, topaz, and the diamond, the beryl, the onyx, and the jasper, the sapphire, the emerald,

and the carbuncle, and gold; the workmanship of thy tabrets, and of thy pipes was prepared in thee in the day that thou wast created. Thou art the anointed cherub that covereth; and I have set thee so; thou wast upon the holy mountain of God; thou hast walked up and down in the midst of the stones of fire.

Thou wast perfect in thy ways from the day that thou wast created, till iniquity was found in thee. By the multitude of thy merchandise, they have filled the midst of thee with violence, and thou hast sinned; therefore, I will cast thee as profane out of the mountain of God, and I will destroy thee, O covering cherub, from the midst of the stones of fire. Thine heart was lifted up because of thy beauty thou hast corrupted thy wisdom by reason of thy brightness, I will cast thee to the ground. I will lay thee before Kings, that they may behold thee. Thou hast defiled thy sanctuaries by the multitude of thine iniquities, by the iniquity of thy traffic; therefore, will I bring forth a fire from the midst of thee, it shall devour thee, and I will bring thee to ashes upon the earth in the sight of all them that behold thee.

Satan was perfect in his ways—he was all right in his way—he was created beautiful—with all those precious stones as ornaments and part of his personality, till the iniquity was found in him.

The fall of Satan after he became narcissus-complexed through pride and worshipped himself. And became self-sufficient unto himself, according to Isaiah 14:12-15, it was on this wise: "How art thou fallen from heaven, o Lucifer, son of the morning, how art thou cut down to the ground which didst weaken the nations. For thou hast said in thine heart, I will ascent into heaven, I will exalt my throne above the stars of God. I will sit upon the mount of the congregation in the sides of the north. I will ascent above the heights of the clouds: I will be like the Most High. Yet thou shalt be brought down to hell to the sides of the pit." There we have the origin of Satan through pride. Jesus speaking of this event in Luke 10:8 said. "I beheld Satan like lightning fall from heaven," thus showing the pre-existence of Christ before his incarnation.

In chapter 3 of I Timothy, verse 6, it says; "Not a novice, lest being filled up with pride, he fall into the condemnation of the devil." So, we find that the basic element of pride is the love of oneself, or the love of one's position. Here in this instance, the novice, through his premature ordination, can be made proud and fall like Satan did.

It is true that sin is our conscious misuse of impulses and instinctive passions which are part of our animal inheritance. In themselves these things are neutral and non-moral; indeed, they are not only biologically but morally necessary to our growth as men. They are the raw materials of our moral life, he very condition and occasion of virtue. Animals can neither sin nor achieve sainthood; man, as a responsible moral agent can and does. But the permanent wound in his nature which needs healing is deeper than anything biology can explain. The central typical, fatal sin is self-sufficient or pride. You cannot account for this as an evolutionary hangover from ape or tiger or even money. It is a completely irrational fact in a world which God has made."

Sin is self-sufficiency. It is putting self above God—building our lives by our own standard, directing the lives of others according to our notion of what is tight or wrong, organizing society to conform to our own wishes, our idea of things. In the final analysis, it is selfness, the antithesis of God-ness—it is the element that makes man think he is self-sufficient unto himself—loves himself, self-conceited, self-motivated So we find that sin, therefore, is selfness.

When one has his center in God, he becomes God conscious. One who has his center in self becomes self-conscious, which is pride. Moreover, he becomes self-conceited, self-willed and self-glorifying. A preacher who will not preach the truth can be considered proud. The Bible says that he that preaches not according tm sound doctrine, be is proud, knows nothing. According to I Timothy 6:2-4, "one can be proud even of his ordination as a Minister." According to I Timothy 3:6... hence we are admonished not to ordain a novice—a beginner—lest he be lifted up with pride. I guess that accounts for a lot of proud preachers, who have been prematurely ordained before they were properly trained, and temperamentally matured sufficiently to be ordained. They have let pride in ordination puff them up.

Alazo-na-ea means boasting. A boastful preacher can be a proud preacher, Anything that emanates from self. A man that talks excessively about himself. For instance, a certain preacher boastfully declares he is the only one preaching the truth. One can be proud of his wisdom or gift or achievements, as such, he becomes obnoxious to God. One ought always consider that they are unprofitable servants.

Pride does not evince itself only in wearing clothes. A certain preacher bases his superiority on the fact that he preaches a woman shouldn't straighten her hair or wear silk stockings, or dress in divers colors. There is such a thing as self-respect—one does not necessarily have to be proud because they are well dressed. People dressed in different kind of colors are not necessarily proud or backslidden. God does not resent people dressing in different colors, I am sure. If it so, why would he put flowers on every hilltop, birds of rare plumage in the trees, and carpet the earth in spring with green, and tack it down with laughing daffodils and daisies.

People are much more proud of their opinions than they are of their clothes. They are much prouder of their homes and fine cars than they are of silk stockings or ring on their fingers.

This preacher preached about a woman not wearing silk stockings or straightening her hair, but he rides in a big car, and even boasts a chauffeur. I think one would be prouder of a fine sleek shining car than one would be of silk stockings. Don't worry yourself about pride. You keep humble, and the Lord will keep you, if you let him. Now people are much prouder of their opinion, prouder of their homes and their cars than they are of silk stockings or rings on their fingers.

What shall we say about wearing rings?

The prodigal son, when he returned home. His father (who represents God metaphorically) put a robe on him and a ring on his finger, put shoes upon his feet (sandals)—and by the by, they were not shoes that were closed in either as we today wear them—they were shoes with the toes out because a person wore sandals back in those days, and My Lord Jesus wore sandals. And I don't think that a woman wearing shoes with her toes out is necessarily wicked carnal or backslid, for they did not have any shoes as we know them—there were no shoes as we know them back in Palestine in those days. When I was in Palestine the folks mostly went barefooted or wore sandals, even with no socks on.

In the 15th Chapter of Luke, you read that the Father put a ring on His son's finger, if God (the Father) could put a ring upon the finger of the prodigal Bon, then I would like to know what is wrong with a husband putting a ring on his wife's finger, or for anyone to wear a ring for that matter.

Now, as to Scriptures speaking about clothes and wearing of jewelry, I would like to call your attention to I Peter 1:14, and 3:1-8, which is the main scripture which this preacher bases his argument. "As obedient children not fashioning yourselves according to the former lusts in your ignorance... But as he which hath called you is holy, so be ye holy in all manner of conversation. Because it is written, be ye holy, for I am holy.

Likewise, ye wives, be in subjection to your own husbands, that, if any obey not the word, they also may without the word be won by the conversation of the wives; while they behold your chaste conversation coupled with fear. Whose adorning let it not be that outward adorning of plaiting the hair, and of wearing of gold, or of putting on of apparel; but let it be the hidden man of the heart, in that which is not corruptible, even the ornament of a meek and quiet spirit, which is in the sight of God of great price.

For after this manner in the old time the holy women also, who trusted in God, adorned themselves, being in subjection unto their own husbands. Even as Sara obeyed Abraham, calling him lord; whose daughters ye are, as long as ye do well, and are not afraid with any amazement. Likewise, ye husband dwell with them according to knowledge. Giving honour unto the wife, as unto the weaker vessel, and as being heirs together of the grace of life; that your prayers be not hindered. Finally, be ye all of one mind, having compassion one of another; love as brethren, be pitiful, be courteous.

I want to make this observation that there is no place in the Bible which speaks against straightening the hair. I want to challenge any preacher that can show me any place in the

Bible which forbids straightening of hair. It says plaiting of hair. You don't need to worry about plaiting the hair—many folks don't have that much.

I desire further to observe that in speaking concerning the wearing of gold and putting on of apparel the 3rd verse, which states, "whose adorning, let it not be," is from a Greek word "OU" (before a vowel OUK) before an aspirated vowel OUCH; does not express full and direct negation or prohibition, independently and absolutely, and not depending upon any condition expressed or implied.

In other words, "Let it not be" does not mean an absolute prohibition. The emphasis of a holiness woman should not be upon her outward adornment, but let it be the hidden man of the heart, in that which is not corruptible, even the ornament of a meek and quiet spirit, which is in the sight of God of great price. She has to have outward adorning. But it should not be on her mind and thought. It should not be the main emphasis—the main emphasis should be on the inner man not the outer man. Whose adorning? The thing she should be proud of, the thing she should cultivate more, the thing that she should esteem and treasure highest, should be the inner man. The adorning should not be so much paint and powder on her face, or what hat she wears. That is all a matter of her choice and taste. But she should be more careful of her inner adornment than her outer adornment.

"Whose adorning it should not be." It does not say she should not have adorning, but don't let it be the outward adorning, plaiting of hair, pompadours, and chignons and all kinds of styles—let it not be that the wearing of gold, etc.

Sometimes you find a woman with a half dozen bracelets on her arm. This is superfluous, vain and should be condemned. But it doesn't read that she shouldn't wear any gold at all—that is she shouldn't even wear a gold ring that her husband puts on her finger as a token of love; or that a man can't have a ring as a token at love from his wife when she marries him. Also, it doesn't mean that if you wear gold you are backslid a transgressor of the will of God. If it means absolute prohibition, then let us be consistent and follow through as the logic of the sentence compels, which reads: "Whose adorning let it not be plaiting of hair; she is forbidden to plait her hair, also to wear any gold or put on apparel, so then she shouldn't wear any clothes; she should go naked—God forbid!

How stupid it is to consider it as absolute prohibition. This is a comparative illustration—that is the outward man with his plaiting of hair. Wearing gold and fine clothes, versus the inner man, with his virtues of love, joy, peace, goodness, faith, kindness—in other words, the fruits of the Spirit recorded in Galatians 5:22-25. That is the ornament of the inner man, the sum total of a meek and quiet spirit, which is a pearl of great price. Now in reference to the phrase, "Let it not be," the chief source of error is in the interpretation of this text. For the language of, the Bible is pervaded by a Hebraistic spirit. Marked by oriental modes of conception which are in many respects quite different from those of our own people. Further, it is to be observed that the language of Scripture is, as a general thing, not philosophical, but poetical.

A poetical language, a language, I mean of a poetical people, delights alternately to diminish and argument, that the imagination of the hearer or reader may be exercised in adding or retrenching. (e.g., Lk 14:26; 16: 15; Eph 5:11 and I Jn 3:9).

It delights by turns to make absolute that which is relative, and relative that which is absolute. (Luke 14:12) "Then said he also to him that bade him. When thou makest a **dinner** or a supper, call not thy friends, nor thy brethren, neither thy kinsmen nor thy rich neighbours, lest "they also bid thee again, and a recompence be made thee. But when thou makest a feast, call the poor, the maimed, the lame, the blind; and thou shalt be blessed; for they cannot recompense thee; for thou shalt be recompensed at the resurrection of the just." This is stated as an absolute prohibition of inviting friends, kindred, rich neighbour's, and a command to invite exclusively the other class.

We know very well that our Lord did not mean to be thus understood, nor does anyone ever thus interpret. Naturally, and as a matter of course, men will invite kindred, the rich and others, and for this, which is done because of mere natural affection or social reciprocity, they will get no religious reward. But it is so much more important on religious grounds alai in hope of a divine reward, to invite the poor and suffering, that our Lord speaks as if compared with this the former must not be done at all; e.g. Proverbs 8:10; Jeremiah 7:22-23. Also, I Timothy 6:17-19 says, as a proof of this:

Charge them that are rich in this world, that they be not high minded, nor trust in uncertain riches, but in the living God, who giveth us richly all things to enjoy. That they do good, that they be rich in good works, ready to distribute, willing to communicate. Laying up in store "for themselves a good foundation against the time to come, that they may lay hold on eternal life.

So, with Matthew 9:13, Hosea 6:6. All this seems obvious. but does not the same principle apply to I Peter 3:1.

Whose adorning let it not be the outward adorning of plaiting the hair, and of wearing of gold, or of putting on of apparel; but let it be the hidden man of the heart... the ornament of a meek and quiet spirit...

The apostle does not mean to be understood as really prohibiting all outward adorning, any more than the other passages prohibit kindred, receiving silver, or offering sacrifices, he means to say emphatically that the most beautiful outward adorning, such as women so highly prize, is as nothing in comparison with that imperishable adorning of the spirit which in the sight of God is of great price.

Another observation is Proverbs 8:10 where it is forbidden to receive gold or silver:

> Receive my instruction, and not silver, and knowledge rather than choice gold, for wisdom is better than rubies and all things that may be desired are not to be compared to it.

I am sure the preacher does not consider this an exact prohibition. Now what I am trying to get to is that the Bible tells you not to receive gold, not to receive money, but it is not an exact prohibition. It is a comparative illustration, showing that wisdom is more to be desired than gold than rubies, and if you have to make a choke between the two, take wisdom. I bound you that that preacher hasn't stopped taking money. It is an absolute statement here, designed to be understood just as in I Peter, 3rd Chapter, in reference to women wearing apparel, plaiting of hair, etc.

In that chapter, what is meant is that in this instance, the most beautiful outward adornment which women so highly prize is as nothing in comparison with the imperishable adorning of the inner man which means that a woman that has an ornament of a meek and quiet spirit is much more beautiful in God's sight than all the hair-do, and all the cosmetics, and all the beautiful gowns, silk stockings, etc., that a woman tan put on her outer personality. It is an absolute statement designed to be understood relatively but also intended by this absolute form to the very emphatic and impressive. If this view of the passage be correct, then thousands of well-meaning Christians, and more than one, organized body, have vainly striven to eradicate the natural love of ornament, merely because they did not consider that the energetic language of Scripture frequently puts absolute for relative; and at the same time thousands of others, through the same mistake, have failed to appreciate the urgent and vehement exhortation to care less for outward. And more for inward adornment. (Lk 18:14) It generalizes that which is particular and particularizes that which is general; takes duty sometimes at its summer, sometimes at its base.

And so, you understand, friends, that God is not objecting to your hair looking nice, nor objecting to clothes that become your personality, so that you may glorify Him in your bodies and your spirit which are His. Of course, the world will object to you if you dress up like a Christmas tree, and look like a freak and carry on like a fool. The Scriptures condemn women wearing clothes of a man. (Deut 22:5)

The woman shall not wear that which is pertaineth to a man, neither shall a man put on a woman's garment; all that do so are an abomination unto the Lord, thy God."

Dress as becomes your personality, with modesty and with decorum, and a certain sense of taste—something to synchronize your personality with your God and that which is proper and that which is up-right and that which is according to I Timothy 2:9:

> In like manner also, that women adorn themselves with modest apparel, with shamefacedness and sobriety: not with braided hair, or gold, or pearls, or costly array, but that which becometh women professing godliness, with good works.

Watch Your Step

In going about the world, we notice on street cars, subways, buses, etc. these terse words, "WATCH YOUR STEP," "SAFETY FIRST," etc., for there is always a danger of being killed; it is good therefore to be watchful. But we should think of these words in a spiritual way. What about your soul? "What shall it profit a man if he gains the whole world and lose his soul." You should see that your soul is saved first. Watch your step. Where shall your soul spend Eternity?

> As the Lord liveth, and as your soul liveth, there is but one step between you and death. (I Sam 20:13)

Death is never idle. Among the millions on earth, there falls on the average, one every second, sixty every minute, 3,600 every hour, 86,400 every day. One in about thirty to thirty-five of the population per annum.

Seventy years is the extreme limit, thirty-five the ordinary limit, with few exceptions. Death is one event that happen to us all. (Eccl. 9:3) It is inevitable. What man is he that liveth and shall not see death? The longest life will come to an end. The young may die; the old must die, for it is appointed unto man once to die, and after death the judgment. (Heb 9:27)

The Time of Death is Uncertain

For man also knoweth not his time; as the fishes that are taken in an evil net, and as birds that are caught in a snare; so are the sons of men snared in an evil time, when it fallen suddenly upon them. Nothing is as sure as death and nothing is so uncertain as time. You may be too old to live; you can never be too young to die; you ought therefore to live every hour as if you were to die the next. For as you live there is but one step between you and death. It flies upon every breeze, in the form of death-dealing germs of disease, that you, even now, may be inhaling, which may take you the final step to death. It lurks around the corner in the form of an enemy, or stalks about in the streets in the form of racing automobiles. It is ever present, even at night when thou art alone at home and all is dark, and thou hast retired, death's sinister approach may be through escaping gas which may make your bed your cooling board, or it may come through defective wiring that may make your home your Crematory, leaving only the ashes of your dead body as witness of the uncertainty of life.

The Cause of Death

"The wages of sin is death." (Rom 6:23) By one man sin entered into the world and death by sin; and so death passed upon all men, for all have sinned. Death is the fruit of sin, its natural result, its inevitable harvest. Oh! sinner, Oh! people, consider your ways.

Can a man take fire into his bosom and not be burned?" Neither can you sin without dying. Stop therefore your self-destructive ways before it is too late. If you walk the earth without God, you will be unfit for heaven. Don't allow sin to destroy you and cast you on the heap of human wreckage. Don't allow sin to have dominion over you. Get rid of sin by coming to Jesus your Saviour. In all times and throughout the world there is none to be pitied more than the man that dies without God, whose heart was filled with ambition and determination, but sad to say, was empty of God. When such a one draws near the valley and shadow, the darkness of death settles down upon him. Soul empty of God has not light to light the way, the earth swings from under him, down he descends through darkness and gloominess and terror. With a wail of despair, he goes to his lone home to wait the judgment. O friends, we ought to be willing to give up sin, yea, glad, because it is the worst enemy of the human race. Sin it is that is destroying our homes; by it, our children are being dragged down to shame, disease, dishonor and death. Sin is the cause of murders, thefts, insanity. Sin fills our jails with criminals, our insane institutions with patients.

Prepare to Meet Thy God!

Considering the above statements to be true, what manner of person ought ye to be? Ye ought not delay one moment to prepare for that ever approaching ever present, uncertain inevitable event, death. If you allow death to come upon you in your unprepared condition you shall be doomed forever. What an interest then attaches to this moment of every man's earthly life—to the parting breath on which the soul passes away from its mortal tenement. As death at the solemn moment finds him—believing or not believing on the only Saviour, reconciled to God or still alienated from Him—

pardoned or unpardoned; so must judgment–yea–so must eternity find him—accepted and saved or cast away and lost. In either case what an END? —MY GOD! But thanks be unto God our Saviour, there is a way of escape; the Word of God says:

"Verily, verily I say unto you, "he that believeth on Me hath everlasting life. (Jn 6:47) He that heareth my words and believeth on him that sent me hath everlasting life and shall not come into condemnation but is passed from death unto life." Jesus said, "I am the way, the truth and the life," His way was to the Cross—when He died for every man's sins. All we as sheep had gone astray; we had turned everyone too his own way and the Lord laid on Him the iniquity of us all. (Isa 53:6)

Yea, God so loved the world that He gave His only begotten Son that whosoever believeth on Him should not perish but have eternal life. (Jn 3:16-17) Our sins have been washed away by the blood of Jesus who died that we might live, yea, and not die, if only we believe on His name and accept His salvation by faith and obedience. For he that believeth not shall be damned. Repent therefore and be baptized every one of you in the Name of Jesus Christ for the remission of sins, and ye shall receive the gift of the Holy Ghost. (Acts 2:38)

Then whatever may betide, if death should come tomorrow, and your body be laid in the cold ground and the worms feed upon it, yea, though after the skin, worms destroy the body, yet in the flesh shall I see God. For when Christ, who is your life shall appear in that day, even the day of the Lord, then shall he a pear with Him in Glory. For the Lord shall descend from heaven with a shout and the voice of the archangel, and the trump of God; the dead in Christ shall rise first: Then we which are alive and remain shall be caught up, together with them in the cloud, to be with the Lord in the air.

Part III - Lawsonian Doctrine on Women and Marriage

Lawson's Stand on Women Ministers

Bishop Lawson built a movement on oneness dogma that included a rigid restriction on women from ordained ministry and other leadership positions. His views on the issue were based on exegesis of Scripture that led him to conclude that women did not have equal rights with men in the ecclesial hierarchy. He believed that female roles established in the Old Testament and echoed by the Apostle Paul are transcultural. So, for him, for women to "assume the role of leadership or equality with men, putting themselves as pastors and administering the rights and duties of the church such as giving communion, baptizing, burying the dead, marrying etc., is an error not so small. [S]he is forbidden by the apostolic rule and order in the sphere of men in the Spirit-filled church, to usurp authority in preaching."[23]

Upon his arrival to Harlem, he ran revivals for Pastor Susan Lightford, founder of the Kings Chapel Assembly When he established his first two churches, he sent for one of Lightford's ministers, Elder Austin A. Layne, Sr. to pastor his St. Louis work. Though he was aware of the women pastors in his parent organization, the Pentecostal Assemblies of the World, Lawson challenged the Pentecostal norms of his day, which allowed the openness for women. And though he had seen strong

---

[23] Robert C. Lawson, "A Woman Shall Compass A Man: Jeremiah 31:22." *For The Defense of The Gospel: Writings of Bishop R.C.* Lawson (New York: Church of Our Lord Jesus Christ, 1971), 26.

women at the helm of other organizations such as Mother Rosa Horn in Harlem, in establishing his denomination, the Church of Our Lord Jesus Christ, restrictions on women have remained intact throughout the life of the organization.

Lawson felt that a true return to Pentecost required that doctrine be "built upon the prophets and apostles." His scriptural understanding was influenced by Cyrus I. Scofield's biblical exegesis. He held to the divine authority and inerrancy of the Scripture.[24] And his hermeneutical process was based on the Bible Reading Methodology used by many of the first-generation Classical Pentecostals and Holiness believers. To develop his position on women in the church he would, "trace out topics in Scripture and then synthesize the biblical data into a doctrine."

He enclosed egalitarianism within a soteriological understanding, teaching that the salvation provided by the blood of Jesus placed men and women into the body of Christ through the baptism of the Holy Spirit. However, he held that this process did not transcend to ecclesial and family relationships. Instead, he saw the submission of the women to the church's male leadership as invoked by the love she has for the church and the church as the bride of Christ loves the bridegroom. For him, this relationship causes mutual submission between male leadership and the women in the church.

Within the Church of Our Lord Jesus Christ, a premillennial theology allowed Lawson to partner with

---

[24] See Cyrus I. Scofield, Scofield Reference Bible, New York: Oxford University Press, 1917.

women congregants for the kingdom of God. They were able to fulfill Acts 2 in light of Pauline doctrines and walk in their evangelistic calling. Since this theology holds to an eschatological vision of the soon return of Christ there is a motivation for both men and women to work to bring souls into the kingdom of God through the baptism of the Holy Spirit.

Missionary Praxis

Lawson allowed and encouraged women who felt the "call of an evangelist" to become missionaries. The Missionary Department was established in 1923 as the Women's Missionary Society. These "called" women assisted pastors in ministering to the needs of the congregation, visiting the sick, preparing females for water baptism, witnessing, tarrying with souls seeking salvation. Their duties parallel those of the third-century deaconess who visited the sick women in their homes, received baptized women when they emerged for the water… and acted as intermediaries between women and male clergy."[25]

Women in Ministry

While restricting women from ordination and ecclesiastical hierarchy, Ethel Mae Bonner contends, that Lawson was building his organization on the backs of

---

[25] Barbara J. MacHaffe, *Her Story: Women In Christian Tradition* Second Edition (Minneapolis: Fortress Press, 2006), 19.

women.[26] Therefore, these women were founders of churches, since several Community Sunday Schools established by senior missionaries evolved into newly planted churches.

Elizabeth Brown served as the first president of the COOLJC Missionary Society from 1923 to 1931. Missionaries had founded and established churches. Isa Robinson co-founded the White City Church of Christ in Hamilton Township, New York. Mildred Brown's home prayer meetings lead to the formation of the Waterway Church in Virginia. Ivy Bell established seven churches through her community Sunday Schools. Louise Virginia Williams founded Churches in Jacksonville and Tampa, Florida. Lillian Fields McCarthy founded Refuge Temple Annex in Bronx, New York through her Williamsbridge Prayer Band. In 1974 Lila Stevenson donated her home to start the Englishtown Community Church in Englishtown, New Jersey.

The first foreign missionary for the denomination was Margaret Giles Johnson who traveled to Liberia. West Africa during World War II to establish the Zuie Refuge Mission among the Gola Tribe. Through Johnson's efforts and sacrifice the COOLJC had seven churches by 1958 and eventually, a school and health clinic would be established.

By 1956 the first church was dedicated in the Dominican Republic through the missionary efforts of Marie Whyte, and by 1988 there were five missions established through her work. The success of COOLJC in

---

[26] Ethel Mae Bonner, *This Is My Story*, S.n.: privately printed, August 25, 1988, 8.

the West Indies and the Dominican Republic was due in large measure also to the untiring and ceaseless efforts of Mother Delphia Perry who also made many trips there, and continually sent clothing, money, and supplies from the Missionary Department."[27] Perry was appointed denominational missionary president by Lawson in 1952 and served as a local missionary for the mother church for thirty years.

In 1926, When Lawson saw the need to establish the denomination's educational arm for the church as a training center for ministers, missionaries, and laypersons, he established the Church of Christ Bible Institute. An overwhelming number of its students have been women. When that institution began offering bachelor's degrees, a female student, Mamie DeSilva, was the first to be awarded the degree. When Lawson was established a boarding school bearing his name for elementary and high school students in Southern Pines, North Carolina, he appointed Isa Winans as a principle in 1959, a position she held until 1969.

The impact of this Lawsonian doctrine is observed through the first-generation denominations that developed from his organization. These groups held to Lawson's theological concept of women's ministry. With Lawsonian restrictions on women in ministry, it was noted in the July 1949 issue of Ebony magazine that Lawson, Sherrod Johnson and Smallwood Williams were the most

---

[27] Mabel Thomas, "The Life of Bishop R. C. Lawson and the History of the Church of Our Lord Jesus Christ of the Apostolic Faith, Inc.," in Arthur Anderson, ed., For The Defense of the Gospel (New York: Church of Our Lord Jesus Christ, 1972), 20.

widely listened to radio preachers within the African American community. With their radio ministry, they proclaimed the Pentecostal message and preached against women preachers.

Lawson's successor, the late Bishop William Lee Bonner, continued to hold that the church's standard for women's ministry in the COOLJC should never change; he believed that if it is changed that it would remove the church from its apostolic setting, Bonner states:

> I direct your attention to some areas of concern, specially the role of women of the Church of Our Lord Jesus Christ. The women by their share numbers, will influence the rise and fall of the Church. The women will influence whether we will be a true Pentecostal body or whether we will compromise and succumb to doctrines and other religious teachings. They will influence whether we will adapt to women and allow them to be preachers. I say this not because I am against women, but because of the tremendous pull external influences can have on them; influences that are diametrically opposed to our biblical position on this... matter.[28]

Bonner held that it is divine order that men hold headship in the home and in the church and that the Women's Liberation movement threatens this divine

---

[28] William L. Bonner, State on Course and Add Thou To It. Unpublished, n.p. n.d), 7.

concept. His view has taken a toll on his personal life. In a letter dated August 10, 1983 his wife, Ethel Mae Bonner mentions being casted "in the traditional COOLJC woman's mold.[29] To which Bonner responds in a letter dated September 14, 1983, to his wife which he states, "you stated that you have rejected the traditional Church of Our Lord Jesus Christ woman's role; and that it was not God's plan for you, nor is it now your desire to permit your life to be governed according to the teachings of the Church of Our Lord Jesus Christ, that which affects on women's role."[30] He further stated that he had to follow the teachings of the church because it is "Apostolic," and that they are on a "collision course."

Bonner codified and attempted to give clarity to the Lawsonian doctrine has complied a Doctrinal Guide for his local COOLJC. In his section on "A Woman's Place in the Church," he defines the word "preachers,"

> There are those who believe a woman can be a preacher as well as a man, this I doubt seriously. Webster says the word "preach" means to proclaim the gospel, deliver a sermon or to urge acceptance of the gospel. According to this interpretation then every saved person is a preach(er) because all of us do urge others to be saved and accept the gospel of Jesus Christ. So, a preacher is more

---

[29] Ethel Mae Bonner, Letter to Bishop William L Bonner. (Flower Pentecostal Heritage Center, Springfield, MO, August 9, 1983).

[30] William L. Bonner, Letter to Ethel Mae Bonner, (Flower Pentecostal Heritage Center, Springfield MO, September 14, 1983).

than just a person who urges an acceptance. He is one that is called to authority over all. So, your biblical meaning of the word "preach" is not what Webster says it is, but is the call of one to a position of authority and power above all.[31]

Pioneer member, Wilhelmena Wheatley contends that Bishop Lawson wasn't against women preaching, he was against women pastoring a church." Indeed, he used women to develop his movement. Despite being refused ordination or the pastorate, many women established churches, became domestic and foreign missionaries or raised funds for the denomination.

Helen Smith was excommunicated for her active involvement in the preaching ministry. Early in her involvement in a South Carolina COOLJC congregation, she felt called to preach. When she began visiting hospitals praying and ministering to the sick, she was informed that restrict her such that [she] could visit the sick, bathe them and feed them, but... not lay hands on them. They said [she] was wrong, and going against the church doctrine if [she] prayed for them. "I went along with this for years..." Smith contended" But later, she offered, that,

> When God saved me, He blessed me with the gift of prophecy, with the gifts of healing and, with a

---

[31] William L. Bonner, The Doctrinal Guide of Solomon's Temple. Unpublished manuscript. Detroit: Solomon's Temple Church of Our Lord Jesus Christ of the Apostolic Faith, n.d.

strange anointing to cast out demons… I did not want to offend these people, so I asked God to take away my gifts and give them to the pastor.[32]

But God did not do that and when Smith, eventually, began preaching, she was disfellowshipped from the church and established the Cainhoy Miracle Revival Center in Huger, South Carolina. She later became Apostle Smith. After establishing fifteen Miracle Revival churches throughout the South and the West Indian island of Trinidad.

Smith was only one among several women who found Lawson and COOLJC's position too restrictive and left to find a more suitable venue for their calling. Rev. Dr. Joan S. Parrott who was raised in the COOLJC under the pastorate of her father, Bishop James Parrott, Sr., currently holds the position of executive minister at the First Baptist Church in Hampton, Virginia. Dr. Phyllis E. Carter, the wife of former COOLJC bishop, Ronald H. Carter, is a professional counselor and family therapist and founder of Living, Learning and Growing Counseling Services. Rev. Jean Bennett is the overseer of True Vine Covenant Remedy Chapel Ministries International which consists of three churches in Liberia, West Africa. Overseer Bennett was ordained by former COOLJC minister, Kent Branch, pastor of Pilgrim Cathedral of Decatur Georgia.

For these women who saw the invocation of the Lawsonian doctrine as hindering the fulfillment of God's

---

[32] Helen Smith, *You're Going to Be Somebody* (Mobile AL: Gazelle Press, 1999), 130-131.

calling in their lives and launched out of the traditional COOLJC role the observations made by Kimberly Alexander, that

> from the beginning of the Pentecostal movement, however, church leaders struggled with the place of women in the church. What began as a dynamic and egalitarian movement where "everybody's a preacher," regardless of race or gender, quickly developed into a more structured and governed network new denominations and organizations, led by strong men.[33]

They saw the strong male dominated leadership intension with the modern-day Pentecostal movement birthed through the Azusa Street Revival under William J. Seymour.

Interestingly, the concept of the Lawsonian doctrine evolved a culture that is not official church dogma because Lawson never established a creed on the subject which has been primarily passed down to COOLJC congregants through an oral tradition (i.e., sermons and Bible classes). The official manual of the COOLJC, the Disciple Book does not address the subject at all though it does contain Lawson's teaching on divorce and remarriage.

---

[33] Kimberly Alexander, The History and Context of Church of God Leadership, Women in Leadership" Women in Leadership: the Pentecostal Perspective, Cleveland, The Center Leadership, 14.

In the following, Lawson addresses those churches and denominations that relied on Jeremiah 31:22 (How long wilt thou go about, O thou backsliding daughter? for the Lord hath created a new thing in the earth, A woman shall compass a man.) to validate the ideology that during this dispensation of grace women can preach the gospel Lawson would respond using his tenets. He challenged their interpretation by exegeting this Scripture within a historical context, interpreting the text, "A woman shall compass a man," as the prophetic restoration of Israel, for he held that the Old Testament prophets did not see the church. For Lawson, "the text in its remotest sense does not suggest women taking leadership away from men, nor of them being on parity with men in the ministry. Indeed, for him, "the context does not deal with the subject of women preachers at all and he insisted that Jeremiah the prophet did not have in mind women preaching or the church; neither did he see the church age or our times."[34]

---

[34] Lawson, "A Woman Shall Compass A Man," 3.

A Woman Shall Compass A Man

The text has reference to Israel's restoration and its conversion to Jehovah, its Messiah in the latter times. The word "compass" has no later interpretation. ln its etymological analysis in any sense as meaning "surpassing," or "supplanting." The Idea that is going around among women preachers, so-called, and the construction that some are putting upon the phase that women shall compass a man." Is that Women preachers shall and are surpassing men; yea, supplanting them, that is, taking their place in the church and ministry of the Lord? The text in its remotest sense does not suggest women taking the leadership away from men: nor of them being on parity with men in the ministry. The context does not deal with the subject of women preachers at all.

Jeremiah the prophet, did not have in mind women preaching or the church, for he did not prophesy concerning the church, neither did he see the church age or our times. He prophesied rather about Israel his people, their then present state, and the immediate going into captivity and despair, and their future restoration and glory. He saw with other prophets the restoration of Israel in the latter times. Like Hosea, who prophesied on this wise, "And my God shall cast them away because they did not hearken unto Him and they shall be wanderers among the nations." (Hos 9:17) "For I will be unto Ephraim as lion and as a lion to the house of Judah.

I, even I, will tear and go away, I will take away, and go away I will take away, and none shall rescue him. I will go and return to my places until they acknowledge their offense, and seek my face. In their affliction they will seek me early." (Hos 5:14) And again, "The children of Israel shall abide many days without a king, and without a sacrifice, and without an image, and without an ephod, and without teraphim. Afterward, shall the children of Israel return, and seek the Lord their God, and David their King and shall fear the Lord and His goodness In the latter days." (Hos 3:4-5) Hosea, in the spirit of prophecy heard Israel exclaiming, "come, and let us return unto the Lord for He hath torn, and He will heal us, He hath smitten and he will bind us up. After two days He revive us; in the third day, He will raise us up, and we will live in his sight, then shall we know, If we follow to know to know will of the Lord, His going forth is prepared as the morning; And He shall come unto us as the rain, as the latter and former rain unto the earth."

This is really what it meant by "a woman shall compass a man," Israel the woman, seeking and wooing her Lord, Jehovah, Who heretofore had sought and wooed her to whom she bad been unfaithful and adulterous, yea, she in her last days shall seek her Lord, shall compass Him as it is recorded further in this book, (2:6-7), therefore, behold, I will hedge up the way the way with thorn and make a wall that she shall not find her paths. And she shall follow after her lovers, but she shall not overtake them; and she shall seek them but shall not find them then shall say, I will return to my first husband; for then was it better than now.

Therefore, through God dealing with her, she shall be brought to repentance and conversion through her chastisement and experiences. From the beginning of time, the Lord has been seeking and entreating Israel; but a new thing shall come to pass in the latter times, Israel shall seek and entreat her Lord; she shall "compass" the man Christ Jesus, who she had denounced and openly rejected, and they chose Caesar, saying, "we have no king but Caesar."

Some may dissent from this interpretation and say that it does not mean what I have set forth in the above, but one thing is obvious, it does not mean that woman shall surpass, or outstrip, or pass by the men in the ministry, because it has no reference to preaching at all, as many so foolishly affirm; their argument is, that men are failing God in these last days by not living, so God must of necessity use women Instead to put over the program. The assertion in itself is absurd, as touching God and the ministry.

First of all, God is all creative Power within Himself, and could thereby create men who would stand, if all who now live had failed to live up to the requirements and qualifications of the ministry. Besides, the fixed eternal standard and counsel of God is, that man is God's glory, and He will not give His glory to another. For He is God and changes not, sayeth His word. Now, for women to assume that they are rising above, or surpassing men in either strength or cleanness of life, and are living better lives than the men, therefore they are superseding them in preaching, being better qualified on the above-mentioned grounds, it is pure presumption in the last degree, and has no basis in the Holy Scripture, of facts, experience, or history.

Experience does not bear out the assumption of the women that are cleaner than men, therefore are more qualified for the ministry. And prophecy is being fulfilled in our day, that a woman shall compass a man; or that God is unable to put His program over through man, because He cannot keep man straight, and has turned, as a last resort last resort, to woman to save the day and the world. To the contrary, experience bears out that women fall and sin more than men; at least, as such, for whenever a man falls in sin, he usually falls with a woman. Wherein then are the women any cleaner than the men? Many times, one man defiles four or five women, on the basis of percentage. Therefore, women fall four to one. In reference to all other ways of falling in sin within each sex, each has its failure to purge them from pride and the "holier than thou attitude," and to affirm their souls again the assertion of Isaiah, "all flesh is as grass."

God and His Word hath not and cannot fail, even if all men should fail. God must, of his own omnipotence, uphold His counsel that He hath declared should stand. That power belongeth to God. He hath said and always will have men who will obey His voice and He can use, or we would limit the power of God to less than that of man.

The Scriptures state definitely that women are the weaker vessels and there is no doubt about it being true. God cannot lie; He said in I Peter 3:5-7, "They shall be subject to their husbands;" the wife being the weaker vessel in every respect should be in subjection, or submission to the will, and obedient to the authority of the man (that is), husband. This conduct will most likely win for them the favor of God and honor from men. God would have a resemblance of Christ's authority over the church held forth in the man over the woman. Christ is the head of the church to protect and deliver it to save and supply it with all good and secure it from evil, and so is the man over the woman, to keep her from error, to provide for and instruct her according to his ability. It is not then an absolute slavish subjection that is required, but a loving subordination and obedience, to prevent disorder and confusion. God in nature, and by His will hath made this subordination. "I suffer not a woman to teach to usurp authority over the man. (1 Tim 2:12), and the reason is added: for Adam was first formed, then Eve. Adam was not deceived, but the woman, being deceived, was in transgression.

It is not permitted unto women to preach in the church sayeth the Scripture (I Cor 1:3), otherwise they may teach, yea, they should teach both by example and good behavior, and by their services by doctrinal instruction among themselves, those whose action and lives becometh holiness. The words of King Lemuel, the prophecy his mother taught him. Such a woman is praised, she openeth her mouth with wisdom, and in her tongue is the law of kindness (Prov 31:26). Their ministry is therefore limited according to the Word of God to teaching, prophesying, and helping in the subordinate role with the minister. But not on equality with or superior to men. (Acts 2:17, Tit 2:3-6, etc.) The word of God and the gospel of Jesus Christ are pure, excellent and glorious by themselves, and their excellency should be expressed in the lives and conduct of His people especially in relative duties; failure in this being disgrace and greatly to the reproach of Christianity, paralyzing the power and effect of the gospel ministry to those whom Christ came to save.

For women to assume the role of leadership or equality with men, putting themselves as pastors and administering the rights and duties of the church and ministry, such as giving communion, baptizing, burying the dead, marrying etc., is an error not so small. She or no one else has any vestige of authority in the Scripture. In the first place, a woman cannot qualify for ordination as a Bishop or Elder, because it is recorded in I Timothy 3:2, "This is a true saying, If a man desires the office of a bishop, he desireth a good work. A Bishop then, must be blameless, the husband of one wife." A woman cannot be a husband; therefore, she can't be a Bishop or an Elder. And in the second place, she is forbidden by the apostolic rule and order in the sphere of men in the Spirit-filled church, to usurp authority in preaching.

What is a Biblical Marriage or How Men and Women are Joined Together by God as One?

First-Vow Made

A vow, or pledge or word or honor, made of your own free will to each other before God, before whom we all stand. You confess your love and promise each other to marry and be one; as a consequence you give a ring or give and receive tokens and presents as a sign of your pledge or engagement. A space of time should elapse, called the "Engagement time," if during that time either one of the contracting parties should prove untrue, by some act of unchastity, which would be "Fornication" and the innocent party is mindful to put her or him away, as the case may be, he or she may do so, they have the right; for fornication is the only grounds upon which they can put (divorce) away their betrothal wife or husband. Jesus said, when asked by the Pharisees, was it lawful to put away one's wife for every cause, limited it from every cause down to one cause—namely fornication. Saying, Moses because of the hardness of your hearts, suffered you to put away your wives; but from the beginning it was not so. And I say unto you, whosoever shall put away his wife, except it be for fornication, and shall marry another committeth adultery; and whoso marrieth her which is put away doth commit adultery. (Matt 19:9) But if they are not disposed so to do then the next step, which is marriage or the legalization of your vow or pledge.

Secondly-Vow Legalized

The law of the land requires people to procure a license, therefore, you must obey the powers that be, and not like some have foolishly affirmed and teach, "that we are not under the law, but under grace, because God hath joined us together in Spirit, we don't have to observe the law." The Scripture says in Romans 13:18.

> Let every soul be subject unto the higher powers. For there is no power but of God: the powers that be, are ordained of God, whosoever therefore resisteth the power, resisteth the Ordinance of God; and they that resist shall receive to themselves damnation. For rulers are not a terror to good works, but to the evil. Wilt thou then not be afraid of power? Do that which is good and thou shalt have praise of the same: For He is the minister of God to thee for good. But if thou do, that which is evil, be afraid; for He beareth not the sword in vain, for He is the minister of God, a revenger to execute wrath upon him that doeth evil.

Wherefore ye must needs be subject, not only for wrath, but also for conscience sake. For this cause pay ye tribute also: for they are God's ministers, attending continually upon this very thing Render therefore to all their dues; tribute to whom tribute is due; custom to whom custom is due; fear to whom fear, honor to whom honor is due.

Therefore you are duty bound to obey the law that requires you to procure a license to marry or live together as man and wife; notwithstanding how much you feel that you are one in heart. Next step is to have the marriage ceremony or

Thirdly-Vow Solemnized

You go to the man of God (the preacher) to whom you give license showing the legalization of your vow made to each other which you reaffirmed before him who is God's representative and spiritual authority in the earth, in the marriage ceremony. Moreover, before the people, as witnesses, and before God to whom you vow as truly as you vowed to each other. The minister upon hearing and receiving our vows made to each other which you have legalized and also solemnized by our reaffirmation before him, the people of God, he proceeds to the next step in a biblical marriage, which is its ratification.

Fourthly-Vow Ratified

Upon hearing and receiving VOW IS made to each other, legalized by, license, solemnized by reaffirmation, the minister ratifies by blessing you and pronouncing you man and wife, in the name of Jesus Christ our Lord. With this declaration "What God hath joined together let no man put asunder."

To the above agree the great biblical authority, Dr. Smith, in his Bible Dictionary, a recognized authority among Bible teachers and preachers on antiquities, biography, geography and natural history, explains this thoroughly on page 382, under the caption of marriage part three. We quote "The selection of the bride was followed by the espousal, a formal proceeding, undertaken by a friend or legal representative of the bridegroom and by the parents on the part of the bride; it was confirmed by oaths and accompanied by presents to the bride; their presents were described by different terms. That to the bride by mohar (A. V. dowry) and that to the relations as 'mattan.' Thus Shechem offers ever so much dowry and gift (Gen 34:12) the former for the bride the latter for the relations. It would be undoubtedly expected that mohar should be proportioned according to the position of the bride, and that a poor man could not on that account afford to marry a rich wife. (I Sam 18:23) The act of betrothal was celebrated by a feast, and among the modern Jew it is a custom, in some parts, for the bridegroom to place a ring on the bride's finger.

"Some writers have endeavored to prove that the rings noticed in the Old Testament (Ex 35:22; Isa 3:21) were nuptial rings, but there is not the slightest evidence of this. The rings are nevertheless regarded among the Hebrews as a token of fidelity, (Gen 41:2) and of adoption into a family (Lk 15:22) between the betrothal and the marriage an interval elapsed, varying from a few days in the patriarchal age (Gen 24:55) to a full year for virgins and a month for widows in later times. During this period, the bride-elect lived with her friends and all communication between her and her future husband was carried on through the medium of a friend, deputized for the purpose, called the friend of the bridegroom. (Jn 3:29) She was now; virtually regarded as the wife of her future husband.

"Hence faithlessness on her part was punishable by death, (Deut 22:23) the husband having, however, the option of putting her away." (Matt 1:10) The above narrative shows two aspects or conditions of marriage, namely, the betrothal or espousal, and the wedded or married state. Now here is wisdom, when a young man and a young lady loved each other, and entered into an espousal contract of betrothal vow, which was ratified by the giving of presents on the part of the young man, after which, according to the above authority, there were reckoned as man and wife, when as yet they had not come together. Now if in that state either one should prove untrue, by committing an act of unchastity, the one that was guiltless was allowed to put the other away, for then fornication was committed, but on the other hand, if after they were married and come together, either one should prove untrue, it would not be reckoned as fornication, but as adultery. That fornication and adultery are not the same can be further seen in reading the works of the flesh in Galatians 5:19 where they are mentioned as two distinct works of the flesh.

"So then, after you are married and come together, there is but one dissolution for your marriage bond, and that is death." (Rom 7:1-3; Mk 10:11; Lk 16:17) "From the beginning of the creation God made them male and female. For this cause shall a man leave his father and mother, and cleave to his wife, and they twain shall be one flesh; so then they are no more twain, but one flesh. What therefore God hath joined together, let not man put asunder.

Whosoever shall put away his wife and marry another, committeth adultery against her. And if a woman shall put away her husband and be married to another, he committeth adultery." To prove the above assertions by precedents we refer you to the experience of Mary and Joseph. ((Matt 1:18-25)

If so be the case, then none of the people who put away their former companions on the ground of fornication are justified, for they were married, and if any unfaithfulness occurred on the part of their companions, it was adultery, and there is no scripture which saith you can put away your wife or husband for adultery, In any case, fornication or adultery, or what not, though it is recorded that Jesus said "except for fornication," yet He did not give any liberty to get married again.

Jesus affirms this eternal principle upon which marriage is based, even your word or vow, by declaring, "By your words you shall be justified, and by your words you shall be condemned." All the experiences, blessings, (Baptism of the Holy Spirit not excluded) revelations, dreams, feelings, spiritual messages and voices, doctrine, divorces and what not, doth not put asunder those who are joined together as mentioned above.

By this the above process, God joins men and women as one in holy wedlock. Wherefore, they are no more twain but one flesh. Not a mere contract, but a condition—one flesh, for this cause shall a man leave father and mother and cleave to his wife.

The Lord being witness to our marriage vow between thee and the wife of thy youth (first wife) if you keep not your vow and divorce one another and marry again to another. Thus dealing treacherously; even though you get saved, baptized with the Holy Ghost, though the preachers and the law justify you contrary to God's word; yet she is thy companion, the wife of thy youth, saith the Lord. (Mal. 2:14-17) Wherein it is asked the question:

> Did he not make one? Yet had he not the residue of the spirit. And wherefore one? That he might seek a godly seed. Therefore take heed to your spirit and let none deal treacherously against the wife of his youth.

For the Lord, the God of Israel, saith He hateth putting away; for one covereth violence with his garment, saith the Lord of Hosts; therefore take heed to your spirit that ye deal not treacherously. Ye have wearied the Lord with your words. Yet ye say, wherein have ye wearied Him? When ye say, everyone that doeth evil is good in the sight of the Lord, and He delighteth in them; or Where is the God of judgment.

An Open Letter on the Burning Question on Marriage and Divorce

Elder Dunlap Chenault
228 Spruce St.
San Antonio, Texas

Dear Brother Chenault:

Greetings in the precious name of Jesus Christ.

As many have taken in hand to write lightly and unadvisedly on the momentous question, "Marriage and Divorce," having given the issue a careful study and observation with much prayer, in answer to your inquiry concerning this doctrine that is causing many to compromise the truth and cause many to stumble at the word; I am sending you this open letter, that you and all saints of like mind who are seeking after truth, may know the certainty of the things wherein you have been taught.

To point you to the truth I have but to refer you to the sayings of the Master when questioned about this doctrine.

The Pharisees came to Him and asked Him, "Is it lawful for a man to put away his wife," tempting Him. And He answered and said, "What did Moses command you?" And they said, "Moses suffered to write a bill of divorcement, and to put her away." And Jesus answered them, "for the hardness of your hearts he wrote you this precept; but from the beginning of the Creation God made them male and female. For this cause shall a man leave his father and mother and cleave to his wife and they twain shall be one flesh... What therefore God hath joined together, let no man put asunder." And in the house His disciples asked Him again of the same matter. And He said unto them, "Whosoever shall put away his wife, and marry another, committeth adultery against her, and if a woman shall put away her husband and be married to another, she committeth adultery." (Mk 10:2-12)

It seems that these words of Jesus ought to be clear to anyone who desires to know the truth. However, we shall consider every text in the New Testament on this subject (Lk 16:15-18):

> And He said unto them, "Ye are they that justify yourselves before men, but God knoweth your hearts; for that which is highly esteemed before men is abomination in the sight of God. The law and the prophets were until John; since that time, the Kingdom of God is preached and every man presseth into it. And it is easier for heaven and earth to pass than for one tittle of the law to fail. Whosoever putteth away his wife and marrieth another committeth adultery; and whosoever marrieth her that is put away from her husband committeth adultery." (Rom 7:1-3):

Know ye not brethren, (for I speak to them that know the law) how that the law hath dominion over a man as long as he liveth? For the woman which hath an husband is bound by the law to her husband as long as he liveth; but if the husband be dead, she is loosed from the law of her husband. So then if, while her husband liveth, she be married to another man, she shall be called an adulteress; but if her husband be dead, she is free from that law...

Some say that she is no adulteress, though she be married to another man.

> The wife is bound by the law as long as her husband liveth; but if her husband be dead, she is at liberty to be married to whom she will; only in the Lord. (I Cor 7:39)

> And unto the married, I command, yet not, I but the Lord, Let not the wife depart from her husband; But and if she depart, let her remain unmarried, or be reconciled to her husband. And let not the husband put away his wife. (I Cor 7:10-11)

It is clearly seen by the above texts that no one has a right to put away his wife and marry another for any cause. Death is the only deliverer from an unhappy marriage, beside getting salvation and then you will love your wife or husband as the case may be and you will be able to forgive him or her and bear with all faults and yet live together. Matthew 5:32 and 19:3-10 are the scriptures people use so much as grounds for divorcing and remarrying. Of texts misunderstood these are the greatest. Let us examine them carefully and see what they say.

> It hath been said, "whosoever shall put away his wife, let him give her a writing of divorcement; but I say unto you, that whosoever shall put away his wife, saving for the cause of fornication, causeth her to commit adultery; and whosoever shall marry her that is divorced committeth adultery;" and Matthew 19:3-10, reads in this wise,

> And I say unto you, whosoever shall put away his wife, except it be for fornication, and shall marry another, committeth adultery; and whoso marrieth her that is put away committeth adultery.

Note it says, "Whosoever puts away his wife except it be for fornication and marrieth another, committeth adultery," not whosoever puts away his wife except it be for adultery and marrieth another committeth adultery. The point is this, there is a vast difference between adultery and fornication. For if this be not true, Paul when writing of the works of the flesh in Gal. 5:19-22, would not have spoken of adultery and fornication at the same time. He would have put only one of them if they both meant the same thing. Fornication cannot be committed by married people, neither can adultery be committed by unmarried people. You will notice by careful reading, that in every relation the word fornication is used, it is in connection with unmarried people, save in the case of the man in I Corinthians 5. He had his father's wife, (his stepmother). On his side it was fornication, on her side it was adultery. Therefore, Paul wrote that is was commonly reported that there was fornication among them. To prove the above statements, I will bring to your notice the modes by which marriage was affected in olden times. And we know that those things were written for our learning and admonition, upon whom the end of the world is come. (I Corinthians 10:11) Smith's Bible Dictionary, a recognized authority among Bible teachers and preachers on antiquities, biography, geography and natural history, gives on page 392, under the caption of marriage, part 3, the following account of the customs of the Hebrews. The customs of the Hebrews and of the Oriental nations in regard to marriage, differ in many respects from those with which we are familiar. In the first place the choice of the bride devolved not upon the bridegroom himself, but upon his relations or a friend deputized by the bridegroom for this purpose. The consent of the maiden was sometimes asked (Gen 24:58); but this appears to have been subordinate to the previous consent of the father and the adult brothers. (Gen 24:51; 34:11)

Occasionally the whole business of selecting a wife was left in the hands of a friend. The selection of the bride was followed by the espousal, a formal proceeding, undertaken by a friend or legal representative of the bridegroom, and by the parents on the part of the bride; it was confirmed by oaths, and accompanied by presents to the bride. These presents were described by different terms, that to the bride by "mohar" (A.V. "dowry"), and that to the relations as "mattan."

Thus, Shechem offers "never so much dowry and gift" (Gen 34:12), the former for the bride, the latter for the relations. It would undoubtedly be expected that "mohar" should be proportioned according to the position of the bride, and that a poor man could not on that account afford to marry a rich wife. (I Sam 18:23) The act of betrothal was celebrated by a feast, and among the more modern Jews it is a custom in some parts for the bridegroom to place a ring on the bride's finger. Some writers have endeavored to prove that the rings, noticed in the Old Testament (Ex 35:22, Isa 3:21) were nuptial rings, but there is not the slightest evidence of this. The ring was nevertheless regarded among the Hebrews as a token of fidelity (Gen 41:42), and of adoption into a family. (Lk 15:22)

Between the betrothal and the marriage an interval elapsed, varying from a few days in the patriarchal age (Gen 24:55), to a full year for virgins and a month for widowed in later times. During this period, the bride-elect lived with her friends and all communication between her and her future husband was carried on through the medium of a friend, deputized for the purpose, called the friend of the bridegroom. (John 3:29) She was now virtually regarded as the wife of her future husband. Hence faithlessness on her part was punishable by death (Deut 22:23, 24), the husband having, however, the option of putting her away. (Matt 1:19; Deut 24:1) We now come to the wedding itself; and the most observable point is, that there are no definite religious ceremonies connected with it. It is probable, indeed, that some formal ratification of the espousal with an oath took place, as implied in some allusions to marriage (Ez. 36:8;

Mal. 2:14), particularly in the expression, lithe covenant of her God" (Pro. 2:17), as applied to the marriage bond, and that a blessing was pronounced sometimes by the parents. (Gen 24:60; Ruth 4:11, 12) But the essence of the marriage ceremony consisted in the removal of the bride from the house of her father to that of the bridegroom or his father. The bridegroom prepared himself for the occasion by putting on a festive dress, and especially by putting on his head the handsome turban described by the term "peer" (Isa 61:10; A.V. ornaments), and a nuptial crown or garland: he was redolent with myrrh and frankincense and "all powders of the merchant" (SS 3:6).

The bride prepared herself for the ceremony by taking a bath, generally on the day preceding the ceremony. The notices of it in the Bible are so few as to have escaped general observation. (Ruth 3:3; Ezek 23:40; Eph 5:26, 27) The distinctive feature of the bride's attire was the "veil" — a light robe of ample dimensions which covered not only the face but also the whole person. This was regarded as her submission to her husband. (I Cor 11:10) She also wore a peculiar girdle called "kishshurim" the attire which no bride could forget (Jer 2:32); and her head was crowned with a chaplet which again was so distinctive of a bride that the Hebrew term "callah" "bride" originated from it. If the bride were a virgin, she wore her hair flowing. Her robes were white and sometimes embroidered with gold thread, and covered with perfumes; she was further decked out with jewels.

When the fixed hour arrived, which was generally late in the evening, the bridegroom set forth from his house attending by his groomsmen or children of the bride chamber (Matt 9:15), preceded by a band of musicians or singers, and accompanied by persons bearing flambeaux. Having reached the house of the bride, who with her maidens anxiously expected his arrival, he conducted the whole party back to his own or his father's house, with every demonstration of gladness. On their way back, they were joined by a party of maidens, friends of the bride and bridegroom, who were waiting to catch the procession as it passed. (Matt 25:6) The inhabitants of the place pressed out into the streets to watch the procession. (SS 3:11)

At the house, a feast was prepared to which all the friends and neighbors were invited, (Gen 29:22) and the festivities were protracted for seven or for fourteen days. The guests were provided by the host with fitting robes and the feast was enlivened with riddles and other amusements. The bridegroom now entered into direct communication with the bride, and the joy of the friend was fulfilled at hearing the voice of the bridegroom conversing with her, which he regarded as satisfactory testimony of the success of his share in the work. The last act in the ceremonial was the conducting the bride to the bridal chamber, where a canopy was prepared. The bride was still completely veiled, so that the deception practiced on Jacob was very possible. A newly married man was exempt from military service or from any public duty that would draw him from his home, for the space of a year; a similar privilege was granted to him who was betrothed.

The above narrative shows two aspects or conditions of marriage, namely, the betrothal or espousal, and the wedded or married state. Now here is wisdom when a young man and a young lady loved each other, and wanted to become man and wife, they first entered into an espousal contract of betrothal vow, which was ratified by the giving of presents on the part of the young man after which, according to the above authority, they were reckoned as man and wife, when as yet they had not come together. Now if in that estate either one should prove untrue, by committing an act of unchastity, the one that was guiltless was allowed to put the other away, for then fornication was committed, but on the other hand if after they were married and had come together either one should prove faithless, it would not be reckoned as fornication, but as adultery. So then after you are married and have come together there is but one dissolution for your marriage bond and that is death. (Rom 7:1-3; Mk 10:11-2; Lk 16:17)

To prove the above assertions by precedents we refer you to the experience of Mary and Joseph. (Matt 1:18-25):

> Now the birth of Jesus was on this wise: When as his mother Mary was espoused to Joseph, before they came together, she was found with child of the Holy Ghost. Then Joseph her husband being a just man, and not willing to make her a public example, was minded to put her away privately. But while he thought on these things, behold, the angel of the Lord appeared unto him in a dream, saying, "Joseph, thou son of David, fear not to take unto thee Mary thy wife; for that which is conceived in her is of the Holy Ghost. And she shall bring forth

a son, and thou shalt call his name Jesus; for he shall save his people from their sins... Then, Joseph, being raised from sleep did as the angel of the Lord had bidden him; and took unto him his wife and knew her not until she had brought forth her first born son; and called his name Jesus.

Joseph when he saw Mary with child, knowing they had not as yet married and come together, thus judged that she had committed fornication; the law commanded that such should be stoned (Deut 22:20, 21), but the Roman government which then held dominion over Palestine, forbade the Jews the power of inflicting capital punishment. The worst Joseph could have done was to make Mary a public example, but not willing to take even so grave a penalty of her, he was minded to put her away privately. And while he thought on these things, the angel of the Lord appeared unto him in a dream, saying "Joseph thou son of David, fear not to take unto thee Mary thy wife." Note the angel called Mary Joseph's wife though they had not as yet come together. So strict were the betrothal vows in those days.

But if they had come together and Mary would have proved untrue then it would have been adultery, as in the case of the woman in John 8:1-12. This woman was caught in the very act of adultery for which the Jews brought her to Jesus and said, "Moses commanded her husband not to put her away, but to stone her. The difference between her and Mary was that she was married, and she and her husband had come together, and then she had proved untrue, which was not so with Mary. Thank God for with the pure (God), all things are pure. The miraculous conception of Jesus Christ did not defile her; yea it rather purified and exalted her above all women that from that time even until now and forever all shall call her blessed, because of being so highly favored by our God; that she should be the medium by which He should come forth into the world as a man, Son of God, Lamb of God, Jesus Christ our Saviour, Emmanuel (God with us), Amen, bless His dear name.

The above case of the woman in John 8, bars forever the way of those that advocate divorcing and remarrying, to justify people who are divorced and remarried, for Jesus said unto the woman who was condemned by the law to be stoned to death and in our day would be condemned by society and divorced by her husband, "go in peace and sin no more," thus overthrowing the doctrine of divorce given by Moses because of the hardness of the heart, and advocating in its stead, forgiveness. Therefore, when Jesus comes into your heart, you forgive all wrongs of your former companion whom you have divorced and take her back and you will also repent of your broken vows unto the Lord and offer unto God thanksgiving for saving you; soul and will not seek to be justified from them but will say as Jephthah, "I have opened my mouth unto the Lord and I won't go back." You will say, I will pay my vows unto the most high even the vow that I made with Him when I told Him, while marrying my first wife, that I would keep her until "death do us part." (Ps

50:14; Eccl 5:4,) Finally, there is no grounds for divorcing and remarrying; the only dissolution of marriage is death. What God has joined together let no man put asunder.

The Plumb Line (Amos 7:8)

"Behold I will set a plumb line in the midst of my people, Israel, and I will not again pass by them anymore." That plumb line is the word of God, that we may know when we are walking uprightly; for saith the scriptures, "How can two walk together except they agree?" There is no altering of God's word for it is settled in heaven forever. He will not pass by us anymore. Therefore, the only thing that we can do is to measure up to "thus saith the Lord." To find out whether the theories following are right, God has given us His word as a pair of scales that we might weigh every theory and doctrine that is put forth. He saith to us in 2 Thessalonians 5:21, "Prove all things, hold fast to that which is good." In 1John 4:1, it says, "Beloved, believe not every spirit, but try the spirits whether they are of God; because many false prophets are gone out into the world. Some say try the spirits by the Spirit, but this is not true nor scriptural, for you will see by reading John 4:1, that these false spirits go out into the world in false prophets,

and it is through their false teachings and doctrines that the people of God are ensnared; therefore to try the spirits means to try the teachings and doctrines of men; the standard by which we must try them is found in Isaiah 8:20. To the law and to the testimony: if they speak not according to this word, it is because there is no light in them.

Many of God's people are being misled having men's persons in admiration because of advantage or reputation or color, etc., they take for granted as true everything certain men say; thinking in their hearts, surely, they ought to know, for they are the great power and wisdom of God. Cease ye from man, whose breath is in his nostrils; for wherein is he to be accounted of? (Isa 2:22) Be thou like the noble Bereans, even though a Paul comes to you and preaches certain things: Search the scriptures to find out whether these things are so, if they are not according to the word, accept them not nor bid him Godspeed, lest ye be a partaker of his sins. (II Jn 10-11)

Yea even though an angel from heaven comes unto you and preach contrary to the word, let him be accursed. Is it not written that even of yourselves shall men arise speaking perverse things to draw away disciples after them, therefore watch... (Acts 20:30-31; Gal. 1:8-9; I Tim 4:1)

> Yea the Spirit speaketh expressly, that in the latter times some shall depart from the faith, giving heed to seducing (that is compromising spirits in false, also true prophets) teaching doctrines of Devils and speaking lies in hypocrisy; having their conscience seared with a hot iron... Therefore, take the scales (the word) that God has given you and everything and doctrine you hear someone preach, and that which you yourself preach and see if it is "found wanting.

To put words in action, we shall proceed to weigh the following theories in the scales, the word of God has given us.

Some Theories Set Forth in Favor of Persons Divorced and Remarried, Also Divorcing and Remarrying

Theory No. 1

When two people are joined together (married) while living in sin and having no knowledge of the law of God; not being under the law of grace they are still permitted by the law of Moses to "put away their wives for the hardness of their hearts" and be joined to another. Then if after being joined to another companion they should be cleansed from sin and filled with the Holy Ghost, they are forgiven of all past unrighteousness and accepted with God. So, what "God has cleansed, call thou not common or unclean." We know that they are accepted of God because we see the anointing of His spirit upon them and the glory of God flooding their souls. Hence the ones who say that such people are living in adultery are bringing or trying to bring innocent souls into condemnation and the Scripture saith, "Who shall lay anything to the charge of God's elect? It is God that justifieth. Who is he that condemneth? It is Christ that died, yea, rather that is risen again, who is even at the right hand of God, who maketh intercession for us." (Rom 8:33, 34)

The above theory in substance was written to me from a brother in central Ohio in defense of a brother who was a deacon in his church, who was also the second husband of his wife. I believe the reason why so many preachers don't stand for the truth of the gospel on this line, is because they are either mixed up in this error or they have some relative or members of their mission who are entangled in the net that has caught and still holds millions in bondage. The above theory when weighed in the scales will be "Found Wanting" when we consider that the marriage institution, or law, was not instituted under the regime or in the inception of the Law of Moses, nor under the law of grace (if there is such a thing as the law of Grace for Grace is not a law, but Grace is God, the Spirit, the Son), (Tit 2:11-14) teaching us to deny ungodliness and worldly lusts, we should live soberly, righteously, and godly, in this present world.

The marriage institution was originated in the garden of Eden in the time of man's innocence long before the Law of Moses or Grace was given or begun. Now after people have been joined together and become one flesh, how can they put one another away and become one again with someone else? when God has said, "What therefore God has joined together let no man put asunder. (Matt 19:6) Roosevelt, Woodrow Wilson, Lloyd George, Clemenceau, Judge Landis nor no doubt [any] man living or dead, not even Moses, for hath not God said, "What therefore God has joined together let no man put asunder"? (Matt 19:6; Mk 10:9)

You will notice that when Moses wrote the precept of divorcement, he did it not willingly but suffered it for the time being because of the hardness of the hearts of the people, he knowing that in the fullness of time Jesus would come and bring Grace that would soften up the heart of the people and enable them to live according to the Word of God; therefore he wrote,

> The Lord your God shall raise up a prophet from among you, like unto me. Thus, saith the Lord. I will put my words in his mouth, and he shall speak unto thee all that I shall command him. And it shall come to pass, that whosoever will not hearken unto my words which he shall speak in my name, I will require it of him. For in what the law could not do, in that it was weak through the flesh, God sending his Son in the likeness of sinful flesh, and sin, condemned sin in the flesh. (Rom 8:3)

Now since Grace has come teaching us and giving strength to do the will of God, shall we not turn that which is lame (that broken vow, that divorced wife) in the way and let it be healed. (Heb 12:11; Eccl 5:3-5)

The brother said the glory of God was flooding their souls, hence anyone preaching that they were in adultery was bringing innocent souls into condemnation. Because a saint is filled with the Holy Ghost and seems to be happy in Jesus, is no sign that they are all right and God is pleased with them and they are walking according to the truth of the gospel. Take, for example, Israel after the flesh in I Corinthians 10. Moreover brethren, I would not that ye should be ignorant, how that all our fathers were under the cloud, and all pass through the sea; And were all baptized unto Moses in the cloud (Holy Ghost baptism, typically) and in the sea

(Baptism in water in the name of Jesus prophetically). And did all eat the same spiritual meat; And did all drink the same spiritual drink; for they drank of that spiritual Rock that followed them; and that Rock was CHRIST. But with many of them God was not well pleased for they were overthrown in the wilderness.

Now these things were our example, to the intent we should not lust after evil things, as they also lusted, neither be idolaters, murmurers, fornicators, adulterers, as some of them were and were destroyed in the wilderness. The Spirit of God in the prophet Hosea seeing that the time would come when the ministers of the gospel would not preach the truth of God on all lines, cried, "My people are destroyed for the lack of knowledge," (why? because the preachers won't preach it) the prophet seeing where the fault was, turned to the preachers and said... because thou hast rejected knowledge, I will reject thee, that thou shall be no more priest to me seeing thou hast forgotten the law of thy God. (Hos 4:6)

Many preachers have been put on the shelf because they would not preach the truth on this line, God has rejected them, though they still go about and preach yet you can see the anointing they once had has left them. Paul seeing that Timothy was somewhat weak on this line wrote to him to "Preach the Word" because the time would come when men would not endure sound doctrine. (Rom 7) Fellow ministers, what are you put in the body of Christ for, if it is not for the perfecting of the saints? (Eph 4:11-14) And if this be so, why should you judge because a person is baptized in the Holy Ghost and the glory of God is flooding their soul that God is well pleased with them, when you know that they are divorced and remarried; and God has said, "Whosoever shall put away his wife, and marry another committeth adultery against her. And if a woman shall put away her husband, and be married to another, she committeth adultery." That whosoever means everyone. Preachers. Laymen, Women and Men, Young and Old, before the law and under the law and after the law.

Jesus Christ spoke in the Garden of Eden when the first couple was married. What therefore God has joined together, they twain shall be one flesh, let not man put asunder. Some say that was under the law, but since Grace has come that has been changed. What Scripture have they for that? Jesus Christ the same yesterday, today and forever. (Heb 13:8) Brother cry aloud and spare not, lift up thy voice like a trumpet, and shew my people their transgression... (Isa 58:1) I know of a woman whom God filled with the Spirit, the glory of God truly filled her soul, but soon after she got mixed up with another woman who taught "Sabbath keeping" and "Purity" and many other errors; well this woman she being on fire for God took to these errors as truths of God, she straightway left her husband in order to be pure, and also she began to observe Saturday as the Sabbath; she also began to teach the errors to everybody she could, she became dishonest and deceitful, yet she spoke in tongues and shouted pretty well all the time and seemingly the glory of God was flooding her soul.

Brother, do you mean that I should not preach against that woman, simply because she is baptized with the Holy Ghost and speaks with tongues? I tell you NAY. When we thus judge we do so after our own understanding, and after manifestations that we see.

But God has said in Proverbs, 3:5, Trust in the Lord with all thine heart; and lean not to thine own understanding. In all thy ways acknowledge him (the Word) and he shall direct thy paths (judgments); again, in Isaiah 11:1-6. Speaking of Jesus, the great shepherd after whom we should pattern, and there shall come forth a rod out of the stem of Jesse... And the Spirit of the Lord shall rest upon him, the Spirit of wisdom, and understanding, the Spirit of counsel and might, the Spirit of knowledge and the fear of the LORD; And He shall make him of quick understanding in the fear of the Lord; and He shall not judge after the seeing of the sight of his eyes (the glory of God seemingly floods the souls of the saints) neither reprove after the hearing of the ears (speaking in tongues) but with righteousness (the Word, I Cor 1:30) shall He judge the poor, and reprove with equity for the meek of the earth... "The only way to judge whether a saint is all right and is well pleasing to the Lord is to judge them according to "Thus saith the Lord." So, we see when the above theory is weighed in the scales, the Spirit of God registers in and through the Word of God "Thou Theory No. 1 thou art weighed in the balance and art found wanting."

Theory No. 2

Not a single passage in the New Testament shows where the apostles had the spirit-filled saints of God to separate and go back to their former companions. There were, no doubt, many of the Jews that had formerly been divorced and remarried. And the Gentiles, without the law, likewise, did the same. In the Old Testament there is but one instance of those who made a mistake in their marriage being compelled to separate. (Ezra 10) This separation was not because of divorcing their former wives and remarrying but because they married heathens as wives. This Scripture is misapplied when used to separate people who have made mistakes in their sinful lives and now have been born again.

The brother in Theory No. 2 says in defense of the people who have their second companion while their former companion still lives, and they don't want to make straight paths for their feet, by going back to their former companion. Not a single passage in the New Testament shows where the apostles had the spirit-filled saints of God to separate and go back to their former companions. There were no doubt many of the Jews that had formerly been divorced and remarried. My answer to the above is this, if they were divorced, it was for fornication and not adultery; for if after they had come together their former companion had proved untrue, they were commanded to stone her, not put her away; if they had not obeyed the command to stone her and she were yet living, they must have gone back of their own accord and taken her back; for she was no worse than they, for both had sinned. She, in that she had committed adultery and he in that he had failed to stone her. (I Jn 3:4)

Therefore, they were both guilty before the Lord and worthy of death. Well if after either had received the Grace of God by being born again, what is more evident of a person being saved and filled with the grace of God, than to see him that is a Jew go back to the wife he wanted to stone and throw his arms around her and forgive her of all her sins against him, and receive her again unto him as Jesus did him; and she asking forgiveness of the man that she had proven untrue to, I say that would show to the world and our former companions that we had truly been changed if we would act in like manner.

But there saith a brother if we follow the law, in this we fail; for the law commanded that after a woman has been divorced from her husband and has gone forth and become the wife of another man, her former husband cannot take her back, for she would be defiled, and that would be an abomination before the Lord. Not so now brother, we have been redeemed from the law by the blood of Jesus, we are now in grace, the gospel of cleansing and forgiveness, now brother you can take your former companion back for she is no more defiled and unclean. For what God has cleansed, call thou not common or unclean. If she is a sinner fear not, for you can go back to her. For a sanctified husband sanctifies the unsaved wife. Amen.

This was brought out in the case of the woman in John 8, who was caught in the act of adultery. When she was brought to Jesus, He said to the Jews, "he that is without sin cast the first stone," and when they had all sneaked out one by one, He said to the woman, "Go in peace and sin no more;" the only way she could do that was by going back to her husband or remaining single.

The brother said the Gentiles without the law did the same thing, that is, divorced and remarried. The Gentiles had no cause whatever to put away their wives for they could have as many as they wanted to, so when Jesus came, he restricted them to one companion, thus putting a stop to polygamy. (Jn 4:1-12; I Tim 3:1-6, 5:9-10) It is evident that the Apostles preached and caused many to go back to their former companion, for in I Corinthians 6:9-11 we read, Know ye not that the unrighteous shall not inherit the kingdom of God? Be not deceived; neither fornicators nor idolaters, nor adulterers, nor effeminate, nor abusers of themselves with mankind, nor thieves, nor drunkards, nor revilers, nor extortioners, shall inherit the kingdom of God. And such were some of you... "Now if I were in jail for a crime and someone comes and pays my fine and comes and unlocks the doors of my cell so that I can go free, if I don't come out from that cell I am still a prisoner, but if I come out and return to my home I am no more a prisoner because I have come out from that cell which I was in. Even so these people must have gone back to their former companions for Romans 7:1-4 says, "For the woman (man also) which hath a husband is bound by the law to her husband so long as he liveth; but If her husband be dead, she is loosed from the law of her husband (wife). So then if, while her husband liveth, she be married to another man, she shall be called an adulteress."

The only way to get from under that condemnation would be for her to leave that man and go back to her husband, or remain single, but by all means she must leave that man or woman as the case may be; for as long as they remain with them, they are in adultery. Now note the woman in Romans 7, Paul speaks of as being joined to her husband by the law or while under the law (that is when they were sinners, without grace) and though she had been born again and was in the church, Paul wrote that if while her husband whom she married when she was under the law (that is in sin) liveth she shall be called an adulteress.

The brother further says in the Old Testament there is but one instance of those who made a mistake in their marriage being made to separate. (Ezra 10) This separation was not because of divorcing their former wives and remarrying, but because they married heathens as wives. This Scripture is misapplied when used to separate those who have made mistakes in their sinful lives and have been born again. Well, the Scripture, (I Cor 10:11) says, "Now all these things happened unto them (Israel) for examples and they are written for our admonition, upon whom the ends of the world are come." Now we understand by the above Scripture, that the things that happened to Israel under the law were examples, types, outlines, and were written for our admonition, that we should not fall into the same error.

Under the law restriction was put upon Israel, not to marry into another nation. But under Grace that restriction is lifted, we can marry into any nation we will; therefore, in no sense can we marry an alien wife, save but to divorce our first wife and marry another. Some say when you marry a sinner companion you are marrying an alien, well surely you would not advocate the putting away your wife because she is a sinner, God forbid.

If this be not true, then the writing of Ezra 10 is of no effect and is in vain; but not so, our God doeth nothing in vain. I believe the book of Ezra was a word-picture-prophecy, showing the church returning from Babylon (the world) after having been carried there captive by Nebuchadnezzar (type of the Devil, the God of this world). After the death of the true prophets and kings the nation backslid from God and went into captivity, after the death of the Apostles and the true saints the Church backslid and went into captivity to the world ruled over by Satan; but bless God, just as he raised up a Nehemiah and an Ezra to bring back Israel from Babylon, God is raising up men with the like spirit that was in those men and they are bringing back the church from the world.

You will notice that in the time of the returning and separation under Ezra, that it was a time of much rain (outpouring of the Holy Ghost, a perfect type of this day of the latter rain). The people being delivered from captivity and in their own land were so grateful that they were willing to do all that was required of them by the Word of God, so that instead of trying to justify themselves before God in the sins that they had committed, they came to Ezra and said: Now therefore let us make covenant with our God to put away all the wives, and such as are born of them, according to the counsel of the Lord, and of (those that tremble at the commandment of our God, and let it be done according to the law. (Rom 7:1-4)... We have trespassed against our God, and have taken strange wives of the people of the land (that is they had followed the custom of the Gentiles in taking as many wives as they wanted). Yet now there is hope in Israel concerning this thing. Thank God there is hope in Israel for you brother who have divorced your former companion and have married again, and have raised a family, if you are willing as these people were to do the will of God you shall receive grace and wisdom from God to do his will. So, we see by the foregoing exegesis that the above theory suffers the same fate of No. 1. Theory No. 2, "Thou art weighed in the balance and found wanting."

Theory No. 3

After preaching so strongly against divorced people, one day a woman came to the altar seeking the baptism of the Holy Ghost. We showed her the Scriptures, but God filled her in spite of it. And she has lived a clean, unspotted Christian life from that day till this (about five years). After she was filled, we pounded Scriptures on her until she separated from her husband. After they separated, he sought earnestly for the baptism, but to no avail. Prayer seemed to do no good. Finally, after they had been separated for several months, she declared that the Lord told her she did wrong in leaving, and so returned to her home. I was puzzled. A few weeks after that, on Sunday night, while preaching to a crowded house, the Holy Ghost fell on the husband while sitting in the congregation near the stove. Everybody saw it. He leaped from his seat shouting and speaking in tongues as the Spirit gave utterance. There and then, I surrendered. "What was I, that I could withstand God." (Acts 11:15-18) He is saved until this day and happy.

Another instance was of a woman who, shortly after that, sought the baptism of the Holy Ghost, and one of the sisters, who was praying with her, learned that she had been divorced and remarried. So, she urged the woman to give up her husband, and then God would fill her with the Holy Ghost. As she sat motionless considering the matter, the sister helping her left, and no sooner had she gone, that the Holy Ghost fell upon the woman and she began to speak with other tongues. Sometime afterward, her husband also was filled, and now they are happy in Jesus and living a blessed life in the Lord. That was my Waterloo.

If I were to follow the above examples of the brother and cease to preach against anyone whom I saw get the Holy Ghost or had the Holy Ghost when I knew that they were living in adultery, according to Romans 7:1-4 [and] Mark 10:12, simply because they were blessed of the Lord, I would be in a dilemma most of the time. I know of a brother who is a preacher, who had a wife who was unsaved; one day his wife took sick in Columbus, Ohio, he left her and was not heard from by her for a long time; in the meantime, this woman got in destitute conditions and had to be sent to the house for the poor. She drew nigh unto death, the saints prayed for her. God raised her up and sometime after that she got saved. Filled with the Holy Ghost. All this time this so-called saint, her husband, was going through the country preaching, he had been gone for about a year and had not sent a penny home to that sick woman, nor had he been back to see her.

So as time went on, she wrote to several of the brothers about how her husband had deserted and was treating her. One brother, an editor of a paper, met or saw the brother in Chicago and learning that he was about to get married to another woman wrote him up in the next issue of his paper well, that caused this preacher to (come home to his wife (his wife lives here in Columbus). When he came home, I met him, and he and his wife and I sat down and began to talk this thing over, and this woman being a noble soul was willing to forgive and forget all and start out anew. After everything was settled and a reconciliation had been effected, in the course of the conversation that followed, he told me of how the Lord had blessed him and how souls had been saved, and how he had built a great work in some place in the north (think of that during that very time when he was treating his wife like a dog). I told him, he that provided not for his own house hath denied the faith, and is worse than an infidel. I told him of his marriage vows, and how God held him to that woman so long as she lived.

He quoted, that because she was a sinner, she was as dead. (I Tim. 5:6) She that liveth in pleasure is dead while she yet liveth. I quickly showed him that text was not of the wife, but of the woman that was a widow. Soon after, he left his wife again (three days), promising her that he would send for her shortly, Well, that was two years ago, and he has not sent for her yet. Until recently we did not know what had become of him, nor where he was; when a brother came to us from North Carolina, and in the course of our fellowship, he asked me did I know the Brother. I told him I did. Well, he said, he certainly is a wonderful preacher.

I met him down in North Carolina, he is having wonderful meetings, people come from miles around to hear him, he has built two or three churches, I preached in one of them; the people come out to hear S.B.D. more than any preacher in town, and many got the baptism. And as he was talking, I was sitting looking with my mouth wide open, and these thoughts kept going through my mind, "How can he do it? How can these things be?" And as he proceeded, he said, "Yes, S.B.D. fell in good, the people are wild about him, he has married a well-to-do widow and is getting along fine."

Well I could have fell over from my chair to think that man who had treated his wife like I had known this man had treated his wife and lied to her and forsook her and without getting a divorce, which the law requires of every man who wishes to marry again, while his former companion liveth, married again. [T]hus [he made] himself a transgressor of the law of the land and stands condemned a bigamist, and before God an adulterer. Yet from the seeing of the eyes and hearing of the ears, [it] seems to them that don't judge him according to "Thus saith the Lord," that he is all right and is the Lord's anointed and no one should touch him for he is the Lord's anointed.

[T]hey imagine there comes floating in on their ears "Touch not my anointed and do my prophet no harm." Instead of this being my Waterloo and my stopping of preaching that a man is joined to his wife so long as she liveth, and if while she liveth, he be married to another he is an adulterer; this proved to be my Fort Sumter experience. And I have unlimbered the guns and unsheathed the sword of God and I intend to fight the forces of darkness on this front until they throw down their arms in unconditional surrender at Appomattox Court House. Amen.

In the case of the woman who was seeking to get her baptism and failed until a sister told her that she would have to give up everything and also her second husband, and as the sister left her, she sat quietly thinking it over. [S]he must have given up everything and was willing in heart to do the will of God, and as soon as she did, God baptized her. [O]r shall we say God baptized her in spite of his word[;] doth not the Spirit and the Word agree? The brother said the Lord baptized the sister in spite of his word. I can't feel safe in saying that, because the sinning Christians in the churches can use the same logic, and say though the Word says "Without holiness no man shall see the Lord, nevertheless he will let us into heaven in spite of the word; thus making the word of God fallible, but God has said heaven and earth shall pass away but my word shall stand forever."

No brother, regardless what I see or hear, the word of God is right. Whosoever putteth away his wife and marrieth another committeth adultery and whosoever marrieth her that is put away committeth adultery. Theory No. 3, thou art weighed in the Balance and found wanting! The brother said in the foregoing theory that the sister was living a clean, unspotted life. According to what standard? Surely not according to the standard found in Romans 7:1-4, Luke 16:17, and Mark 10:11-12. Again, the brother said that after he had preached the word to her, she separated from her husband, and after remaining sometime in that estate, she declared that the Lord told her that she did wrong in leaving her husband, the brother said he was puzzled. Well, that would not have puzzled him if he had kept his eyes on the Word of God, the Scriptures say believe not every Spirit but try the Spirits whether they are of God or not.

The way to have found out whether it was God that spoke to the sister or not was to go to the Word of God, and know this one thing that anything that is not according to the Word is not of or from God. To the law and to the testimony if they (the Spirits) speak not according to this word, there is no light in them. (Isa 8:20)

In the days of old, a prophet of God had the Word of God to come unto him, telling him to go unto Bethel and cry out against King Jeroboam and his idolatrous worship and also to warn him of the impending judgment of God that was about to come upon him and the nation of Israel. As long as he obeyed the Word of the Lord, God protected him from all danger, even the wrath of the king had no power over him, for God dried up the uplifted hand of the king who sought to do him harm, the altar was rent in twain, the king repented of his madness when he saw the power of God manifested in behalf of the prophet who dared to obey the word of God.

And he beseeched the man of God that he might be healed; God healed him at the request of the prophet. (O, that ministers of God would preach as this prophet did, they too would have the power of God to protect them as this man had, and also, they would have power to heal all manner of diseases.)

> Then said the king to the man of God, Come home with me and have some refreshments and rest and I will give thee a reward. The prophet in answer to his invitation: "If thou wilt give me half thine house, I will not go with thee, neither will I eat, nor drink water in this place. For so it (was charged me by the word of the Lord) saying, Eat no bread, nor drink water, nor turn again by the same way that thou comest." So, he went another way, and returned not by the way that he came to Bethel. Now there dwelt an old prophet in Bethel; and his sons came and told him all the works that the man

of God had done that day in Bethel: the words which he had spoken unto the king, them they told also to their father.

And their father said unto them, what way went he? For his sons had seen what way the man of God went, which came from Jordan. And he said unto his sons, saddle me the ass. So, they saddled him the ass: and he rode thereon, and went after the man of God, and found him sitting under an oak, and he said unto the man of God that came from Judah, saying, Thus unto him, Art thou the man of God that cometh from Jordon? And he said, I am. Then he said unto him, Come home with me, and eat bread. And he said, I may not return with thee, nor go in with thee; neither will I eat bread, nor drink water with thee in this place; for it was said unto me by the word of the Lord, Thou shalt eat no bread nor drink no water there, nor turn again to go by the way that thou earnest. He said to him, I am a prophet, also as thou art; and an angel spoke unto me by the word of the Lord, saying bring him back with thee into thine house, that he may eat bread and drink water. But he lied unto him.

So, he went back with him, and did eat bread in his house and drank water. And it came to pass as they sat at the table, that the word of the Lord came unto the prophet that brought him back. And he cried unto the man of God that came from Judah, saying, Thus saith the Lord, Forasmuch as thou has disobeyed the mouth of the Lord, and has not kept his commandment which the Lord thy God commanded thee, but comest back, and hast eaten and drunk water in the place, of the which the Lord did say to thee, Eat no bread, and drink no water; thy carcass shall not come into the sepulchre of thy fathers.

And it came to pass after he had eaten bread, and after he had drunk, that he saddled for him the ass, to wit, for the prophet whom he had brought back, and when he was gone, a lion (the type of the Devil) (I Peter 5:8) met him by the way, and slew him; and his carcass was cast in the way, and the ass (a type of selfishness and stubbornness) stood by it, the lion also stood by the carcass. And, behold, men passed by, and saw the carcass cast in the way, and the lion standing by the carcass, and they came and told it in the city where the old prophet dwelt. And when the prophet that brought him back from the way heard thereof, he said, It is the man of God, who was disobedient unto the word of the Lord, therefore the Lord has delivered him unto the lion (Devil),which has torn him and slain him, according to the word of the Lord, which he spake unto him. (I Kgs 13:1-27). [35]

---

[35] Read 2 Thess 2:11-14

The above is a warning of what will befall us (spiritually) if we don't adhere strictly to the word of God, trust not to what people say or to dreams nor visions or spirits not even though an angel from heaven come unto you speaking anything contrary to the word of God let him be accursed. Had not God said that even though a prophet rises up among you and give a sign or a wonder. And the sign and the wonder come to pass, whereof he spake unto thee, saying, Let us go after other Gods (that is anything contrary to the word of God) which thou hast not known, and let us serve them, thou shall not hearken unto the words of that prophet or that dreamer of dreams: For the LORD, your GOD, proveth you, to know whether ye love the Lord your God with all your heart, and with all of your soul. Ye shall walk after the Lord your God and fear him. O how God has tried and proven many of his people and found that they because of the people they will go contrary to the word of God, therefore He has left them to go their way until they know that the words of the Lord are pure; as silver tried in the furnace, purified seven times; and that it changeth not forever.

Theory No. 4

Therefore, if any man be in Christ, he is a new creature; old things are passed away; behold, all things are become new. (II Cor 5:17)

When Jesus spake in Matthew 5:31-32; 19:4-9, He had reference to the Church and its dealings with the people after they had come into it. No man under the law could abide the words spoken on the mount. Note, he did not say, "Whosoever hath put away his wife and married another committeth adultery," but whosoever SHALL put away his wife and marrieth another committeth adultery." From this I begin to see that when a man has been "born again" and made a "new creature in Christ Jesus "God began to reckon his life from that time on. From that time forward his life and conduct is judged by the church. (I Cor 5:12) In the church there is to be no divorcing and remarrying among the children of God. Our past life is forgotten. God remembers it no more. A [crucifixion] has taken place (Gal 2:19-20) and a new life has begun. Having been born again God has forgiven all our trespasses and started us off anew. Thank God for His abundant grace! If we all had to make right all the wrongs done in the past, who then should be saved? "If thou, O Lord, shouldst mark iniquities, who shall stand? But there is forgiveness with thee that thou mightest be feared."

Is it true when Jesus spoke in Matthew 5:31-32; 19:4-9, he had reference to the church and its dealings with the people after they had come into it? If so, where are there any scriptures that bear that out? To say that Jesus said in Mark 10:11, Whosoever shall put away his wife and marry another committeth adultery against her, and not "Whosoever hath put away his wife and marry another committeth adultery against her" does not mean anything at all in this matter for it will be seen by the preceding verses, 6-9, that Jesus had reference to the original marriage institution when he said "From the beginning of the creation, God made them male and female. For this cause shall a man leave his father and mother and cleave to his wife; and they twain shall be one flesh; so, then they are no more twain, but one flesh.

What Therefore God Hath Joined Together Let Not Man Put Asunder

The above is simply a play of words to the support of them that are in this life. Dr. R. F. Weymouth in his translation of the New Testament renders the above passage on this wise, "Whosoever divorces his wife and marries another woman commits adultery against his first wife; and if a woman puts away her husband and marries another man, she committeth adultery." Also, in the Douay version of the Bible, Luke 16:18, "Everyone that putteth away his wife and marrieth another committeth adultery; and he that marrieth her that is put away from her husband committeth adultery." All the theories set forth in defense of men and women who have their second husband or wife as the case may be, regardless who the men may be, or in what age they lived, that set them forth; they are overthrown by the saying of Jesus that he uttered when the Pharisees came to him with the theory of Moses. He said, "But from the beginning it was not so." (Matt 19:8) So, brother, whatever is put forth that is not according to the word, regardless of how plausible it seems, Jesus says unto you, From the beginning it was not so.

The brother wrote that from the above theory when he saw it, he began to see that when a man was "born again" and is made a new creature in Christ Jesus, God began to reckon from that time on. Our past life is forgotten. God remembers it no more. A crucifixion has taken place. And a new life has begun. Having been born again God has forgiven all our trespasses and started us off anew. Thank God for his abundant grace. Without going into details of the theory, I simply will point you to the evil that it is leading to.

A preacher that I know has been going around teaching the married women that have sinful husbands that they were not joined to their husbands because they had broken their marriage vow and had proven untrue to them, and they, being saved, could depart and marry again; and when this said preacher saw the above theory in print, he said I believe the same. You see what evil people will go to when you give them such a chance as this. If a crucifixion has taken place, they thus judge I married when I was a sinner, and now I am saved. God has forgiven and forgotten my past life and started me out anew. I can get a new husband and everything new; for the scriptures say if any man is in Christ, he is a new creature old things have passed away and behold all things are become new.

The theory speaks that "No man could stand the word spoken on the mount" true enough; but the marriage and divorce law was not given from the mount, neither was the marriage institution; one (marriage institution) was before the law was given, and the other (marriage and divorce law) was after the law (the Ten Commandments) was given. The divorcement law and. other handwriting of ordinances which was contrary to us was nailed to the cross (Eph 2:15; Col 2:14), For we are they that have been redeemed from the law and from sin and we are in a spiritual sense back in the beginning as it were when Jesus spoke, "It was not so." What

God has joined together let not man put asunder; for they twain are one flesh.

If a crucifixion has taken place and a new life begun, having been born again God has forgiven all our trespasses and started us out anew, that is, don't require us to restore or make right as far as in our power the things that we have done in the past. What it is then meaneth the word of God in Ezekiel 33:14-17. Again when I say to the wicked, Thou shalt surely die; if he turn from his sin, and do that which is lawful (Rom 7:1-4) and right; If the wicked restore the pledge (vow, perhaps the marriage vow) give again that he has robbed, walk in the statutes of life, without committing iniquity; he shall surely live, he shall not die, none of his sins that he has committed, shall be mentioned unto him (why?) he hath done that which is lawful and right; he shall surely live, Yet the children of thy people say,

THE WAYS OF THE LORD ARE NOT EQUAL; but as for them, their ways are not equal. Truly I believe though a crucifixion has taken place yet I know that God requires us to make straight paths for our feet by measuring up to the word of God on all lines, the crucifixion mentioned in Galatians 2:19-20 have reference to the things of sin in death, but not to the things of sin in life, for Paul said I am crucified with Christ nevertheless I live. If you will notice the crucifixion spoken was a crucifixion to death from the law that we might live unto God; but the marriage institution or law was before the law was given.

Truly God has given us abundant grace sufficient to enable us to do the will of God from the heart. God gives the Holy Ghost to us so that we might have power to do his will that before we were too weak to do. "For the earth which drinketh in the rain (type of the Spirit) that cometh oft upon it, and bringeth forth herbs meet for them by whom it is dressed, receiveth blessing from God. But that which beareth thorns and briers is rejected, and is nigh unto cursing, whose end is to be burned. But, beloved we are persuaded some better things of you, and things that accompany salvation, though we thus speak." (Heb 6:7-9)

Dear saints of God, if we don't do the will of God after we have been filled with the Holy Ghost we shall surely be lost. Some say, if I was an adulterer and wasn't right, would God dwell in me? When the word says, God will not dwell in an unclean temple. Now we know that when we taught three Gods and the second work of grace theories, we were all liars, yet because we were ignorant, God did not depart from us, but blessed us, not because we were right but in spite of our being wrong for we were blind, but now after we have come to the light on these things, if we refuse then we would be found sinners before him and then He would depart from us.

Even so, saith Jesus to the Jews, that If I had not come and spoken unto you these words you had not sin, but I have spoken unto you these words, therefore you have no cloak for your sins; so it is today in regards to the marriage and divorce question when people don't know the truth on this line they still have the Holy Ghost to abide in them, but when they have seen the light there is no minister who they have more confidence in than they have in the word of the Lord who would teach them to see differently, thus blinding them and causing them to think they are right when they are wrong.

So, God in his great mercy will let his Spirit remain with them striving with them to make them see the light e'er it be too late; they, I say, who see the light will invariably walk in the light or the Holy Spirit will depart, and they will backslide. In conclusion, I will say that this and all other theories are overthrown by the saying "In the beginning it was not so." Theory No. 4, thou art weighed in the balance and found wanting.

Theory No. 5
What God has cleansed, that call not thou common. (Acts 10:15)

The above text has been a puzzle to many because they fail to see that the text was not spoken in relation or in regard to the marriage and divorce question, but was spoken in regard to the universal acceptance of God in the great plan of salvation of all people regardless of nationality. "But in every nation; he that feareth him, and worketh righteousness, is accepted with him." (Acts 10:35) Now to use that text to the support of those in adultery is, to my mind, wresting the scriptures to those souls' destruction who would otherwise be saved perhaps from their condition. I know some will, no doubt, think that I am rather harsh, but my heart is tender towards all them that are in this sin, and I speak out in no uncertain tone in this matter because I love them and desire to see them saved. It will be seen we are not perfectly cleansed when we consider I John 1:7. But if we walk in the light, as he is in the light, we have fellowship one with another, and the blood of Jesus Christ His son cleanseth us from all sin. So, to call such a one that is living in adultery an adulterer is not calling what God hath cleansed common; for as long as they have not walked in the light on this truth they are not cleansed from that sin. It is by walking in the light we receive cleansing from sin. So, Theory No. 5 thou art weighed in the balance and art found wanting.

Theory No. 6

The preacher that left his wife sick and almost dead, because she was a sinner, when I told him he could not marry again, because he was joined to his wife as long as she lived, he quoted I Timothy 5:6, "But she that liveth in pleasure is dead while she liveth." But if you will notice the preceding verses you will find that he is giving instruction to Timothy in regards to taking widows in the number (a home that was supported by the church for women who had lost their husbands and could not make a living for themselves) and also how he should treat them in general. He instructed him concerning their age and other requirements that they should measure up to. But he said younger widows refuse because they would break their vows when they would wax wanton against Christ (11th and 12th verses), so you can see the above quotation in favor of divorce and remarrying is like the many theories put forth: It is weighed in the balance and found wanting.

Theory No. 7

Some say we were not joined together by God, for if we had we would have loved each other, and would not have separated. The only one that God requires you to stay with until death do part, is the one that you love; which is the one that he joined you.

N ow we know that God has given to man to be his own free moral agent (Deut 15:20), and he can take his choice in any matter pertaining to this earthly life, when therefore man chooses a woman to be his wife, and comes before the powers that be whom God has ordained for that same purpose, and says I want to marry this woman, or in other words, I am allowed by God to take one woman to wife; therefore of all the women of earth I have chosen this one as my companion for life until death do us part. The powers that be issues him a license thus giving him power to take the woman to wife. He turns from the powers and proceeds to the minister's house and gets him to solemnize what he has done, thus binding himself of his own free will by the powers that be and by a vow to God unto the woman until death do them part. Now to say that God did not join you to the woman because you did not love her, is to tell a lie, and thus condemn yourself; for you said you loved her. By your words thou shalt be justified, and by your words thou shalt be condemned. (Matt 12:37) Again if you will notice any standard form for the solemnization of matrimony you will notice that when you repeated after the minister you said that you took (wife or husband) to love, so if after you have married you find out that you don't love her (or him) remember you promised to love her, so go ahead and love her, thus fulfilling your promise.

The marriage ceremony is equivalent to a vow, for you promise therein that you would keep her through sickness and through health and through wealth and through woe until death do thee part; therefore God has said in his word in Ecclesiastes 5:4-7, When thou vowest a vow unto God; defer not to pay it, for he hath no pleasure in fools: pay that which thou hast vowed. Better is it that thou shouldst not vow than that thou shouldst vow and not pay. Suffer not thy mouth to cause thy flesh to sin; NEITHER SAY THOU BEFORE THE ANGEL THAT IT WAS AN ERROR (I made mistake in my marriage, therefore God has forgiven me and I have married again) wherefore should God be angry at thy voice, and destroy the work of thy hands?... But fear thou God. (Gal 6, 7) Be not deceived; God is not mocked, for whatsoever a man soweth, that shall he also reap. For he that soweth to his flesh, shall of the flesh reap corruption; but he that soweth to the Spirit (word) shall of the Spirit reap life everlasting.

Therefore, David in the Psalms 50, 14 and 15 verses said, God said, Offer unto the Lord thanksgiving; and pay thy vows unto the most high; And call upon me in the day of trouble; and I will deliver thee and thou shalt glorify me. Amen. The above fallacy from the pit under fire of God's word has retreated back thereto, and has suffered the same fate that all others of its kind or will suffer when they come un against the word of God, they shall be bound as all others, "Weighed in a balance and found wanting."

Theory No. 8

The law permitted divorcing and remarrying (I Jn 1:17), But under Grace these things are prohibited. The Law is yet in force to every unsaved man and woman today. Christ is the end of the Laws only to them that believed. (Rom 10:4) The law still grants divorces, "because of the hardness of the hearts." There are many today trying to force the regulations of the church of God upon an unregenerate world. You cannot put new wine in old bottles. Not everyone that professes Christianity has been born of God. There's where our judgment failed. The precepts in Matthew 5 are for those who have been made partakers of the Holy Ghost, and not for the world. And no man is under grace until he is born of God's Spirit. God is making no mistake in baptizing those who have been divorced and remarried, but we are erring, not understanding the scriptures, and have driven many precious souls into despair, for whom Christ had died and even given His Holy Spirit. There are cases where God pours out His Spirit on such people at home and they are happy and blessed of the Lord until they come into contact with some mission or someone preaching on the marriage and divorce question, then they are put under pressure, and in many cases give up and go back to the world. My judgment is as it is revealed to me through the word of God, that we let them alone who have come to God, being accepted of him bearing witness by giving them the Holy Ghost.

It is useless to bring in an argument which has the law for its basis in defense or justification of people divorced and remarried. For it is clearly seen that the marriage institution was before the law was given, therefore when man breaks the marriage vow he is condemned by his vow apart from law; for it was in the time of man's innocency before sin came into the world by transgression that the law of marriage was given; therefore when we are saved, we return back (in a spiritual sense) to the beginning, and under the covenant given to Adam in his innocence we are placed. Therefore, shall a man leave his father and his mother and shall cleave unto his wife; and they shall be one flesh. (Gen 2:24) Therefore, what God has joined together let not man put asunder. (Matt 19:6)

It has been said that Jesus when he was preaching to the people on the marriage and divorce question was talking not to the world, but to the church; therefore, it is not lawful to force the laws of the church on the unregenerate world. Well, that is not scriptural, for at that time there was no church; for Jesus said in Matthew 16:18, Upon this rock I will build my church and the gates of hell shall not prevail against it. The church was not built until the day of Pentecost. (Jn 7:37-39; I Cor 12:13; I Peter 2:5; Eph 2:18-22; 1:22-23) On one occasion, Jesus said, "What I say unto one I say unto all." And in Matthew 13, we read, The same day Jesus went out of the house, and sat by the seaside, and great multitudes gathered together unto him; so that He went into a boat and sat, and the whole multitude stood on the shore. And He spoke many things unto them (note it doesn't say He spoke many things unto the church).

But now, to be fair with our brethren, I will grant them that point that He was speaking to the church and not to the world. We will read what He told the church in His final commission just before His ascension into heaven. (Matt 28:17-20) Notice that in verse 17 says that some were in doubt, but Christ assured them He meant what He said while with them on earth, when He said in the verse 18, "All power is given unto Me in heaven and in earth," thus showing that He was able to back up what He had said. Then He said unto them, "Go ye therefore and teach all nations, baptizing them in the name of the Father and of the Son and of the Holy Ghost; teaching them to observe all things whatsoever I have commanded you; and I am with you always even unto the end of the world."

It can be seen that we are not making a mistake when we preach the laws of the church to an unregenerate world, we do not put new wine in old bottles, but we break the old bottles with the hammer of God (His word) that they may be made anew (new birth) and filled with the new wine (Spirit). To let people alone because God has given them the Holy Ghost when we know they are wrong according to His word, would be sparing them. God has said, "Cry aloud and spare not, lift up your voice like a trumpet, and shew MY PEOPLE their transgression.

What is sin? John said that sin was a transgression of the law. I John 3:4, Know ye not, brethren, (for I speak to them that know the law) how that the law has dominion over a man as long as he liveth? For the woman which hath a husband is bound by the law to her husband as long as he liveth (one brother said when you come to Christ you die to sin, therefore you are loosed from the husband if he is a sinner, because you have died), but if the husband be dead, she is loosed from the law of her husband. So then if while her husband liveth, she be married to another man, SHE SHALL BE CALLED AN ADULTERESS (not a sister or saint). But if her husband be dead, she is free from that law; so that she is no adulteress, though she be married to another man. (Rom 7:1-4) We know that God is making no mistake in baptizing people with the Holy Ghost; but we also know that He has made no mistake in giving us the word, and in placing in the church apostles and prophets and evangelists and pastors for the preaching of the word to the saints that they may perfect themselves by walking in the light.

I will not accept the doctrine that a saint is all right because they talk in tongues and seem to be living happy when I know they are not living according to the word. I have seen too many talk in tongues and there wasn't a bigger devil than they. Of late, there comes to my attention a man who has been preaching and is now, and shouting, and talking in tongues, and as it were supposed having wonderful meetings. He has been found out to be, living in the sin that Joseph fled from while in Egypt. Oh, no, brother; I must not lean to my own understanding, I must take the word of God to mean what it says and to say what it means.

We know that they that have not heard the word on "Jesus is God," go on fine until they come in contact with a mission that is preaching the message and if they don't walk in the light they will come under condemnation and backslide, even so them that get the baptism of the Holy Ghost in their homes; God gives it to them so they might walk in the light; and when they come in contact with some mission preaching the light on this truth, they will either walk in the light or fall into condemnation and finally backslide. If we are going to leave them alone, let us leave the liars and whoremongers and thieves, drunkards, etc., alone;

let us not become Antinomians who taught the doctrine that a saint of God is free from the obligation to keep the precepts of the moral law. The tendency to this error appeared early, and is referred to by St. Paul in Romans 6:14-15.

The Holy Ghost is given for the saints of God to work out their salvation with fear and trembling. The church is being judged today. Beware that you neglect not so great a salvation, and won't be accounted worthy to escape (rapture). Judgment has begun at the house of God, and if the righteous scarcely escape, where shall the sinner and the ungodly appear? To be certain about this thing, instead of taking a chance with my soul's salvation, if I were mixed up in that life I would leave, and I if after I found I had made a mistake then I will be saved anyhow, but if I remain in that condition and after I stand before the judgment bar, find I had been living in sin I would be lost.

So, in order to play "safety first" I would leave my present companion and go back to the first one, or if I could not get the first one back, I would remain single. (1 Cor 7:10-11) For it would be better I suffer here than to suffer yonder. God pity the people that are caught in this life. I know that the yoke of Jesus is easy, and if they will only take it, they will find that God will grant the grace to do His will. He will also provide for them who cannot provide for themselves, if they will only step out on His promise like Abram did, not knowing where he was going. O, fellow ministers, woe, woe, woe be unto us if we rock souls in the cradle of carnal security by not preaching the truth, God shall surely judge us in that day.

My soul trembles when I think of what our judgment will be because we preached not the truth on this line, thus causing souls to be lost. Jesus said, "Therefore ye shall receive the greater damnation;" Paul, "Woe is me if I preach not the gospel." Jesus said again, "If the blind lead the blind they both will fall into the ditch" (hell), According to the above theory we should not preach this gospel to the sinners, because that would be forcing the laws of the church on the unregenerate world; and we should not preach it in the church where there are people who are mixed up with their second companion, because that would drive many precious souls into despair for whom Christ died and has given His Holy Spirit. What are we going to do? Hold our peace? No! No! No! A thousand times No! When there comes to our ears the voice of God (the Spirit) in His word, (Isa 62:6-7), "I have set watchmen on thy walls, Jerusalem, which shall never hold their peace day or night: YE THAT MAKE MENTION OF THE LORD KEEP NOT SILENCE." Again, in Isaiah 58:1, "Cry aloud and spare not, lift up thy voice like a trumpet, and shew my people their transgression."

Brethren with all love I have purposed to preach this truth and let the people take the judgment upon their own heads and not me take upon my head by presuming that the Lord meant this, and that, when he meant just what He said and said just what He meant. (Mk 10:11-12; Rom 7:1-4) It is a presumptuous sin to tell a soul they are all right (when the word of God condemns them), simply because God has given them His Holy Spirit. I am preaching this and if they obey it or not that is their own affair: my mission is to preach the word. And when they come to me, I tell them what the word says. If it is wrong, God put it there; and I don't have to account for it; I did not put it there; and if God had not wanted it preached, He would not have put it there.

There are many other theories put forth in defense of marrying and divorcing and of people divorced and remarried that time and space would fail me to make mention of in this brief treatise on this subject. But though there be many their overthrow is accomplished in the one saying of Jesus, "In the beginning it WAS NOT SO. (Matt 19:8) Therefore, beware lest ANY man spoil you through philosophy and vain deceit, after the traditions of men, after the rudiments of the world, and NOT AFTER CHRIST. (Col 2:8) Theory No. 8, thou art weighed in the balance and found wanting.

The Ministry of John the Baptist was a Type of the Holy Ministry of Today

You will notice that John came preaching water baptism unto repentance presaging the revelation of God in the flesh, in the person of Jesus Christ, after God was revealed in the flesh. John's next message was the marriage and divorce question, when he told that old adulterer, King Herod, it was not lawful (Rom 7) for him to have his brother's wife. (Matt 14:4, Mk 6:18) Though he lost his head, he did not draw back from the truth, but preached it to the world (Herod was of the world, a gentile, yet John preached to him it was not lawful to have his brother's wife). He died and went to Glory with the smile of God upon his soul and the testimony of Jesus Christ ringing down the years of time saying,

Of men born of women there hath not risen a greater than John the Baptist." He had finished his course and had kept the faith (the word) a perfect type or example for us to follow.

The Comparison

One of God's ministers began preaching the water baptism in the name of Jesus Christ according to Acts 2:38. This led the brethren to see if there was but one name, there was but one God. So, the preaching of water baptism in Jesus' name for the remission of sins proved to be the forerunner, like John the Baptist, presaging the revelation of God in the Spirit. God revealed in the flesh is Jesus Christ, and Jesus Christ revealed in the Spirit is God almighty. Hallelujah to his precious name. Now as John, after the revelation of God was seen by the chosen few who had submitted themselves to the righteousness of God by being baptized of John, took up the ministry of the marriage and divorce question and lost his head, and went on to Glory, even so should the ministry of the church take up this marriage and divorce question and say unto the world and to the saints in the church and everywhere, "It is not lawful for you to have your brother's wife" or your sister's husband" regardless if we lose our head (reputation, superintendent head, etc., or our natural head). If we do, we will sweep through the gates of Glory with the smile of God upon our souls, and will hear the welcome approbation of Jesus Christ, our God and Saviour, "Well done, thou good and faithful servant; thou hast been faithful over a few things, I will make thee ruler over many things, Enter thou into the joys of the Lord," prepared for you from the foundation of the world. Of a truth the next message to take up is the marriage and divorce question.

The Evil Results of the Divorce Laws and Doctrines

Of all the sins that the world is guilty of, "Adultery" stands at the head of the category. (Gal 5:19) Well, then, seeing it is the leading sin, we should "Cry aloud and spare not, against this serpent of lust" until by the word of God we shall bruise its head to death. The Apostle John said we know that we are of God, and the whole world lieth in the arms (Selah!) of the wicked One. The hydra headed monster of adultery has the human race in its slimy arms, and its greenish eyes of false doctrines are charming many souls into its coils of lust. God help the ministers to preach the word and deliver the people. The evil of this beast was seen and spoken of by Christ, when He said, "But as the days of Noe were, so shall also the coming of the Son of Man be. For as in the days before the flood they were eating and drinking, marrying and giving in marriage, until the day that Noah entered into the ark; and knew not until the flood came and took them all away; so shall also the coming of the Son of Man be. Jesus knew the beast would have great power upon the people, and that many of his people would be ashamed of the word against the people who are guilty of this sin; therefore He said, "Whosoever therefore shall be ashamed of me and my words in this adulterous and sinful generation;

of him shall the Son of Man be ashamed when He cometh in the glory of his Father with the holy angels." (Mk 8:38)

Some Statistics Taken from Pastor A. L. Frazier's Tract, Marriage and Divorce

The results of investigations covering several thousand cases indicates that there are practically only two purposes in obtaining divorce, viz.: to protect property interests and for the purpose of marrying again. For other purpose than these two, separation would be just as good. But they cannot tolerate anything of that sort. They want to be free and pursue their wicked ways and go further from God, even unto the very gates of hell. Let us quote a few figures. A fair estimate is that 95 per cent of all divorces are due to immorality and the percentage of the divorces for the state of Illinois for the year 1897 and 1900 was about 10 1/2 of all marriages in the state, while the national figures for the same averaged about 13 1/2 per cent of the total number of marriages. The proceedings of the Juvenile Court in this city (Chicago) have brought out some remarkable facts. It has been found that the parents of 90 per cent of the children that come under the jurisdiction of the Juvenile Court are either divorced or separated. Isn't that an astounding fact? Isn't that its own commentary upon the moral effect of divorce, that 90 per cent of the children who come to the Juvenile Courts in these days are the offspring of parents who are either separated or divorced. Since the establishment of this court in 1899, there have been 53,358 petitions for the care of children. Of this number 33,750 were brought into the court as the result of divorces or because of the iniquity of the fathers through drunkenness and desertion, which formed sufficient ground for divorce on the part of the wife.

Just to see where the hammer falls! It does not fall on the man and the woman; it falls on the helpless child. That is where the curse falls, on the innocent children. (My God how long!) That is where the blight of divorce and drunkenness is felt most. In 1912, in the Circuit Court alone in this city (and the Superior also had jurisdiction over the divorces) there were 2,038 decrees granted, 1,515 of which were secured by women plaintiffs. Of 2,038, 1,644 went by default; that is one party brought a suit for divorce, the other party failed to show up. What an awful commentary on the condition of affairs in this wicked city Judge Petit is authority for the statement that about 5,000 divorces are granted annually in Chicago. There were 2,849 suits for divorce, separate maintenance—or annulment of marriage in the first six months of last year, and of these 2,660 cases, 482 of the disagreeing couples had BEEN MARRIED LESS THAN A YEAR; 260 had been married less than two years, and so on.

The court of domestic relations was established some four years ago in Chicago. It is accomplishing some good, but much more good can be effected. The divorce laws must be made more stringent. Their laxity is responsible for many evils, such as uncontested cases. This is the great field of the divorce abuse. If the plaintiff swears that he does not know where the defendant lived, "service by publication" is permitted, and notice of the filing of the suit printed in some legal newspaper with a small circulation. But men will often perjure themselves, and women, too, just to secure the divorce. A further evil is found in the infectious nature of the divorce. Some plead why not give them a divorce if they are determined not to live together? Why maintain a legal fiction regarding a condition no longer existing? For the simple reason divorce spreads like disease? Yea for stronger reason than that, God forbids. (Rom 7:2-3) It is infectious, and where you find one case you will generally find a crop springing up around. Separation may be permissible for sufficient reasons, but Divorce is different. Easy divorces are demoralizing to both young and married people.

Divorce is simply a license to remarry. Men are frequently divorced and set free to get somebody else in a tangle. Sometimes a pre-arranged marriage is the cause of the whole trouble, and in many cases, money is paid to women to help secure the divorce and pave the way for remarriage. At the same time, unscrupulous lawyers and ministers, for the sake of a fee, contribute much to this regrettable state of affairs.

The trivial causes upon which divorce suits are based, is contempt of the word of God and consequently an abomination to God, when we vow before God that we would keep one another until death do us part, and then before one year is over we are in court getting a divorce on such trivial grounds as "He's constantly provoking quarrels," "She hit me with her fist," "The biscuits were burnt," "Extreme cruelty," "He spent his money in gambling and riotous living," etc. Be not deceived, God is not mocked, whatsoever a man soweth that shall he also reap; he that soweth to the flesh shall of the flesh reap corruption, but he that soweth to the Spirit shall of the Spirit reap life everlasting. Whosoever putteth away his wife and marrieth another committeth adultery against her; and he that marrieth her that is put away committeth adultery. Now, it makes no difference who it is, man or woman, Pentecostal or Presbyterian, Baptist or Methodist, if you have legally married and have left your husband or wife for another, you are AN ADULTERER IN THE SIGHT OF GOD, regardless of what the laws of the land say. God's laws are superior to the laws of the land. The many that have died from a broken heart because of the divorce laws and doctrines cry out, though dead, they speak against this damnable evil.

The many children who have been made homeless by this traffic cry unto the ministers of the land to rise up and speak against sins that are making the land mourn, and the beasts of the field languish, and the blood of men break out and blood touch blood. (Hos 4:1-2) My God, judge thou the ways of men. If a man is an adulterer before he gets baptized in water and gets the Holy Ghost and if, after he is baptized and gets the Holy Ghost, he goes back and lives just like he lived before; is he not an adulterer?

Yea, he that covereth his sins shall not prosper, but he that confesseth and forsaketh the same shall have mercy. Shall we continue in sin that grace may abound? God forbid! How shall we that are dead to sin live any longer therein? Know ye not that so many as were baptized into Jesus Christ were baptized into His death? Therefore, we are buried with by baptism into death that like as Christ was raised from the dead by the glory of the Father, Even so we also should walk in the newness of life, not in the old life, but in the life that is given in the word.

Startling Exposure of People Divorced and Supposed to be Married

There are many people living together, men and women, upon the supposition that they are married, and are husband and wife, because they had a wedding ritual performed by a minister joining them together. They would be surprised to find out they never were married, for the very ceremony that was supposed to join them together was too weak in that it acknowledged that if they were joined together otherwise than God's word doth allow, they were not joined together by God, neither was their matrimony lawful.

I will quote verbatim from the standard form for the solemnization of matrimony that is used more or less by all ministers in performing weddings. Dearly beloved, we are gathered together here in the sight of God, and in the presence of the witnesses, to join together this man and this woman in holy Matrimony; which is an honorable estate, instituted of God in the time of man's innocency, signifying unto us the mystical union that exists between Christ and His church; which holy estate Christ adorned and beautified with his presence, and first miracle that He wrought in Cana of Galilee, and is commanded by St. Paul to be honorable among all men; and, therefore, is not by any to be entered into unadvisedly, but reverently, discreetly, and in the fear of God. Into which holy state these two persons present come now to be joined. Therefore, if any can show just cause why they may not be joined together, let him now speak or else hereafter forever hold his peace.

Speaking to the persons that are to be married, the minister shall say:

I require, and charge you both, that if either of you know any impediment why you may not be lawfully joined together in matrimony, you do now confess it; for be you well assured, that so many are coupled together OTHERWISE THAN GOD'S WORD DOTH ALLOW, ARE NOT JOINED TOGETHER BY GOD, NEITHER IS THEIR MATRIMONY LAWFUL.

If no impediment be alleged, then shall the minister say unto the man, (and the woman alternately), Wilt thou have this woman to be thy wedded wife, to live together after God's ordinance (Word) in the holy estate of matrimony? Wilt thou love her, comfort her, honor and keep her, in sickness and in health; and forsaking all other, keep thee ONLY UNTO HER, SO LONG AS YE BOTH SHALL LIVE?

(The man and woman as these questions are put to the man first and the woman next, answer I will.) Then the minister causes them to join hands and repeat after I, M; take thee, N; to be my wedded wife, to have and to hold, from this day forward, for better, for worse, for richer, for poorer, in sickness and in health, to LOVE and to cherish, TILL DEATH US DO PART, ACCORDING TO GOD'S HOLY ordinance (His word); and therefore I plight thee my troth. (Then the minister prays.) Then the minister joins their right hands together and says: For as much as M. and N. have consented together in holy wedlock, and have witnessed the same before GOD and this company, and therefore have pledged their faith either to other, and have declared the same by joining of hands, I PRONOUNCE THAT THEY ARE HUSBAND AND WIFE TOGETHER (that is, if they have no living companion) in the Name of the Father, and of the Son, and of the Holy Ghost, THOSE WHOM GOD HAS JOINED TOGETHER LET NO MAN PUT ASUNDER. AMEN. (And the minister adds his blessings.)

So, you see, dear one, the glaring inconsistency of the present-day ministry. For the sake of fees and gaining and holding members, they will allow people to think they are married when they themselves know differently. Many people today feel condemned about their marriage, but they allow themselves to be rocked in the cradle of carnal security by some minister, and they will reject the word of God. But be this known unto you that "Whosoever putteth away his first companion and marrieth another, committeth adultery, and as long as they stay together they, are living in adultery, In praying over this problem of causing people to go back to their former companions, the Lord spoke to me and said in regards to baptism in water, You all cause saints to divorce themselves from the baptism in the name of the Father, and of the Son, and of the Holy Ghost, and go back and be married to the baptism in the great name of Jesus, even though they are saved, you tell them if they don't walk in the light and go back and be baptized again they won't make the rapture. Why don't you send back those people who have living companions and make them straighten up the marriage life, as you make others straighten up their baptism. I then took fresh courage and resolved to preach this truth everywhere I go. The Church divorced herself from the baptism in the name of Jesus Christ after the Apostles died, and she married herself to the baptism in the Name of the Father, and of the Son, and the Holy Ghost, but now the light is come calling her to return to her first baptism, which was in the Name of Jesus Christ. (Acts 2:38)

A Call to a Higher Standard

Russelites (Jehovah Witnesses) try to make to bible fit science. The Seventh Day Adventists try to make the Bible fit history. The Protestant world (i.e., Methodist, Baptist, Lutheran, etc.) tries to make the Bible fit their several traditions. The Catholics try to make the Bible fit Romanism. The Rationalists try to make it fit reason. But we, the people of God, take the Bible just as it is, and try, by the Grace of God, to make our lives fit the Bible. Jesus said, "Take My yoke upon you and learn of Me;" a yoke has two places in it, one for each ox, even so Jesus is in one yoke and we are in the other. God is one, not two or three; it is one with God all the way. One Lord, one Faith, one baptism, (Eph 4) One way, (Jer 32:39) One mind, I Cor 2:16) One Name, (Acts 4:12) One body, (Eph 4:4) One Spirit, (Eph 4:4) One hope, (Eph 3:4) One God and Father of all, (Eph 4:6) One Church, (Eph 5) One husband, one wife. If the Church should not have but one H us band or God, then they that are of the Church should not have but one husband or wife. Awake, O church of God and contend for the faith once delivered to the saints. Preach the word. Fear not men. God will be with thee.

The Inconsistencies of the Present Day Ministry

In the Minute Book of a certain body of Pentecostal people, there is in substance these words:

whereas there are certain people in our midst who have been divorced and remarried, we advise that we let them alone and let them walk in the light as God shines it upon their pathway. Be it further resolved that no minister be given credentials who has divorced and remarried, for that would be a stumbling block to others.

"Consistency, thou art a jewel." In the first place, if everyone that is filled with the Holy Ghost is a saint, why should they designate those who have second companions as "certain people in our midst," and, if so, why should they not preach to the people about their sins and not try to put the job on God. How can God shine the light (word) on their pathway if the ministers don't preach the word to the people, so God can witness to the word, and so shine the light on their pathway. How can they ever find out they are wrong? And, if it is a stumbling block for a minister to have a second companion, what about the saints? Surely God hasn't one standard for the laity and another standard for the clergy; when he has said in His word, Hosea 6:9: Like people, like priest," and again a husbandman must be first partaker of the fruits. (2 Tim 2: 6) Once more He said: "Be thou an example of the believers." (I Tim 4: 12. I Cor 1:10) "Now, I beseech you, brethren, by the Name of our Lord Jesus Christ, that ye all speak the same thing, and that there be no divisions among you; but that ye be perfectly joined together in the same mind and the same judgment. Now we know when we say that the ministers should not have a second companion while the first one lives; but the saints may; that we are not perfectly joined together in the same mind and the same judgment. Consistency, thou art a jewel.

A brother, some time ago, brought out a wonderful message and revelation on the 13th Matthew chapter 13 and the 1st, 2nd, and 3rd chapters of Revelation, showing that the seven parables found in Matthew 13, correlated with and meant the same thing as the 1st and 2nd and 3rd chapters of Revelation. And as the brother went on comparing parable after parable with the several church periods, he came down to the Laodiceans, which he compared to the seventh parable in Matthew 13, which is the Dragnet parable. Now, if that be true, let us look at the dragnet parable and compare it with the subject at hand. (Matthew 13:47-48) The kingdom of heaven is like unto a net (Gospel) that was cast into the sea (people), and gathered of every kind (adulterers, drunkards, thieves, murderers, etc.), which, when it was full (after the revival), they drew to the shore (word of God), and gathered the good into vessels (missions), BUT CAST THE BAD AWAY. According to the above theories we should keep all we gather, for, if they were not good, we would not have caught them, or, in other words, God is making no mistake in baptizing them, "Let them alone." Consistency, thou art a jewel. Brethren, if we will be consistent, we will cast back every adulterer we have preached to and got in the mission who will not walk in the light. Why if a man is a drunkard and gets saved, if he continues to live as a drunkard, we put him out. What about the man living in adultery? If he gets saved, why should we not tell him to quit his life of adultery? And if he doesn't, why should we say, "Let him alone"? Why don't we put him out as we would a drunkard? Sin is sin; there is no difference with God. Again, if a thief gets saved, straightway we teach him to stop stealing and to give back the things he has stolen, and, if he doesn't, we put him out... Paul said, "Let him that stole steal no more, Let him that lied lie no more," and I say, "let them that was living in adultery live in it no more." Tell me, do you think that when John told old Herod it was not lawful for him to have his brother's wife, if old Herod would have got saved, do you think that what it was not lawful for him to do before he was saved, it would be lawful after he was saved?

The Patriotism of the World—Versus—the Patriotism (Love to God) of the Saints

Behold the love (patriotism) the people of the world have for their respective countries; look what sacrifices they will make to uphold the laws. And in the time of war they will give all that they have, yea, and their lives if need be, that the principles contended for by their country may be maintained. One young man, in order to join the army and fight for his country, underwent an operation to remove an impediment that hindered him from answering the call of his country. This shows that we should be willing to suffer anything for the kingdom of Heaven's sake, yea, for our own sake, that we may be accounted worthy to escape all the things that are coming upon the earth, and to stand before the Son of Man.

Behold the devotion of Bismarck to the Prussian Throne: He would not stop at anything in amalgamating, the German Empire. You may hang me said he, "so long as the rope you do it with binds Germany to the Prussian Throne." Shall his zeal for the Prussian Throne surpass our zeal for the Throne of our God.

The throne of Prussia is temporal, but the Throne of our God is eternal. Well, might we say, I will leave this man or this woman who is an eye or hand which causeth me to offend, (i.e., stumble) because l am, unlawfully joined and I will walk with God even though I will have to leave my home and brave the cold world alone: (yet not alone for God will be with thee) And though l walk through the vale of poverty, yea, even the valley of the shadow of death; I will fear no evil, so long as I am lead to and bound thereby to the Throne of God on high. Amen, bless his Great Name forever.

Listen to the testimony of Apostle Paul, our beloved, father in the faith when facing bonds, afflictions and death for the word of God; being entreated with much tears and warnings, said:

> What mean ye to weep and break my heart for I am ready not to be bound only, but to die for the Name of our Lord Jesus Christ. Even so, we must suffer the loss of all things and count them as dung; that we might win Christ, and be found in him at that day, not having our, own righteousness (our ways and doctrines), but the righteousness of God that came by faith and obedience to his Word. Amen.

Part IV: Entreating for Justice

The Social Activism of Robert Clarence Lawson

Robert Clarence Lawson was one of the few early black Pentecostal leaders, who used his intellect and influence not only to preach the gospel but also to engage in social justice activism to combat the entrenched racism that impacted his parishioners and community. Born in segregated Louisiana, that institutionalized white supremacy, Lawson migrated North only to find that Jim Crow was alive and well there also challenge the normalcy of Jim Crow.

Seeing racism as a social injustice issue condemned by God as sin, he observed on one occasion,

> It is bad enough to preach prejudice and uphold the iniquitous custom of segregation, but to make God a party to it is a monumental sin. Is God the minister of sin? To the contrary ...[36]

In a 1947 essay, Lawson insisted that "The hydra-headed monster of prejudice rears its ugly head as a challenge to the Holy Spirit, who says that brotherly love should continue regardless of race or color—that each one should esteem his

---

[36] Robert C. Lawson, *An Open Letter to A Southern White Minister on Prejudice* (New York: Privately Printed, n.d.), 12.

brother better than himself—that he that is greatest among you, let him be servant of all..."[37]

Afro-Hermeneutical Development

Lawson employed the Bible Reading Method[38] used by Holiness and Pentecostal preachers of his day, as a starting point for his exegesis. However, in contrast to other Pentecostals, he supplemented this simplistic technique using other lines including Ethiopianism. The ideology of Ethiopianism provided an ancestral link between African Americans and Africans during the eighteenth through the mid-twentieth centuries. As a component of the Harlem Renaissance, it employed religion and literature to link those from the African diaspora with the mother continent of Africa.

The movement, derived from the prophetic understanding of Psalms 68:31, "Princes shall come out of Egypt; Ethiopia shall soon stretch out her hands unto God," saw Africa as an example and contributor to the development of Christianity. According to John Gruesser, "Ethiopianism in America during the nineteenth century and

---

[37] Robert C. Lawson, "Sparks From The Anvil," *For The Defense of the Gospel* (New York: Church of Our Lord Jesus Christ, 1972), 326-327.

[38] Hermeneutics is the method one employs to exegete, interpret, and contextualize Scripture. Hermeneutics seeks to understand why the author wrote what he wrote; and how did his contemporary audience understood it, what was its intended meaning and how to we appropriate it for contemporary society. Lawson was unique among early Pentecostal with a working knowledge of the Greek and Hebrew and ancient history.

the first decade of the twentieth was certainly more religious than politically oriented."[39]

Lawson's embrace of Pan-Africanist ideology was evidenced in his work as spiritual advisor for the United African Nationalist Movement and involvement with the Ethiopian World Federation, for which he served as president in 1951. He encouraged African Americans and Caribbeans to support the Ethiopian cause during Mussolini's invasion and to purchase land in that nation. He also sponsored Ethiopian youths to study in the United States, some at his R. C. Lawson Institute. For his effort, Lawson, one of the few African Americans who had a close relationship with Emperor Selassie who awarded the prestigious, Star of Ethiopia.

From his congregation in one of New York City's poorest communities, Lawson determined not only to prorogate the gospel, but to instill ethnic pride within his community. He used Scripture to demonstrate how African Americans were not inferior to their white counterparts, and, therefore, should not accept Jim Crow social values or racial discrimination.

Historical theologian, Douglas Jacobsen saw Lawson as, "drawing on new developments in anthropology and his knowledge of world history and the Bible... [to] outline an Afrocentric critique of Western culture and a theological

---

[39] John Cullen Gruesser, *Black on Black: Twentieth-Century African American Writing About Africa* (Lexington, KY: University of Kentucky Press, 2000), 9.

critique of racist Christianity [and] develop his own multiracial theology of Christ and the atonement."⁴⁰

His June 1957 sermon, The Greatest Evil in This World Is Race Prejudice, lauds African trailblazers, including Imhotep, the Father of medicine; African descendent and Greek storyteller, Aesop, and Cleopatra. In this message Lawson stated,

> It is the Church's job not to foster, aid and abet white supremacy, through segregation, but to eliminate it, as God said to Jeremiah, to root out, and pull down, to build, and to plant in the human heart through the new birth, the doctrine of the Fatherhood of God and the brotherhood of man. ⁴¹

For him, segregation didn't only separate races, but yielded economic exploitation and degraded black personhood. As product of the oppressive system, Lawson noted that racism made it,

> ... extremely difficult [for black people] to maintain, even in the Church, a semblance of human dignity. At every turn he is hindered at

---

[40] Douglas Jacobsen, *A Reader in Pentecostal Theology Voices from The First Generation* (Bloomington IN: Indiana Universality Press, 2006), 200.

[41] Robert C. Lawson, "The Greatest Evil in This World Is Race Prejudice," *For The Defense of the Gospel the Writings of Bishop R.C. Lawson* (New York, 1972), 255.

places he cannot enter because of his color; churches, schools, restaurants, theatres, lunch counters, rest rooms, not to mention the widespread job barriers. Living is made like a convict serving out a sentence.[42]

However, Lawson saw the church as inclusively open to all with no distinction of race or gender. In a sermon, Letter to The Laodicean Church, preached January 1949, he noted,

> You need to be in a spiritual Church. The spiritual church makes you welcome—it is for white, for black, for rich, for poor, ignorant or educated—a universal Church—not denominational—but spiritual Church—not a lukewarm Church, but a spirit filled Church, triumphant are you in that Church, the Saviour's Bride.[43]

While in the British West Indies, Lawson perused a pamphlet by American minister, J.A. Lovell entitled, Predictions for 1949. In a section on the "Negro," Lovell used scriptures to attempt to demonstrate the inferiority of African Americans. His contention greatly disturbed Lawson, who responded with a 15-page open letter entitled, An Open Letter to A Southern White Minister on Prejudice.

---

[42] Ibid, 253.
[43] Robert C. Lawson, "Letter to The Laodicean Church," *For The Defense of the Gospel the Writings of Bishop R.C. Lawson* (New York, 1972), 137.

In it, he used Lovell's own Scripture references to refute his contentions.

From example, where Lovell used Genesis 24:3-4, to forbid interracial marriages, Lawson responded:

> For every white girl attacked, there are one hundred Colored girls that have been seduced by white men. That is proven by the fruit —mulattoes, quadroons, creoles, and other light colored Negroes, who obviously are children of white men, adulterers and seducers. Moreover, God would much prefer intermarriage, rather than bastardy, adultery and fornication, of which the Southern white most is most guilty.[44]

He further turned to the Scriptural to propose a genealogy of Christ that included Africans in His legal blood. He insisted that segregation hinders the Body of Christ being in unity and that God has no respect of persons.

A Multiracial Message

Within Ethiopianism, Lawson saw the Gospel as universally ministering to all races, in obedience to the great commission of Christ. Following the example of his father in the gospel, Haywood, he also led a multiracial congregation (which Talmadge French concludes "expanded quickly") and

---

[44] Lawson, *An Open Letter to A Southern White Minister On Prejudice*, 8.

asserted, "I have pastored a mixed congregation of white and black folks ever since I have been pastoring, and they can bear me witness that I write the truth when I affirm that I have at all times showed the same love to all, regardless of race or color. For God has shown me to esteem all men alike in as much as all are made in His image."[45]

When Lawson saw discrimination impacting the economy of African Americans, by not affording them the educational and employment opportunities given he provided employment opportunities in New York. Lawson used his business acumen entered into several business enterprises at a time when most holiness pastors felt that the saints should not delve into secular matters."[46] From 1926 to 1938, he founded several shops and service locations including a book store, record shop grocery store restaurant, a five-story apartment building and three funeral homes and a cemetery. He also established the Church of Christ Publishing Company, with a printing press that produced the official organ for the denomination, The Contender for the Faith, as well as books and tracts.

Lawson viewed education as a resource of upward mobility during a climate of discrimination. Ministering in poor segregated communities, he observed the disparities in the public educational system for African Americans and was

---

[45] Robert C. Lawson, *The Anthropology of Jesus Christ Our Kinsman* (New York: The Church of Christ Publishing Co., 1925), i.

[46] Mable L Thomas, "The Life of Bishop R. C. Lawson and the History of The Church of Our Lord Jesus Christ of the Apostolic Faith, Inc.," in *For the Defense of the Gospel,* ed. Arthur Anderson (New York: Church of Our Lord Jesus Christ, 1972), 10.

motivated provide quality elementary and secondary education for the youth in his African American community. In 1930, the Methodist Church, gave Lawson The Industrial Union Training School and Orphanage in Southern Pines, North Carolina which he subsequently renamed the R.C. Lawson Institute. Lawson envisioned a school that would take children of working parents off the streets and train, their hearts, head, and hands. He wanted the school to have a tuition fee low enough so [to be] within the reach of even the poorest"[47] The school not only provided education but sought to instill racial pride and self-worth among the student body.[48] In an August 1931 article the New York Age reported,

> ... this school and orphanage [are] an important factor in the work that Bishop Lawson is doing. Several children without parents have been there, and on August 1 it is planned that another carload will be taken down. From the New York headquarters, Bishop Lawson is constantly sending quantities of food and clothing for the poor dependents entrusted to his care, together with such monies as are raised to help in this most commendable work.[49]

---

[47] Ibid., 11.

[48] Robert C. Lawson, *A Short Sketch of the Industrial Union of America, West Indies and Canada Its Objects, Etc.* (New York: Privately Printed, 1932), 2.

[49] New York Age, August 1, 1931.

Civil Involvement

During the 1920s, Lawson aligned with important civil rights leaders such as Adam Clayton Powell, Jr. and ecumenical associations. Powell, the pastor of Abyssinia Baptist Church, represented New York as the first African American to Congress. He preached at the twelfth anniversary of the Church of Our Lord Jesus Christ, and his choir rendering the music.[50]

African Freedom Day was established in 1958, held in Accra, Ghana it commemorated the first Pan-African meeting of African countries. It marked the freedom of colonized Africa, from European rule, and celebration included those of the African diaspora. In the United States the selection of the 1959 conference, was Lawson's, Refuge Temple. African and American speakers included the Nation of Islam minister, Malcolm X.[51]

Community Ecumenism

Lawson's attempt to impact social justice led him to cross denominational lines and associate with clergy and movements outside the Oneness fold to benefit his community both economically and politically.

In 1948, when a white man, William Horner was killed in his furniture shop in Trenton, New Jersey, his common-law wife who had also been beaten, reported to police, that a

---

[50] "12th Anniversary of the Refuge Church of Christ." *The New York Age,* August 1, 1931.

[51] "Refuge Temple Picked for 'Freedom' Day.' *The New York Age,* April 4, 1959.

group of young African American men had killed her husband. Though the young men who were apprehended for the crime had alibis, their lack of access to counsel among other issues forced a major case.[52] The case caused an uproar in the Northern African American communities.[53]

When the Civil Rights Congress (CRC), became involved case of the Trenton Six, the Harlem branch of the CRC made Lawson an honorary co-chairman on their committee to free the Trenton Six.[54]

Lawson applauded the religious organizations that supported civil rights and condemned Pentecostal Churches for their lack of involvement since he held that it was the churches responsibility to condemn racism and that Pentecostals should be in the forefront.[55] He notes,

> ... not a word from the Pentecostal brethren. No outstanding minister of the Assembly of God or the United Pentecostal Church has raised his voice in approval of the Supreme Court decision and in disapproval of the traditional concept of segregation.

---

[52] Knepper, Cathy D. "The Crime and the Trenton Six." In *Jersey Justice: The Story of the Trenton Six*, 1-22. New Brunswick, NJ: Rutgers University Press, 2011. http://www.jstor.org/stable/j.ctt1b3h9rr.4.

[53] L. A. Parker, "Recalling infamous case of Trenton,'" The Trentonian News, February 4, 2005. Accessed April 3, 2018. www.trentonian.com/article/TT/20050204/TMP02/302049993

[54] "On Committee for Trenton Six," *The New York Age*, March 19, 1949, 2.

[55] Robert C. Lawson, "Prejudice," *For The Defense of the Gospel* (New York, 1972), 329.

He further states, "

> ... I hoped and trusted that the Pentecostal movement would have been the church which should redeem Christendom from the virus and plague of race prejudice and segregation as an established order of society.[56]

For Lawson, the stand against racism was orthopraxis - correct ethical and moral practice that aligns itself with one's orthodox doctrinal teaching and proclamation. The brotherhood of humankind and the Fatherhood of God has no room for discrimination. His entreaty for social justice reflected his theology.

---

[56] The Greatest Evil In This World Is Race Prejudice, 249.

An Open Letter to a Southern White Minister on Prejudice: The Eating Cancer of the Soul

Dr. Lovell, D.D.

While on a trip to the West Indies in the month of February, I picked up one of your pamphlets captioned Predictions for 1949. Having been intensely interested in prophecy for the last twenty-five years, it for natural for me to easily peruse pages of your booklet, until I came to page five and the article below captioned under "The Negro" Genesis 14:3-4.

What I then read grieve me so that I laid down your booklet and read no further. Why you should send this to the West Indies to an island 95% Negro is beyond me. Such sentiments which distort the Scripture and misrepresent God should not be exported as a religious of the New Testament.

Someone truly said that prejudice is a great timesaver. It enables one to form opinions without bothering to bothering to get the facts. You truly did not get the facts when you wrote the following article on the Negro:

> The Negro: Genesis 14.3-4. "And I will make thee swear by the Lord, God of all the earth that thou shall not take a wife unto thee of the daughters of the Canaanites among who I dwell. But thou shall

go unto my country and my kindred and take a wife unto my son Isaac.

From the above Scriptures you will notice that God told his people Israel not to marry outside their own race; to do so would be violating one of his strictest laws, carrying with it the death penalty. Contrary to what the modern preachers tell us, and shame on them for telling us such unscriptural things. This and other of God's laws still hold true and are for us as a nation today.

I have no prejudice in my heart against the colored people. I employ a precious Christian colored in our home whose work is just as faithful and satisfactory and whose Christian life is just as beautiful as any worker I have. There would be no PROBLEM where the colored race was concerned if all of them were Christian like the one who works for us. If they didn't get mixed up with the Communist and listen to a lot of false propaganda, and if they didn't attack white girls. The average colored person doesn't want to intermarry with the white race any more than a white person wants to intermarry with the colored.

Henry A. Wallace, who should have learned his lesson in the recent election, recently advocated marriage between colored and white people. However, Mr. Wallace, as much as we disdain this in him, should not be blamed as much as when some modernistic preacher, who certainly should know better, advocated such mixed marriages. Shame on the whole bunch!

So while we are scoring the Communist for bringing on the whole trouble with the colored race, and while we censor any individual colored person for doing that which he should not do, let us also censor, without restraint, the modernistic, unscriptural, infidel preacher who advocates mixed marriages among colored and white people, thus encouraging the colored people in doing the things the rest of white people blame them for doing.

This Article I am Answering Categorically

In this period of world history, a wrong move or delayed action policy by diplomats or the generation of wrong sentiments by ministers can bring a holocaust of total war using the many devastating missiles and devices for the destruction of humankind.

It is unthinkable that you, a minister of the Gospel should generate, perpetuate or condone prejudices of any kind or use the Bible to justify it. You are definitely prejudice though you deny that you have any prejudice in your heart against Colored people (1) You are definitely prejudice if you believe one race is more with more ability, more xx or more character than any other race (2) You are prejudice if you believe that members of your church are good and most others are queer and bad. If you accuse or judge a whole race of people, if you repeat rumors or gossip about other races, if you believe that members of other races should be restricted in their opportunities, employment or education, then you are prejudices. (3) You are prejudice if you keep your children, friends or members of your race from associating with members or friends of others races or creeds. "But if you have respect to persons, ye commit sin, and are convinced of the law as transgressors. Whosoever shall keep the whole law, and yet offend in this one point, he is guilty of all. (Jas 2:9-10)

You make the statement that God told Israel not to marry outside their own race, but to have not one scrap of Scripture to prove it. The Scripture you did use was not God speaking to Israel, but Abraham speaking to his servant. Secondly, it was restricted to the peoples of the land and to the daughters of the Canaanite descendants of Canaan, the youngest son of Ham who begat the Sidonite, Hittites, Jebusites, Amorites, etc. Whereas Ham was the father of three other sons: Shem, Mizriam, the Egyptian and Cush, who, intern, begat many sons. Cush, for instance, begat Nimrod, the first man to wear a crown. He was mighty in the earth, a leader and a mighty hunter before the Lord. He founded the Kingdom of Babylon. (Gen 10-12) Mizriam was the father of Egypt in our Bible. Ham was his father and the father of the so-called colored races, for instance, the Libyans, Philistines, etc., out from whom empire builders who built the Kingdoms of Assyria, Babylonia, Ethiopia, etc.

Most of the people of the East and Far East are Negroid, that is, Colored people, who married and intermarried with the Children of Israel. This is proven by JUDAH and SHUAH, DAVID and BATHSHEBA, SOLOMON and RACOB, and MOSES, for instance, who married an ETHIOPIAN woman.

The Hamitic contribution to the anthropological development of Jesus Christ comes in at the incipiency of the tribe of Judah out of which Christ came, for it is written in

Genesis 49, "That the scepter should not depart from Judah until Shiloh came.

The beginning of the tribe of Judah is recorded in Genesis the 38th Chapter which reads on this wise:

> And it came to pass at that time that Judah went down from his brethren and turned into a certain Adullamite whose name was Hirah, and Judah saw there a certain Canaanite negro woman whose name was Shuar whom he married. And she conceived and bore him a son and called his name Er. She conceived again and bare him a son, and she called his n a. me Onan, she bore him yet another son whose name was Shelah... (Gen 38:1-5a)

In a process of time Judah took a wife for his first-born Er whose name was Tamar, but Er, Judah's first son was wicked in the sight of God, so the Lord caused him to die. Judah consequently said to Onan, marry the wife of your brother and raise up an heir for your brother, but Onan knew that the heir would not be his own, therefore, before he approached his brother's wife, he did the unspeakable thing, wasting the seed of his brother. What he did was wicked in the sight of God, therefore, he caused him to die. Not only was it wicked of him to do such an abominable act, but his wickedness was great in that he refused and resisted the will and purpose of God in the mingling of the blood of the Hamitic or negro race, with Shem and that of Japheth in the anthropological development of Jesus Christ. It was necessary in the plan of God to develop the most perfect man of the human race, to mingle and to intermingle the blood of the three branches to produce the best and most perfect man. Our Saviour who would be our kinsman redeemer by virtue of birth for all humankind.

Of course, all of this is out of gear with the pseudo-scientific teaching of the day, especially relative to the Colored race in regard to miscegenation; that is, the mixing of the blood of black and white races. They say that this would deteriorate the white races, but the Bible infers that it would be just the opposite. Surely in the case of Our Lord Jesus Christ, this is evident for he had Negro blood in his veins, yet he was the fairest of ten thousand of whom it is said, even his enemy and judge, Pilate said, "Behold the Man." He was indeed the holiest among the mighty and the most mighty among the holiest. He lifted off the gates of empires and turned the river of human history and changed time to A.D. The spirit of Onan still lives today in many of his children who still resist the truth and purpose of God, but His will shall be done, and men shall know at least, that all flesh is grass.

> Judah said to Tamar, his daughter-in-law who was a Canaanite woman as his wife was... "Remain a widow at my father's house, till Shelah, my son, be grown," for he said, "Lest peradventure he dies also, as his brethren did." And Tamar went and dwelt in her Father's house. And in process of time, the daughter of Shuah, Judah's wife, died; and Judah was comforted and went up unto his

sheepshearers to Timnath, he and his friend Hiran the Adullamite. And it was told Tamar, saying; "Behold thy father-in-law goeth up to Timnath to shear his sheep." And she put her widow's garments off from her, and covered her with a veil, and wrapped herself, and sat in an open place, which is by the way to Timnath; that she saw that Shelah was grown, and she was not given unto him to wife.

When Judah saw her, he thought she was an harlot, because she had covered her face. And he turned to her by the way and said, "Go I pray thee le e come unto thee" (for he knew not that she was his daughter-in-law). She said, "What will you give me that thou may come in unto me?" And he replied, "I will send you a kid from the flock." And she said, "Wilt thou give me a pledge until you send it?" He said, "What is the pledge that you I shall give you?" And she answered, "Your signet and thy bracelets and the staff you have in your hand." And he gave them to her and came in unto her and she conceived of him, then she arose went away and laid by her veil from her and put on the garments of her widowhood.

And Judah sent the kid by the hand of his friend, the Adullamite to receive the pledge from the hands of the woman, but he found her not. Then he asked the men of the place saying, "Where is the harlot that was openly by the wayside?" And they said, "There was no harlot in this place.

And he returned to Judah and said, "I cannot find her and also the men of the place said that there was no harlot in this place. And Judah said, Let her take it to her, lest we be shamed. Behold, I sent this kid, thou hast not found her. And it came to past about three months after, it was told Judah saying, "Tamar, your daughter-in-law hath played the harlot," and also, "Behold she is with child by her whoredom." And Judah said, "Bring her forth and let her be burnt." When she was brought forth, she sent to her father-in-law saying, "By the man whose these are, am I with child; and she said, Discern, I pray thee, Whose are these, the signet, and bracelets, and staff."

> And Judah acknowledged them, and said, She hath been more righteous than I; because that I gave her not to Shelah my son. And he knew her again no more.

> And it came to pass in the time of her travail, that, behold, twins were in her womb. And it came to pass, when she travailed, that the one put out his hand; and the midwife took and bound upon his hand a scarlet thread, saying, This came out first.

> And it came to pass, as he drew back his hand, that, behold, his brother came out and she said, How hast thou broken forth? This breach be upon thee; therefore, his name was called Pharez.

And afterward came out his brother, that had the scarlet thread upon his hand; and his name was called Zarah. (Gen 38:11-30)

There was born to Judah by the two Negro women the children who were the progenitors of the "TRIBE OF JUDAH. If any race has wherewith to boast as touching the things of the flesh relative to Our Lord Jesus Christ, the Colored race has more for they gave to the world, the two mothers of THE TRIBE OF JUDAH out of which Christ came. So, I may say, they were the first mothers of Our Lord, for as touching the flesh. He was at that time in loins of His father, Judah, to whom pertaineth the pre-eminence among the twelve Tribes of Israel, to whom was given the adoption and the glory, and the covenants, and the giving of the law, and the service of God, and the promises; whose of the fathers, and of whom as concerning the flesh, concerning the flesh, Christ came, whom is over all, God blessed forever, Amen. (Gen 38; 49:8-13)

For fear that it may be reasoned that Judah has other children and out of that branch came Jesus, we will trace his genealogical descent to I Chronicles 2:3-5, where it is recorded: "The sons of Judah; Er, and Onan, and Shelah: which three were born unto him of the daughter of Shuah the Canaanitess. And Er, the first-born of Judah, was evil in the sight of the Lord; and He slew him. And Tamar his daughter-in-law bare him Pharez and Zerah. All the sons of Judah were five.

So, you see Judah had no other sons than by these two Negro women. Three by his wife and twins by his daughter-in-law. Matthew clinches this in his Gospel of the genealogy of Jesus, "The book of the generation of Jesus Christ, the son of David, the son of Abraham. Abraham begat Isaac and Isaac begat Jacob, and Jacob begat Judas and his brethren Pharez and Zerah of Tamar. (Matt 1:1-4)

Is it a surprise to you to know that a Colored woman was the first mother of the Tribe of Judah? Let me add some more to this surprise! Following her was (b) Tamar; then in the process of time, (c) Rahab of Jericho, a Canaanite woman was married into the genealogical development of Judah and became one of its mothers. Then there was Bathsheba, the wife of Urias, a Hittite, whom David saw bathing one day and brought her into the house while her husband was in the front fighting with the Army of Israel in defense of the throne of David. David humbled her, and she conceived and sent word and told David, "I am with child.

David, in order to cover up his sin, sent for Urias from the front, ostensibly to inquire how the battle was going on, but, in reality, to have Urias to go to his own home to his wife, so that he, David, would be sheltered from the shame of his sins. But Urias slept at David's door, and in the morning said unto him, "The ark, and Israel, and Judah abide in tents; and my lord Joab, and the servants of my lord, are encamped in the open fields; shall I then go into mine house, to eat and to drink, and to lie with my wife? as thou livest, and thy soul liveth, I will not do this thing.

Then the basest act of David was committed, when he conspired with Joab against the life of Urias and ordered that Joab should put Urias in the front of the battle in the thickest of the fight so that he would be killed. It so happened that

Urias was killed, and after Bathsheba, his wife had mourned for him certain days, and after the days of her mourning were over, David sent and took her for his wife. Her first-born died, notwithstanding that David prayed that it should be healed. However, she bore David another child whose name was Solomon, who reigned in his stead after David's death, as King. He was reputed to have been the wisest man that ever lived.

If so be the case, to the everlasting honor of the Colored race, he was a Negro (that is a half-breed), who according to the laws of the South and the standards of the Ku Klux Klan, of whom a lot of our white ministers seem to be under the influence of or a member of, he was a Negro, for he had more than one-sixteenth Negro blood in his veins—so also, anyone who has the blood in his veins of four Negro (Canaanitish) women, (l) Shuah, (2) Tamar, (3) Rahab and (4) Bathsheba. According to that standard, therefore, if Our Lord would return to the earth in the flesh and go down South incognito, He would be Jim-crowed and segregated for he had more than had more than one-sixteenth of Negro blood in Him.

Solomon in his songs, (SS 1:5) singing to the bride of his love, said, "I am black, but comely. Note the process of miscegenation in the genealogical development of Christ. Pharez and Zarah (Gen 38:29-30); Tamar (Gen 38:11-30) the first four women in the genealogy of Matthew 1. The other three were Rahab, verse 5; Ruth, verse 3, and Bathsheba, verse 6. Note the introversion, Hebrew, Gentile, Gentile, Hebrew, showing the condescension of Christ in taking His nature from all races.

Publuius Letus, the Roman scribe is said to have given a description of our Saviour:

> He was a man in stature of about six feet. His hair being wine-colored and overflowing the shoulders. His countenance convincing to behold yet with a note of tenderness and authority. He was the color of a filbert (a nut of reddish hue)," thus making Jesus neither white nor black. This record of Publuius Letus, is, only to be found in ancient church histories.

The idea contained in Genesis 24:3, 4, is not so much for Israel not to marry out of their own race, as to marry out of their own religion of worship of the one true God. Moreover, the restrictions imposed upon Israel not to marry outside of their own nation was specifically directed against the Canaanite alone, but rather all Gentiles which includes all people, any color, white or black. This restriction was not to be induced or persuaded to worship idols or go whoring after them. Note Exodus 34:10-17, particularly the 15th to 17th verses, also Deuteronomy 9:1-2 and 12th verse. Moreover, if any one of a race became a proselyte to the Jewish religion, he became numbered in Israel, and it was permissible for an Israelite to marry with him.

You make an erroneous statement concerning the above prohibition when you state, "This and other of God's laws still hold true and are for us as a nation today. Kindly tell me what scriptures you have. Do you claim that you are a Jew and that this nation is a Jewish nation to whom this law is given? Moreover, you state that "if all Colored people were as your Christian Colored servant, there would be no problem where the Colored race was concerned, if they did not get mixed up with Communists and listen to a lot of false propaganda, and they did not attack white girls. Is not this a call to race violence and a misrepresentation of the Negro, who has less Communists among them than the white people. And is not this an indictment of the entire race for the act of a few licentious, ignorant Negroes that may attack white girls occasionally, but are there not thousands of intelligent, educated Negroes that are not guilty of any such crime. But on the other hand, would it not be helping to solve the problem if all white people were as good as that fine Christian Colored woman you mention. Then there would not be bastardy in the South. For every white girl attacked, there are one hundred Colored girls that have been seduced by white men. That is proven by the fruit—mulattos, quadroons, Creoles, and other light-colored Negroes, who obviously are children of white men, adulterers, and seducers. Moreover, God would much prefer intermarriage, rather than bastardy, adultery, and fornication, of which the Southern white man is most guilty.

Another false and vicious statement you made is that They (Colored people) as well as we, realize such intermarriages would represent a violation of the laws of nature and the teachings of God.

I am sure the Colored race knows no such law, and I challenge you to prove it—that it is a violation of the nature and the teachings of God. You ought to know that all this is a lie, and you have neither chapter nor verse.

Henry Wallace, whom you propose to disdain, shows more honesty, breadth and vision than you who are presumably a Bible fundamentalist preacher who abrogates to yourself the inferring that they are infidels because [of] the things the white people blame them for doing.

If you are looking for the soon-coming of Our Lord and expect to be numbered among those in the Kingdom Age during the period of the Millennium, you will be wholly unfit, for during the Kingdom Age, there will be a people of all races, and there will be no segregation. It is such white people as you who are embarrassing your country, diplomats and leaders before Russia and her satellites and the world of Colored people, such as India, Africa, China, and the Isles of the Sea, who point to the inconsistency of the Church and of democracy in their treatment of the Negro, and their professing of religion, principle and democracy.

Thank God the light is breaking for better understanding and the honest facing of facts. To save our civilization we must break down all barriers of segregation and discrimination if we aspire to moral leadership of the world. In the New York Herald Tribune, one young leader of tomorrow, Mr. Summerfield came out with the following:

> The problem which seems to be claiming the first consideration of more people every day is that the United States is engaged in a death struggle for the moral leadership of the world. And I would say also,

that more people every day are coming to realize as I am that there are some areas in which we may be doing things to jeopardize our chances for that position of leadership." Citing the case of Herman Marion Sweatt, applicant to the Texas University Law School (International News Service, January-February 1948) and Ms. Ada Louise Fisher Sipuel still seeking admission through the courts to the University of Oklahoma's all white law school, Mr. Summerfield (young white progressive) scored those Texans who... still find ways to rationalize their prejudices and whose misinformation had led them to think that some great disaster would occur the moment segregation was broken down at any point. It is this group, I think, which is responsible for the testimony of many school officials and politicians on behalf of segregation.

I am certain that many of these leaders know the facts of the situation better than they seem to, and I don't see how anybody can believe one thing and profess another, without eventually injuring his integrity... I believe any American who considers himself educated and still denies equality of opportunity to anyone, is either making an excuse for some exclusive privilege, or he isn't educated to the democratic facts of life.

The so-called superiority of the white race, or any other race for that matter, above any other group is purely hypothetical and has no basis in fact. The leading anthropologists of the world have agreed as recently as last year, 1948, at least 85% of them, that there is no such, thing as pure race upon the earth that is distinct, separated and different from any other of the human species.

Such terms as Hamitic for the Ethiopians, and Semitic for the Jew—these terms, if they have any meaning at all, are only as language groups; precisely as Latin, Anglo-Saxon, Arabian. It is as nonsensical to talk to the Jewish race as it is to talk of a Christian one.

What ethnologists have to say on the alleged inferiority of certain people, remind(s) one of a Haitian proverb, "When the rooster and the cockroach come to court, you don't have to guess which one will win." What ethnologists need most is emancipation from exploiting capitalism and complete divorce from the slave master's legend of the Negro as being subnormal and inferior to the white race

This is definitely discounted and proven to be a false premise by history that records illustrious names of great men of color: for instance, Imhotep, God of medicine; Thomas III, conqueror of the then known world. Akhenatom, first Messiah; Lockman, the first great fabulist of the world; Aesop, whose proverbs influenced the world's greatest thinkers; Cletus, comrade of Alexander the Great and also his chief cavalry leader. Hannibal of Carthage had the reputation of being the greatest military leader and strategist of all times. Napoleon, after selecting the seven supreme military geniuses of the world, ranked him as the first in daring... and this Hannibal, said he, "is the most audacious of all, the most astonishing; so bold, so sure, so great in everything, who, at twenty-six conceived what is highly inconceivable what one may truly call the impossible."

Cleopatra, the seventh Queen of Egypt has come down to us through twenty centuries as the perfect example of the seductive art in women. She was unique, excelling in licentiousness, a woman of great charm and force and education.

It is reputed that she spoke Greek, Egyptian, Latin, Hebrew, and Arabic. Dion Cassius wrote of her:

> She was splendid, to see, and was capable of conquering the heart that resisted most obstinately against the influence of love; and those that have been frozen by age. Her charms of speech were such that she won all who listened to her.

Among the many who fell in love with her, the first and most notable is Julius Caesar, who was debonair, and one of the world's greatest orators and a beloved ruler.

The second was Mark Anthony, the Magnificent, the Don Juan of his time and a great orator. To these two men she gave birth to several children. She became within an inch of becoming the mistress of the world but for a misunderstanding of the outcome of the Battle of Actium; mistaking the battle to be lost, she left the scene in her ship of war, followed by Mark Anthony who died in her arms in her own mausoleum. Afterwards, she followed in death from the bite of an asp smuggled to her by slaves, conveyed to her in a basket of figs.

In Asia, following her was the noted Zenobia Queen of the East. So much for warriors —now for scholars. Antar, poet and chivalrous figure of the East and the literature of the East. He is known as Abdul Fauras, and there is also a famous writer of the Ninth Century, Al ahiz, the most genial writer of the age (A.D. 778-888) if not in Arab literature, and the founder of Arab prose. He was the grandson of a Negro slave.

According to Christopher Dawson, Al ahiz was the greatest scholar and stylist of the Ninth Century. Ykub Al Mansur, greatest of Spanish caliphs, Amou Hassan Ali, the black Sultan of Morocco, Chaka Zulu, conqueror and despot, and Tippo Tib, African trail blazer, are among the other great warriors.

In religion, Samuel D. Crawford, Bishop of Niger, Menelik It was the Lion of Judah, who defeated the Italians with overwhelming slaughter; Alfred A. Doggs French General and empire builder, Isaac Wallace Johnson, African and indomitable labor leader, and Emperor Haile Selassie, the Dauntless of Ethiopia. Time would fail me to make mention, of course, of the great Saints, like St. Augustine of Carthage, an African, and St. Benedict, the Moor, the Saint of the Catholic Church, born in Sicily; Abraham Hannibal, Russian General and chief, and Jean Louis, the world's greatest swordsman and duelist, George H. Bridgetower, prodigy on the violin; Alexander Dumas, the world's greatest romancer, and Alexander Dumas... the remaker of the French Theater; Ira Aldridge, the greatest of the Othellos, and Samuel Coleridge Taylor, world's musical sensation;

Toussaint Louverture, Negro of whom Napoleon was jealous; Dessalines, liberator of Haiti and its first emperor.

Time would fail me to make mention of medieval and modern men of color. The great poet Robert Browning had Negro ancestry. Beethoven, the great musical genius had definite strains of Negro blood in him. These all, until the rise of the doctrine of white superiority, were generally pictured as Colored, especially Cleopatra. Shakespeare, in the opening lines of his Anthony and Cleopatra, calls her tawny. In his day, mulattos were called tawny. Captain John Smith, the Governor of Virginia and a contemporary of Shakespeare used tawny as a synonym with mulattos. Writing of a chief of Morocco, it was, "King Mully Hamet was not black as many supposed but mulatto or tawny as many of his subjects." (True Travels, Vol. 1, p. 45). Also, in Act 1, Scene 5, Cleopatra calls herself black, made by the sun, Phoebus. The above is sufficient to explode the myth of the so-called inferiority of black or mixed people.

> In the last analysis, we see only what we hope to see, what we have been taught to see; we eliminate and ignore everything that is not a part of our prejudice, says J. M. Charcot.

This is true, and perhaps, Reverend sir, your whole outlook on the race problem is the result of your Southern antecedents and background which warps your judgment and colors your vision to such an extent that you read even into the scriptures the postulates of white supremacy and the inferiority of the Negro race. You seek to certify these false assumptions or prejudices by the sanction of Scripture to make them to say these things are of divine origin and are the Will of the Creator, not thinking that this would make God the Author of inequality, and the author of partiality and injustice. For God to create men unequal, and demand the same responsibility and standards of them, would be a rank injustice. God forbid! This cannot be true, for it is incompatible to His divine nature.

No, beloved of God, God is not the author of inequalities or injustices. There is but one human race. Though there may be many nations, there is but one race. There are different languages and customs, but there is no basis for differences between men, for God hath made one blood all nations of men to dwell on the face of the earth. It is not enough to preach prejudice and uphold the iniquitous custom of segregation, but to make God a party to it is a monumental sin! To the contrary, the Scripture states that God has through the Cross of Jesus broken down the middle wall between Jew and Gentile and all other nations, for that matter, and has purposed that through the new birth a holy nation should be Jew nor Greek bond nor free, black nor white, a classless nation where all distinctions and differences are obliterated. (Acts 17:26; Eph 2:11-22; I Peter 2:9)

The Church is the divine agency through which this is to be brought about by the preaching and practice of the Gospel through the ministry. But, alas, through your type of ministry, this will never be brought about, for you are a preacher who builds again these things which Christ destroyed. Until there are ministers who are saved through and through, baptized with the Holy Spirit, who know no difference, and who have a vision of God's one world and His new order, that will never be brought about.

Not mere separation of races is involved in segregation, but the economic exploitation, the selfishness, and pride, which is the capital sin that caused Satan to fall from his holy state as a covering cherub known as Lucifer. It is in the design of segregation, the vicious and wicked psychology that fosters pride and arrogance on the part of the white man. God resists the proud, but giveth grace to the humble. It demeans the Negro, stuns the growth of his manhood, hinders his development, retards his initiative, courage and cooperation, and makes it extremely difficult for him to maintain even in the Church a semblance of human dignity. At every turn, he is hindered at places he cannot enter because of his color; churches, schools, restaurants, theaters, lunch counters, rest rooms, not to mention the wide-spread job barriers. Living is made like a convict serving out a sentence.

Moreover, segregation hinders fellowship of equally with other members of the family of God of other races. This is equivalent to raising a family, praising one child and berating or humiliating the other, which is unfair. This a true minister of the gospel should not condone or practice in the Church of Christ. To these sentiments agree H. G. Wells, a noted historian. Says he, "I am convinced myself that there is no more evil thing in this present world than race prejudice. None at all. I write deliberately. It is the worse single thing in life now. It justifies and holds together more baseness, cruelty and abomination than any other sort of error in the world."

It is the Church's job to foster, aid and abet white supremacy, through segregation, but to eliminate it, as God said to Jeremiah... to root out, and to pull down, to build, and to plant..." in the human heart through the new birth, the doctrine of Fatherhood of God and the brother hood of man. For the grace of God that bringeth salvation hath appeared to all men, teaching us that, denying ungodliness and worldly lusts, we should live soberly, righteously, and godly, in this present world; looking for that blessed hope and the glorious appearing of the great God and our Saviour Jesus Christ. (Tit 2:11-13)

Someday, perhaps, you will realize that all men are individuals, and should not be judged by the layer of skin which is only one hundredth of an inch thick. A wise man does not judge a car by the color it is painted, but by the motor it has. Were we all blind! What difference would it make if our neighbors were black or white. There is nothing respecting which a man may be so long unconscious as the extent and strength of his prejudice, but as Addison has said, "Prejudice and self-sufficiency proceed from inexperience of the world and ignorance of mankind."

Very small groups of people have the extreme characteristics of white, yellow and black races; the great majority of the people of the world are the "in-betweens" those with various shades of tan and brown. Man's greatest adventure was his spread from somewhere in Asia to all corners of the world.

Originally man was neither light nor dark. As he advanced into the areas of hot sunlight and long summers to the South, those with darker skins were better able to survive. The short wide nose developed as the best means of inhaling the moist warm air, and body hair disappeared. As he advanced into the North those with lighter skins were better able to absorb the sunlight in the short months of summer, and so store up a quantity of Vitamin D against the long dark winter to come. Here too, the long thin nose was better adapted to inhale and warm the cold air, and a large amount of body hair was some protection against the cold. In some places in Asia, a fold of skin developed over the inner corner of the eyes to produce what we call the slant eye. The geographical differences between men are however of small magnitude when one considers the fundamental likeness.

The population of the world was small in the days of early man, and differences, once begun, tended to persist through isolation and in breeding. Each so-called race became functionally adapted to living in the area in which it found itself. There was no question of superiority or inferiority for the white man would have suffered in the hot tropical sun as much as the Negro would have suffered in the cold north.

With the growth of civilization, man has been enabled through the use of proper clothing and scientifically prepared food and vitamins, to move into all areas of the world, no matter what his color. The-so-called racial differences are superficial and man is, essentially, the same and has the same potentialities wherever you find him, be he light, dark, tall, short, fat or thin, long headed or round headed

Dr. Chisholm says, "Our danger and other people's unresolved hates, and that of the world lie in our own and their antagonisms; our and their undiscriminating obedience; our and their tendency to find acceptable whatever concepts may fit the emotional state of the moment." Chief Justice Charles Evens Hughes said, "Rancor and bigotry, racial animosities and intolerance are more dangerous than any external force, because they undermine the very foundations of democratic effort."

R. R. Moton states that, "The thinking Negro refuses to accept the idea or even the theory that race prejudice is natural and inevitable; that it is inherent in the child, either white or black." He insists that it is acquired and cultivated, and that the greatest single aid to its cultivation is segregation.

Dr. Ernest A. Hooton of the Department of Harvard University has stated that "Racial prejudice is little more than the cloak to cover an apparently universal desire of selfish and morally low-grade human beings to dominate their fellow beings.

Allegations of racial inferiority or superiority were not based on scientific findings and had never deceived any except the ignorant and the mentally inferior, but these, unfortunately, included an enormous proportion of individuals of whatever race or nationality.

Racial difference provides the most obvious excuse for antagonism that really springs from sheer selfish desire to "dominate others, and especially to justify rivalry that is political, social or economic.

The hatreds that arise from human competition easily shift their emotional expressions from race to nationality to economic class to "religious affiliation, or to any other handy pretext whereby an ugly sentiment, a sordid motive or downright viciousness may be rationalized or whitewashed.

It is for this reason that racial prejudices will persist in spite of scientific demonstrations that there are no hierarchies of physical, mental, or cultural ability in human races, and no rank lists of virtues and vice.

We shall have to improve individual human quality before we can get an amelioration of group behavior as manifested in race discrimination, class rivalry, religious persecution and welfare. But in my opinion, the greater part of such human betterment will have to come about by segregating and preventing the reproduction of criminalistic, mentally defective, insane and constitutionally deteriorated individuals of whatever race, nationality and creed, and by studying human inheritance so that it will provide a knowledge that will enable us to breed better men.

Specifically, we shall have to have better quality of whites before Negroes will receive the justice that they deserve, and for which they clamor; and generally, before we achieve lasting peace for the world, we shall have to breed Born Again Christians, a majority of human individuals that are sufficiently intelligent to behave decently and not like packs of baboons. Repeated mouthings of political and moral aspirations whether remitted by idealist individuals or uncomprehending.

Dr. Harry Emerson Frosdick says,

Race prejudice is as thoroughly a denial of the Christian God as atheism is, and it is a much more common form of apostacy. Race prejudice denies the universal Fatherhood of God; it denies the New Testament insistence on the equality of all souls before God; it denies the central affirmation of the Gospel that God so loved the World that He gave His son. And as for Jesus of Nazareth, who took His Hero, the man of Samaria from a despised race, anyone who harbors race prejudice parts company with him.

Barrow says,

None are too wise to be mistaken, and few are so wisely just as too acknowledged and correct their mistakes, and especially the mistake of prejudice.

I trust that you ae among those wise enough to correct those mistakes and prejudices as set forth in your "Predictions of 1947.

I remain,

Yours in the yoke of the Master
Bishop R.C. Lawson, Th.B., D.D., LL.D.
Senior Bishop and Apostle of the
Church of Our Lord Jesus Christ of the Apostolic Faith

The Anthropology of Jesus Christ Our Kinsman

Dedicated to the Glory of God
and to the
Help of Solving the Race Problem

"Pardon's the word to all! Whatever follies they commit, their shortcomings or their vices what they may, let us exercise forbearance; remembering that when these faults appear in others; it is our follies and vices that we behold. They are the shortcomings of humanity, to which we belong whose faults, one and all, we share; yes, even those very faults, at which we now wax so very indignant, merely because they have not appeared in ourselves. They are faults that do not lie on the surface. But they exist down there in the depths of our nature; and should anything call them forth, they will come and show themselves, just as we now see them in others. One man, it is true, may have; faults that are absent in his fellow; and it is undeniable that the sum total of bad qualities is in some cases very large; for the difference of individuality between man and man passes all measure." - - Schopenhauer.

"Go Then My Booklet Whither The Providence
of God Leadeth Thee."

Preface

The purpose of this little volume is not to foster race prejudice in the heart of no one against the white race; nor is it prejudice in the heart of the writer that is the reason for the publication of this book. I have love in my heart for all my brethren, white or black. I have some of my very best friends among the white race, I have pastored a mixed congregation of white and black folks ever since I have been pastoring, and they can bear me witness that I write the truth when I affirm that I have at all times showed the same love to all, regardless of race or color. For God has shown me to esteem all men alike, in-as-much as all are made in His image. But the cause that has led me to write this book, has been brought upon me on all sides, everywhere I have gone in this country and many other places of the world, I have beheld the pitiful condition of the white race as the passion of prejudice, blinds, binds, and dominates them; causing them to hate, and in turn be hated by their brethren. Prejudice to my mind is the greatest enemy of mankind, a breeder of division, murderers, wars, and every other evil. Prejudice is caused by false knowledge of each other, in other word[s], misunderstanding.

One race is puffed up over another because of a misconception of that race, therefore, the only thing to kill race prejudice is to give truth knowledge and understanding to races that are prejudice against each; other. To love a race worthily we must esteem that race properly. The false conception of the black race by the white race has brought about pride and prejudice in the white race, because of false knowledge which puffeth up, and in the black race the

"Inferiority Complex" which are in both cases injurious to the Church and the world, and hateful to God.

The question of race relationship is affecting not only international affairs, but also the status of Christianity before the world. Largely because of color prejudice the Christian missionary movement is at a standstill in India, China, Japan and Africa, the great pagan reservoir for proselytes. Indeed, it appears that Africa is destined to become a great Mohammadean empire. The darker races have reached a point where they will not kindly accept a gospel of love and brotherhood when the denial of their essential manhood is by Christian people negates the tenets which they are asked to accept.

When some like Dr. W. A. Plecker, the registrant of Vital Statistics of Virginia advocates the suicidal philosophy of race hate, even against the plain teaching of the Bible when he writes; "let us turn a deaf ear to those who would interpret Christian brotherhood to mean racial equality" It is time to protest. If the white brethren don't preach the fatherhood of God and the brotherhood of man irrespective of color or nationality, and exemplify the true spirit of brotherhood and equality to all, their civilization is doomed. However, God will bring deliverance from another quarter, and will raise up a people who will preach it and exemplify it in their lives and relationships with their fellowman.

By separating themselves like Peter did at Antioch, they are not walking according to the truth of the gospel; and having respect of persons, they sin, and break step with God, but perhaps this must be, that Ethiopia having stretched forth her hand for fellowship and help to her white brothers and been released shall turn to God; and then shall be brought to pass the saying, "Princes shall come out of Egypt, and Ethiopia shall stretch forth her hands to God. (Ps 69) It may be that God will use her to bring the gospel to the nations, because she will not spurn or hate any, for she knows what it is to be hated and set aside, and furthermore, she, being black, will love the darker races.

The Anthropology of Jesus our Kinsman

Our brethren of the white race are laboring under a handicap in their spiritual life to their great disadvantage. In their relationship to, and love for the brethren of the colored race, their spiritual condition is deplorable. To see them laboring under the two ideals, one racial and the other spiritual, trying to adjust themselves according to two different principles, makes them cowards in one sense and hypocritical in another.

I think the root of the matter lies in the fact of their civilization, that is their education, which should not be confounded with true knowledge. Ignorant education is the worst ignorance. To love a thing or one worthily, we must esteem a thing or one properly. They cannot love, respect, and esteem their colored brethren as themselves according to the scriptures, because they look upon the darker races as inferior both in blood and in intellect. This is the result of their civilization which is biased toward the Negro in every phase and department, but especially in the four main departments, History, Art, Science and Religion.

Our white brethren being the product of this civilization, it naturally follows that they are biased too, in their mental and spiritual makeup. They have been taught to glory in the contributions of their race which indeed have been and are wonderful; yet they are ignorant or forgetful of the fact that they are heirs, as also others were, of the civilizations that have gone on before. There is nothing new under the sun.

The newspaper logic and propaganda, is a point in hand. Newspapers are current history. I need but to mention this one point—when a white man is arrested for murder or rape the papers state that a man was arrested for murder or rape. When another man is arrested for murder or rape, the same papers declare that a "Negro" was arrested for murder or rape. When a white man steals something, it is the thing stolen which is of interest to head writers and reporters. When another man steals something, it is his race which is of paramount importance. Only when a black man makes a great discovery or does something especially commendable is his racial identity forgotten by head writers and reporters. This is newspaper logic—white American logic. The answer is obvious.

Tactics such as these serve to keep before the white race the delusion that we are a race of thieves, murderers and rapists. It is a deliberate plan to vilify a humble God-fearing race. When the white child reads history, or the newspaper, he thinks of the negro somewhat on this manner, "He never has been anything, is nothing now and never will be anything, because he is of an inferior race," to get away from the fact of the contributions of the colored races to the sum total of civilization as we now have it, their historians have either passed over or colored-white everything of importance touching the contribution of the darker races and in anything otherwise that they could not pass over or color, they have minimized as of no importance, thus giving to the white child a feeling of contempt and impression of inferiority about the colored races.

H. G. Wells in his "Outline of History" is a notable example of this practice. He gives credit to the Nordic Aryans for most of the progress of civilization. Over and over again he writes of the dark whites, Indo-European, Iberians, the Dravidians and of course he makes the Egyptians white, and of these he claims civilization receives her origin and main developments, but when he came to that ancient civilization of Babylon, called the Sumerian civilization, including the Sumerian language, he has this to say in Volume one, Chapter 16, Section 2 A, Pages 188-190.

> Perhaps the earliest people to form real cities in this part of the world or indeed in any part of the world, were a people of mysterious origin called the Sumerians. They were neither Semites nor Aryans, and whence they came, we do not know. Whether they were dark whites, or Iberians or Dravidian affinities is less certain to be denied.
>
> They used a kind of writing which they scratched upon clay, and their language has to be deciphered. It was a language more like the unclassified

Caucasic language groups, than any others that now exist.

These languages may be connected with Basque language—that is an African tribe—and may represent what was once a widespread group extending from Spain and Western Europe to Eastern India and reaching southwards to Central America. These people shaved their head and wore simple tunic-like garments of wool. They settled first on the lower coasts of the great river and not very far from the Persian Gulf which in those days ran up for a hundred and thirty or more miles beyond its present head. They fertilized their fields by letting water run through irrigation trenches. Therefore, they gradually became very skillful hydraulic engineers; they had cattle, asses, sheep, and goats, but no horses; their collections of mud huts grew into towns and their religion raised up tower-like temple buildings. Clay dried in the sun, was a very great fact in the lives of these people. This lower country of the Euphrates-Tigris valleys had little or no stone. They built of brick, they made pottery and earthenware images. They drew and presently wrote upon thin tile-like cake[s] of clay. They do not seem to have had paper or to have used parchment. Their books and memoranda, even their letters, were potsherds.

At Nippur they built a great tower of brick to their chief god, El-lil (Elil), the memory of which is supposed to be preserved in the story of the tower of Babel. They seem to have been divided up into cities and states which warred among themselves and maintained for many centuries their military capacity. Their soldiers. carried long spears and shields and fought in close formation.

Sumerians conquered Sumerians. Sumeria remained unconquered by any stranger race for a very long period of time indeed. They developed their civilization, their writing, and shipping through a period maybe twice as long as the whole period from the Christian era to the present time. It reached, says an inscription at Nippur, from the lower (Persian Gulf) to the upper Mediterranean or Red Sea. Among the mud heaps of the Euphrates-Tigris valley, the record of that vast period or history that first half age of civilization is buried. There flourished the first temples and the first priest ruler s that we know of among humankind. The first of all known Empires was that found by the high priest or the god of the Sumerian city of Erech. [57]

Instead of being honest and frank, Mr. Wells speaks of the mysterious origin of people, called the Sumerians, who he admits were neither Semites nor Ayrians—Japhethites—and rather than say they were Hamites or Cushites, descendants

---

[57] H. G. Wells *A Plain History of Life and Mankind* (Toronto: Doubleday, 1929).

of Ham, he says that concerning them, and whence they came we do not know. Like unto the Pharisees of old, who opposed Jesus when He pressed them to give an answer concerning the baptism of John, rather than admit that it was of Heaven, they said, "We do not know.

He further says that the first of all well-known Empires was that founded by the High Priest of the god of the Sumerians city of Erech; rather than say, as the Bible plainly teaches that the sons of Ham were Cush, Mizriam, Phut and Canaan, and that Cush begot Nimrod, and he began to be a mighty one of the earth. He was "A mighty hunter before the Lord." Wherefore it is said. "Even Nimrod the mighty hunter before the Lord and the beginning of his kingdom was Babel (afterward was known as Babylon) and Erech and Accad and Calneh in the land of Shinar. The Bible plainly teaches that Nimrod, the son of Cush, who was the son of Ham, the father of the Negro race, was the founder of Erech.

If the Sumerians were neither Semites nor Japhethites, which he admits, there is but one other branch of the human race they could have come from, and that is Ham, who was the father of the Hamitic or the Negro race. There was another example of this abuse or true history by modern historians in a New York paper not long ago.

Negro Civilization of Babylon

In the New York Times of Monday, May 11, 1925, in bold type I found these words, "Palace of the kings of Kish reveals splendors [from] three thousand years B. C." "Field

Museum—Oxford expedition unearths colossal capital of the Sumerians. One hall is seven hundred feet long. Ladies hand mirrors, vanity cases, manicure sets, paints and fishhooks also were found. Toy horses in nursery and many other things reveal the struggles and vanity of men and women who, three thousand years B.C., built a mighty dual empire in the now barren sand of Mesopotamia.

Prof. Lankdon who headed the expedition excavating at Kish, discloses the vastness of the ancient city before it was buried by the desert. He describes in detail the recent discovered palace of the first kings of Kish, which, he says, covers three acres with stairs and platforms flanked with chambers leading to adjacent temples wherein were found works of art, throne rooms, baths and even women's boudoir jewels and ornaments, etc." But the thing that I would like to call your attention to is the slightest alteration in the word, "Kish" which, evidently by any true principle of etymology, is a derivative or corruption of the word "Cush," but of course it must not be "Cush" because then it would point to a Negro Civilization. Therefore, the historians, in order to still perpetrate this injustice, both to the Negro and their own descendants—to one not giving due credit and the other not giving true knowledge, they change and twist words to keep up this historic fraud. The fact of history is that Babylon Contemporary with Egypt boast of a civilization of most primitive origin as far as 3000 years B.C. Like in Egypt the Anglo-Saxon has tried to claim and rob the Negro of credit of his civilization.

The ancient Sumerians, the founders of Babylon were children of Nimrod who was the oldest son of Cush, the son of Ham. The eleventh chapter of Genesis reveals this. Like their cousins, the Miziamites, their father's brother's children, the Sumerians came from Ethiopia or Sudan. The language, gods, and customs are akin to those in Egypt and Ethiopia. Nimrod, whose image is on Babylonian coin characterized in the Bible, "A mighty hunter before the Lord," said to be Romulus, the founder of Babylon, was a negro as I aforesaid. Read the above quotation from the Bible. The Babylonians were beautiful to behold, being a mixture of many Negro complexions and shades. Think of Nebuchadnezzar, King of Babylon, as a Hamite, a Negro.

Another instance of this practice is found in "Ancient History" by Myers, a standard work in our educational system, on page 15; chapter 16, under the caption "The Black Race"—Africa south of the Sahara is the home of the peoples of the Black Race. But we find them on all the other continents and on many of the islands of the sea, whither they have migrated or been carried as slaves by (the stronger races; for since time immemorial they have been "hewers of wood and drawers of water" for their more favored brethren."

Under [the] caption "The White Race and its Three Groups" reads like this, "The so-called White Race embraces the historic nations, The chief peoples of this division of mankind fall into three groups: the Hamitic, the Semitic, and the Aryan or Indo-European. The members forming anyone of these groups must not be looked upon as kindred in blood; the only certain bond uniting peoples of each group is the bond of language. The ancient Egyptians were the chief people of the Hamitic branch. In the grey dawn of history, we discover them already settled in the valley of the Nile, and there erecting great monuments so faultless in construction as to render it certain that those who planned then had had long previous training in the art of building. The Semitic family includes among its chief peoples the ancient Babylonians and Assyrians, the Hebrews the Phoenicians, the Arameans, and the Arabians. Most scholars regard Arabia as the original home of this family and this peninsula certainly seems to have been the great distributing center."

What a shame! What dishonest scholarship to refer to the black race as hewers of wood, and drawers of water, and their only contribution to civilization was labor, and that in slavery. And to make the Hamitic race a group of the white race is an open and willful distortion of historical facts or in other words—lying. How can the white race love and respect the black race, when they are taught in such a prejudicial way, made to believe a lie; hating their brother of the darker race, for who m Christ died.

But thank God there is now and then, and here and there, an honest scholar like Dr. Spiller who said, "The status of a race at any particular moment of time offers index to its inherent capacities." This shows honesty, for as everybody that pretends to know, know[s] that because a race has been, or is in bondage to another that, that is no true index to their capacities, nor is it proof they have always been in slavery since time immemorial, and at no time have been anything but "hewers of wood and drawers of water" for their more favored brethren. Dr. Spiller further says, Civilizations are meteoric, bursting out of obscurity only to plunge back again. Macedonia, for example! In our own day we have seen the decline of Aztec and Inca civilizations.

Of the early history of man, we know nothing definite. Prior even to paleolithic man there might have been civilizations excelling our own. In the heart of Africa, explorers may yet unearth marks of some extinct Negro civilization in a manner similar to the case of Assyria forgotten for two thousand years, and finally discovered by accident under forty feet of earth. For instance, the Chicago Evening Post of October 11, 1916, speaking editorially of the recent discoveries made at Nepata by Dr. Reisner of Harvard says,

> To his amazement he found even greater treasures of the Ethiopian past. Fragment after fragment was unearthed until at last, he had reconstructed effigies of no less than eleven monarchs of the forgotten Negro empire. [58]

Since then the tombs of fourteen other kings and fifty-five queens have been unearthed by the Reisner expedition. Among them is that of King Tirkaqua mentioned in the book of Isaiah. Thank God for such honest men as Dr. Spiller, Dr. Reisner of Harvard and Mr. Boas, of Columbia University.

But here of late I find that even Dr. George A. Reisner, the eminent Harvard scientist, who has spent 26 years exploring ancient Egypt, has been influenced somewhat by the evil genius of prejudice, when if newspaper reports are

---

[58] J. A. Rogers, *From Superman to Man* (Self-Published, 1915), 19.

true, he is quoted as saying that the Ethiopians are not African Negroes. The answer comes: For the benefit of these learned scientists we might add that there is not now, nor has there ever been a tribe on the continent of Africa ethnologically classified as Negroes. The term "Negro" originated with the Portuguese and means black.

Scientists, not above prejudice always try to rub out Negro (or black) history. I met Dr. Reisner in Egypt, he seemed a fair and impartial man. The report seemed hardly true; I somehow believe it is a distorted account. However, if Dr. Reisner said it as reported of him, it does not alter the case that the Ethiopian was and is a black man. The Bible plainly affirms this in the book or Jeremiah, the prophet, chapter 13:3, viz., "Can an Ethiopian change his skin, or a leopard his spots? Then ye may also do good, that are accustomed to do evil." The very word "Ethiopian" is a general translation of the word Cush, which means black or burned face. It follows that the American Negro (black man) is an Ethiopian, in as much there is no ethnological distinctions other than color. To all of the so-called ethnological sophistries, the bible gives the only true answer, viz., "God hath made of one blood all nations of men for to dwell on all the face of the earth, and hath determined time before appointed, and the bounds of their habitation." (Acts 17:26)

The Negro Civilization Of Egypt

Historically speaking, Egypt is the second born of time, the mother of all subsequent civilizations the longest lived among the nations of the earth. The teacher of Art,

Philosophy and Religion. Before the Roman or Grecian or the Anglo-Saxon civilization, was the Negro's. The ancient name of Egypt is Kimet or Kern, the root word, means black and swarthy. The Hebrew is Miraim, the Greek or modern name is Aiguptus or Egypt. The language and letter, on hieroglyphics are different from that of other races. They are Coptic and Ethiopian in language and character.

The ancient Egyptians themselves claimed their origin in Punt of Ethiopia. According, Pinder and Herodotus their religion and gods were Sudanese and from Ethiopia, Prichard, the world's greatest ethnologist, says, "They were like negroes." The white man has tried in every way to rob us of Egypt because she is the mother of his modern civilization. Negro faces and characteristics are still left to be seen in Egypt to prove they were Negroes. The Sphinx of Gyek, the world's greatest monument and work of art is the face and monument of a black Negro Pharaoh.

There are 7,000 years of known history of the valley of the Nile during which three great Ethiopian dynasties arose. The first 2000 years; the second 2,400 years; the third 1,500 years. Think of the duration of these civilizations and compare them with the transitory kingdoms and civilizations of the white man of today. Go today to the museums See for yourself the mummies and paintings of Egypt preserved through ages, if they are not Negroes. At the University of Pennsylvania, Rahotep, father of the recent find, Tut-Ankh-Amen, with his heavy features; Neferet, with the nose and lips of a Zulu; Aahrnes, and Nefertain are unmistakably Negroes.

We have been reading of late in our newspapers and magazines or the discovery of the tomb of Fur-Ankh-Amen by the Earl of Carnarvon, Pharaoh, of the 18th dynasty, who lived about 2,400 years ago and is said to have been contemporary of Moses. The civilization and splendors which are being unearthed in this tomb have no rival in the world. The works of art are said to have been among the finest found and are intact. A close examination of a photograph published in the New York Sunday Times of February 11 upon a close examination from his Negro features and black face show he is unmistakably a Negro. In all this great excitement of today though unearthed and preserved" very few Negroes or people will ever know Tut-Ankh-Amen to be a Negro. Time and space will not permit us going further into detail.

Negro Civilization on West Coast

Egypt and Ethiopia are not the only contributions Africa has made in the beginning of order and culture. There are evidences that the valley of the Congo has also had a great civilization that once flourished on the coast of the Gulf of Guinea, that even Egypt learned in culture from Sudan, the land of her cradle, and the Southern lure drew masses there even to the ends of South Africa co found a government of some sort of culture.

In the 14th century, Cibn Batura, the greatest Arabian traveler of his day, visited Kilwa, a city in East Africa which had three hundred Moguls. Its houses were beautiful and well-built. The Negro empire during the reign of Ale-Ghajidena, that not only were the pots, dishes, and drinking vessels of his household of pure gold, but that the spurs and bridles of his dogs were also gold. That was the golden age of Central African Negro culture. Here a Negro empire around

Lake Chad and embracing 8,000,000 people was then the Rome of her day, dominating a great area.

We might mention Melie and Sanghay in Northwest Africa, arid Yorula. Hemin of Banghirimi, Wadea, Darfur, Zeg-Zeg and the Borun peoples. These have been great African States whose civilizations were remarkable in their day. Read Ezekiel 26, 27, and 28 chapters for the biblical history of the greatness of the Hamitic civilization.

The Negro Civilization in Ethiopia, Sudan, or Now Modern Abyssinia

Abyssinia, remnant of ancient Ethiopia o Sudan, claims a civilization and past dating back to 11,000 years. Her history and civilization have been preserved through her priests and written and handed down to her priests from generation to generation. No man outside of their priests has been able to obtain or write her past.

She claims the oldest lineage or rule of any nation or country to exist and stand, though broken through intervals; the present king, relative of Menolik, claims direct descendance of King Solomon and the Queen of Sheba, They claim Judaism, their present religion, was introduced to them by the Queen of Sheba from the courts of King Solomon. The Ethiopian eunuch mentioned in Acts 8:26-38, was from Abyssinia or the Ethiopian kingdom. Tradition tells us that Ethiops, Son of Ham, was the founder of Ethiopia; Christianity was introduced there after the conversion of the Eunuch by Philip. The Coptic Bible (Old and New Testaments) and church both of which date back to our earliest versions and are now used in the interpretation of our Bible, came from Ethiopia. Negroes, then, can rightfully now claim Abyssinia, a remnant of Ethiopia, not only the oldest surviving Christian nation, but the oldest kingdom on the earth.

Historical Proof that Egyptians Were Black People

The black man, like the Aztec, was civilized when the dominant branches of the Caucasian variety were savages. Herodotus, the father of History an, eyewitness, distinctly mentions the black skins and wooly hair of the Egyptians of his day. In Book 11, Chapter 14, of his history he says:

> I believe the Colchians are a colony of Egyptians, because like them they have black skins and woolly hair.

> The ancient Egyptians were real Negroes of the same species as the other present natives of Africa.

A glance at the Sphinx or any of the ancient Egyptian statues in the British Museum will confirm these statements. When I saw the statue of Amenhotep Ill, I was immediately struck by the facial resemblance of Jack Johnson. I have seen Negroes here and in Africa, who bore a striking resemblance to King Sahure of the V Dynasty. By the light of modern research, it does appear a white-skinned humanity got its civilization from the black-skinned variety, and even its origin." Volney says:

> To the race of Negroes—the object of our extreme contempt—we owe our arts, science and even the very use of Speech.

Each of the three branches of the human race with many of their ramifications of nationalities have been great in their day (if ruling the world. Ham first; Babylon, Egypt, Ethiopia, then Shem with Palestine, and adjacent nations with his Davids and Solomons, Japhetite with Europe and all of the present Anglo-Saxon civilization. Ham went down because of pride and arrogance and forgetting God. Because that, when they knew God, they glorified him not as God, neither were thankful; but became vain in their imaginations and their foolish heart was darkened. Professing themselves to be wise, they became fools. And changed the glory of the incorruptible God into an image made like to corruptible man, and to birds, and four-footed beasts, and creeping things. The result was the Gentile world apostasy. Wherefore God also gave them their own bodies between themselves, who changed the truth into a lie, and worshipped and served the creature more than the Creator, who is blessed forever. Amen.

Shem the Jew, his kingdom fell, and his rule was overthrown because he forgot his God and turned to idols, therefore God gave them over to their enemies, scattering them among the nations of the earth, saying through Hosea 3:4-5, "The children of Israel shall abide many days without a king and without a prince and without a sacrifice and without an image, and without an ephod and without teraphim. Afterward shall the children of Israel return and seek the Lord their God and David their king; and shall fear the Lord and his goodness in the latter days."

This is Japheth's day, and the indications are that he with his civilization are doomed to go the same way, because of his pride, arrogance and the present drift away from God. The scriptures prophesy of his downfall with graphic outline. He shall be overturned as others were for so sayeth the scriptures. "I shall overturn it, overturn, overturn: (Ezek. 21:27). Three times there shall be an overturning significant of Shem. Ham and Japheth's reign over the earth. All have made an utter failure of the job. Instead of lifting up one another, they have made slaves of the weak hating them.

They have kept them down, but the scriptures states that this overturning "shall continue until He comes, whose right it is. Isaiah, seeing the coming of Him whose right it is to reign, wrote:

> Behold a king shall reign in righteousness and princes shall rule in judgment." They shall not hurt nor destroy in all his holy mountain; fur the earth shall be full of the knowledge of the Lord, as the waters cover the sea. And in that day, there shall be a root of Jesse, which shall stand for an ensign of the people; to it shall the nations seek; and his rest shall be glorious (Isa. 11:9-10, 32:1).

This king is none other than Jesus, our kinsman, Saviour and God, who shall give for a thousand years an example of righteous government, and from Him, Ham, Shem, and

Japheth shall learn how they should have governed the world.

The Negro in Bible Art and History

The negroes have not been given but very little part or place in the Bible or Biblical art. All the pictures of Jesus and illustrations and scenes of the Bible are credited to the Anglo-Saxon. The original inhabitants of the Promised Land before the Jews took possession, were negroes. (Exodus 3:8) The land of the Canaanites was the land given to Canaan, who were children of Canaan who was the youngest son of Ham, the father of the negro race as it is written in Genesis 10:15, Canaan beg at Sidon his first born, and Heth, and the Jebusite, and the Sinite, and the Girgasite, and the Hivite, and the Arikte, and the Sinite, and the Arvadite, and the Semarite, and the Hamathite; and afterward the families of the Canaanites spread abroad. And the border of the Canaanites was from Sidon as thou comest to Gerar unto Gaza; as thou goest, unto Sodom and Gomorrah and Adman and Zeboim, even unto Lashia.

The Jews after taking possession of the land of Canaan intermarried with the Canaanites as it is recorded in Judges 3:5-6. The children of Israel dwelled among the Canaanites—and they took their daughters to be their wives and gave their daughters to their sons, and served their gods, thus, making them a negroid race or Semitic mixed, which we shall speak of farther on, Zipporah, the wife of Moses, was a negro. The Egyptians claim that Moses father was the prince of Egypt, and his name was recorded as one of the princes of Egypt. He was a brown man in color and not white,

Read Exodus 4:7. It is certain that his father-in-law. Jethro was a negro, for it is recorded that Aaron and Mariam spoke against Moses because of the Cushite woman who he had married, for he married an Ethiopian woman. (Num 12:1)

I met a Jew in London, whom I told in the course of a conversation about the Holy Land, that the Jewish race was a kindred to the negro because of their much intermarriage in ancient days, and that they were indebted to us fur the idea of their Sanhedrin Court which was given to Moses by Jethro, his father-in-law, when he came to him in the wilderness and saw him endeavoring to judge ail the people, thus wearing himself out and also the people. Exodus 18th Chapter, therein you will find that Jethro had heard of all that God had done for Moses in the land of Egypt and had come to bring him his wife and two sons, and seeing Moses judging the people, said unto him in the 19th verse, "Harken now unto my voice, I will give thee council and God shall be with thee."

Be thou for the people God-ward that thou mayest bring the causes before God—Teach the people the laws and ordinances wherein they must walk and must do. Moreover provide out of all the people able men, such as fear God, men of truth, hating covetousness, and place such over them, rulers of thousands, hundreds and fifties; let them judge the people at all seasons, and it shall be that every great matter they shall bring unto thee, but every small matter they shall judge, so that it shall be easy and they shall bear the burden with thee.

It is recorded that Moses hearkened to his father-in-law and made a great feast unto him after which his father-in-law departed unto his own land. Thus, indirectly our white brethren are indebted to us for_ their supreme court, for the laws of this civilization are more or less based upon the law of Moses. In the art of today on our Sunday School cards, and in our art galleries, the darker races are always put in a servant's position. For instance, Solomon is pictured white with black slaves fanning him with huge fans. In the Methodist Episcopal Centenary exhibition held in Columbus six years ago, they had a white woman representing the Queen of Sheba and a negro preacher thinly clad with brass rings on his arm, and a spear in his hand representing her guard-slave.

How did this white woman get over in Abyssinia and become queen of all those black folks and how could Solomon be pure white when his mother, Bathsheba, the wife of the Hittite Urias, whom David married, was a full-blooded negro woman? In our art galleries the pictures we see of the Lord's Supper, all of the Disciples are white, when the scriptures plainly infer that at least one was black, Matthew 10:4, Simon, the Canaanite. (See Mk 3:18, Gen 10:15, 20)

We seldom, if ever, see a picture of Simon, the Cyrene, bearing the cross of Jesus up Golgotha Hill. We think if he had been an Anglo-Saxon, we would have heard much of this great honor that he brought upon their race? His glory would have been sung by poets and bards, and no doubt he would have been canonized as a saint and people by this time would have been praying to him; but of course, such is impossible because he was black.

Two of the foremost teachers of the Gentile church at Antioch in the 13th chapter of the Acts were black, according to Dr. R. F. Weymouth.[59] "Now there were in Antioch, in the Church there as Prophets and teachers—Barnabas, Symeon surnamed, 'The Black,' Lucius, the Cyrenean, with Barnabas and Saul." Dr. Weymouth adds a footnote with reference to Symeon possibly the man who bore the cross behind Jesus. It is evident that Rufus and other children of Symeon were leading Christians in the early church.

The Evangelist calls Simon the Cyrenean the father of Alexander and Rufus. (Mk 15:21, Rom 16:13) Evidently the two sons were well known to all whom Saint Mark was writing, and Paul speaks of them intimately and calls their mother, Simons wife, his mother, saying in Romans 16:13. Salute Rufus chosen in the Lord and his mother and mine. Paul evidently was dead to the color line. St. Augustine, one of the later church fathers, was an African and of Africa and negro blood.

The Anthropology Of Jesus

This is the first division of our main subject matter. The word anthropology means the science of physical facts concerning man and his development and history. After the fall of man through the transgression of Adam, God came seeking the lost; His voice was heard, upon the wind of the day by Adam, who was afraid and hid himself in the thickets of the garden, but finally sought out and found by the great

---

[59] Richard Francis Weymouth, *Resultant Greek New Testament* (Boston: Pilgrim Press, 1909).

Jehovah—Saviour, who after eliciting out of him the confession of his guilt, promised him, a Saviour, "the seed of the woman that would bruise the head of the serpent." (Gen 3:15) In order to fulfill this promise, the Lord set about the development of the seed. He chose Abraham of the branch of Shem, the father of the Semites.

Abraham had inherent, those fundamental qualities that make for the highest spiritual attainments and developments namely, faith and a spirit of obedience. Moreover, his quest for true knowledge of God brought him into contact with the Infinite who said unto him, "Abraham, get thee out of thy country and from thy kindred, and from thy father's house, unto a land that I will show thee."

Believing the voice that spake with him to be God, the God of Gods above all, he obeyed, not knowing where he was going, thus becoming the father of faith and the reservoir of psychic forces, the inheritor of Adam's lost inheritance; the possessor of the covenants and promises of God. God through the obedience of Abraham, by his wanderings and journeys, developed those psychic forces and ideals of faith, also multiplying his promises, brought Abraham to the stage of spiritual development that he become a worthy progenitor of the seed that would afterward bruise the serpent's head.

Under the emotion of the ideal of a universal kingdom in which all nations of the earth would be blest through the promised one, Abraham waxed strong in faith not considering Sarah's body now dead, nor yet his own body. He staggered not at the promises of God but was strong in faith giving glory to God. God, therefore, being pleased, gave him a seed saying in Isaac, that all nations would be blest, therefore multiplying the seed of Abraham, Isaac, and Jacob, and the transmission of those spiritual ideals and promises along with the emotional and psychic inheritance to the twelve sons and their children which compose the family (or nation) of Abrahams, so to speak. Out of which Christ came, who is God over all, blessed forevermore, Amen.

The Development of the Nation of Jesus

In passing, it is good to note the continuous development of the physical virgin stalk out of which Abraham and Christ came, and the intensifying of those psychic qualities along with the renewing of the promises and covenants of God to each succeeding generation. Abraham married his half-sister (Gen 10:12), Sarai. Nahor his brother, married Milcah his brother Haran's daughter. (Gen 27:30) Abraham, after he entered into the land of Canaan, sojourneying there, when the time drew near to his" death, sent his servant, Elezur back to the land of Mesopotamia, unto the city of Nahor, the land of his fore-fathers and his people, to get his wife for his son Isaac, who was Rebecca, his brother Nahor's daughter, Isaac's second son, Jacob, also returned to the land of Ur of Chaldee when he fled from the face of his brother Esau upon the entreaty of his mother, to take a wife not like Esau did of the Canaanites, but of his father's house. Therefore, he returned to the land of his fathers into the house of Laban, his father's brother's son of whom he took a wife, yea two, Rachel and Leah, his second cousins who bore for him the twelve patriarchs who form the national anthropological background of the physical foundation of Jesus Christ.

The second layer on this foundation is the development of the tribe out of which Jesus came—(Judah). The above deals strictly with the Semitic contribution to the anthropological development of Jesus Christ.

The Hamitic Contribution To The Anthropological Development Of Jesus

The Hamitic contribution to the anthropological development of Jesus Christ comes in at the incipiency of the tribe of Judah out of which Christ came, for it is written in Genesis 49 that the scepter should not depart from Judah until Shiloh came. The beginning of the tribe of Judah is recorded in Genesis the [38th] Chapter which reads on this wise:

> And it came to pass at that time that Judah went down from his brethren and turned into a certain Adullamite whose name was Hirah, and Judah saw there a certain Canaanite negro woman whose name was Shuar whom he married. And she conceived and bore him a son and called his name Er. She conceived again and bare him a son, and she called his name Onan, she bore him yet another son whose name was Shelah... (Gen 38:1-5a)

In a process of time Judah took a wife for his first-born Er whose name was Tamar, but Er, Judah's first son was wicked in the sight of God, so the Lord caused him to die. Judah consequently said to Onan, marry the wife of your brother and raise up an heir for your brother, but Onan knew that the heir would not be his own, therefore, before he approached his brother's wife, he did the unspeakable thing, wasting the seed of his brother. What he did was wicked in the sight of God, therefore, he caused him to die. Not only was it wicked of him to do such an abominable act, but his wickedness was great in that he refused and resisted the will and purpose of God in the mingling of the blood of the Hamitic or negro race, with Shem and that of Japheth in the anthropological development of Jesus Christ. It was necessary in the plan of God to develop the most perfect man of the human race, to mingle and to intermingle the blood of the three branches to produce the best and most perfect man.

Of course, all of this is out of gear with the philosophical and pseudo-scientific teaching of the day, especially relative to the colored races in regard to miscegenation, that is, the mixing of the blood of the black and white races. They say that this would deteriorate the white races, but the Bible infers that it would be just the opposite, surely in the case of our Lord Jesus, this is evident, for he had negro blood in his veins, yet he was the fairest among ten thousand, of whom it is said even of his enemy and judge, Pilate, "Behold the man." He was indeed the holiest among the mighty and the most mighty among the holiest. He lifted the gates of Empires and turned the river of human history and changed time to A. D.

The spirit of Onan today still lives in many of his children who still resist the truth and purpose of God, but his will shall be done, and men shall know at last that all flesh is grass. Judah said to Tamar, his daughter-in-law, who was a Canaanite woman as his wife was, "Return as a widow to your father's house until Shelah my youngest son grows up, for he reflected" perhaps she shall also kill him, like his brothers. Therefore went and returned to her father's house.

Now, as time went on, Shuar, the wife of Judah, died. Judah grieved for her. He went up with Hirah, his partner, to shear the sheep at Timanth and it was reported to Tamar that her father-in-law was going up to shear his sheep, so she put off her widow's garments and concealed herself in her veil and dressed in the attire of a harlot and went down and sat at the wells which is on the way to Timanth. For she saw that Shelah was grown up and he was not given to her as a husband. Judah saw her and thought she was a harlot, for she had hidden her face, so he turned from the road to her and accosted her as a harlot.

She said, "What will you give me?" and he replied, "I will send you a kid of goats." She replied, "if you will give me a pledge that you send them." He said, "What is the pledge that you I shall give you?" And she answered, "Your ring and stick that you have in your hand," so he gave them to her, and she consented to him, then she arose and put off her veil and dressed herself in a widow's garments and went away, but Judah sent the kid of goats by Hirah, his partner, who was to receive the pledge from the hands of the woman, but he could not find her. He therefore inquired of the men of the place asking, "Where is the harlot of the wells by the road?" but they replied, "There is no harlot by there," so he returned to Judah and replied, "I cannot find her." Three months later it was reported to Judah, "Your daughter-in-law, Tamar, has prostituted herself, "Bring her here and burn her." They brought her. But she produced the ring and walking stick and said, "By the man that these belong to, I am with child," and she continued, "To whom belongs this ring and its motto, and this walking stick." Then Judah replied and said, "You are more virtuous than I, for I did not give you Shelah my son." He therefore proceeded no further to examine her. When however, the time for her delivery came, there were twins in her womb, and it happened in her travail, one put out his hand, so the mid-wife and tied a scarlet thread upon its hand, remarking, "This came first," but it occurred that he drew back the hand, and then his brother was produced when she said, "What, have you broken? The breach be upon yourself." Therefore, she called his name Pherez. After thread, so she called his name Zarah.

Thus, was born to Judah by the two negro women the children who were the progenitors of the tribe of Judah. If any race have whereof o boast as touching things of the flesh, relative to our Lord Jesus Christ, the colored race has more, for they gave to the world the two mothers of the tribe of Judah, out of which Christ came, as I may so say, were the mothers of our Lord, for as touching the flesh he was at that time in the loins of his father Judah to whom pertaineth the pre-eminence among the twelve tribes of Israel, to whom was given the adoption and the glory, and the covenants, and the giving of the law, and the service of God, and the promises; whose of the fathers and of whom as concerning the flesh Christ came, who is over all, God blessed forever, Amen. (Gen 38 and 49:8-13)

For fear that it may be reasoned that Judah had other children, and out of that branch came Jesus, we will trace his genealogical descent. I Chronicles 2:3-15 where it is recorded; The sons of Judah; Er, and Onan, and Shelah; which three were born unto him of the daughter of Shua, the Canaanitess. And Er, the first born of Judah, was evil in the sight of the Lord; and he slew him. And Tamar, his daughter-in-law, bore him Pharez and Zerah. All the sons of Judah were five. So, you see Judah had no other sons other than by these two negro women, three by his wife, and twins by his daughter-in-law. Matthew clinches this in his gospel of the genealogy of Jesus, 1st, chapter, verses 1-4. Which reads "The book of the generation of Jesus Christ, the son of David, the son of Abraham. Abraham begat Isaac; and Isaac begat Jacob; and Jacob begat Judah and his brethren; and Judah begat Perez and Zerah of Tamar."

It is interesting in studying the genealogy of Jesus in St. Matthew in the revised version that though Judah had no other Children save by these two colored women, yet there were at least two other negro women who gave their blood in the royal line and veins of our Saviour, Jesus. Matthew further says that Perez begat Hezron; and Hezron begat Ram; and Ram begat Amminadab; and Amminadab begat Nahshon; and Nahshon begat Salmon; and Salmon begat Boaz of Rahab who was the next colored woman who gave her blood in to the royal line. She was of Jericho, the first Canaanite city captured by the Israelites under Joshua, evidently a negro woman, for the people of Jericho unto this day equal in blackness, the darkest tribes in Africa.

I never will forget, months ago, when I was in Palestine having made a pilgrimage to the River of Jordan, on my returning to Jerusalem, we passed by modern Jericho, and after buying some oranges of the natives, preparatory to shipping them back to America, we took our leave of them and proceeded on our way up the beautiful palm tree shaded road leading towards the ruins of ancient Jericho, upward of a mile away, In passing, I beheld some black folks laboring in the vineyard to the left of the road, and some working around a house, Upon inquiry of my guide, I asked, "Who are they?"

He answered readily, "They are the people of Jericho- that is the Aborigines—the people of the land." There remained no doubt in my mind, therefore, when I make the assertion that Rahab, the harlot, was a black woman who had the warm sympathetic heart for {he foreigners who came to her house in Jericho to spy out the land. Perhaps, it was this wonderful attribute that is innate in the heart of the black race; that warm loving, peaceful, sympathetic trait and blood that the Lord desired to mingle with the highly developed spiritual and psychic emotional nature of the Shemites to that merciful warm-blooded, tender-hearted race of Hamite.

When Israel settled in the land, Rahab, the harlot, was spared and was not given to the edge of the sword because she received the spies in peace. She was numbered with the children of Israel and married Salmon who begat Boaz, who in turn married Ruth, the Moabite, who is a representative of the Anglo-Saxon, the Japhethic branch of the human race. But before we shall dwell upon this, we shall make mention of the fourth Negro woman who gave her blood in the anthropological development of Jesus. This woman is Bathsheba, the wife of Uriah, the Hittite who David saw bathing one day and brought her unto the house while her husband was in the front fighting with the army of Israel in defense of the throne of David. David humbled her and she received and sent word and told David, "I am with child."

David, in order to cover up his sins sent for Uriah from, the front, ostensibly to inquire how the battle was going, but in reality, to have Uriah to go to his own home unto his wife, so that he, David would be sheltered from the guilt of his sins. But Uriah slept at David's door, and in the morning, said unto him, "The ark of Israel abides in the tents and Joab and the servants of the Lord are in camp in open fields; shall I then go into my house to eat and to drink, and to lie with my wife As thou liveth and thy soul liveth, I will not do this thing."

Then the basest act of David was committed when he conspired with Joab against the life of Uriah, when he ordered that Joab should put Uriah in the front of the battle, in die thickest of the fight, so that he would be killed. It so happened that Uriah was killed and after Bathsheba, his wife, had mourned for him, certain days, after the days of her mourning was over, David sent and took her for his wife. Her first-born died, notwithstanding that David prayed that it should be healed. However, she bore him another child whose name was Solomon, who reigned ill his stead, after David's death, as King. He was reputed to have been the wisest man that ever lived. If so be the case, to the everlasting honor of the colored race, he was a Negro, that is a half-breed who according to the laws of the south and the standard of the Ku Klux Klan of whom lot of our white brethren seems to be under the influence, he was a Negro, for he had more than Vile-sixteenth Negro blood in him, and according to that standard, if our Lord would return to earth again in the flesh and would go down South incognito, he would be Jim-crowed and segregated, for he himself had more than one-sixteenth of Negro blood in him. Solomon in the songs he wrote, 1st Chapter, 5th verse, in singing to the bride of his love, said, "I am black but comely."

Publuius Lentus, the Roman scribe, who is said to have given a description of our Saviour:

> He was a man in stature of about six feet. His hair being wine-colored and overflowing the shoulders. His countenance convincing to behold, yet with a note of tenderness and authority. He was the color of a filbert, a nut of reddish hue.

Thus, making Jesus neither white nor black. This record of Publuius Lentus is only to be found published in the ancient church histories.

Japhethitic Contribution to the Anthropological Development of Jesus Christ

You may ask, "Why are you so concerned to prove that Jesus Christ had Negro blood in him?" It is vitally necessary and helpful, especially when the wave of prejudice is causing so many to sin through the egotism of race pride, thinking themselves better than other people because of race, and separating themselves in the body of Christ through shame of their brethren of the colored races, bringing upon themselves spiritual leprosy as typified by that which came upon Mariam who murmured against Moses because of his Ethiopian wife.

There are many of them murmuring today, especially among our white brethren of the South because of colored brethren occupying prominent positions in the church of Christ. Some even go so far as refusing to take credentials signed by a Negro. What a shame! It seems that this issue has arisen time and again in the history of the church in America, and all have failed lamentably to measure up to the high Christian idealism of the "Fatherhood of God and the brotherhood of all men." They did run well, at first, but when this issue came up between the black and the white races, they were hindered because of not accepting their colored brethren upon absolute equality.

The Baptists have failed in this issue; therefore, we have black and white Baptist. The Methodists likewise have let this issue separate them from the Jove of God, therefore, we have white and colored Methodists, etc. This is something that Paul knew not, when he said, "Nothing shall separate us from the love of God." But today we find that this color proposition is the one thing that is separating many from the love of God. Whenever a people or a movement have come up to this proposition and have failed to walk according to the truth of the gospel, they have lost power with God, and have failed, as an instrument in his hands in saving the world for Christ

How can we love and abide in God who we have not seen, if we love not without respect of persons our brethren, and be with them, not separating on any grounds or reasons? All of these various churches have failed this issue on color, misrepresenting the spirit of Christ, but when God poured out his spirit here some fifteen years ago, culminating in the movement called "The Apostolic Faith" we thought surely if ever there were a people of God that would love one another regardless of race, color or nationality, these were the people, namely, The Pentecostal People, possessors of the faith of the Apostles.

We thought, surely, that now had Come upon the stage of action, a people who would rise above prejudice and measure up to the high ideals of the "Fatherhood of God and the brotherhood of man," regardless of color, or race. We thought sure that wherein the other churches had failed upon the issue of "color line" and had divided into race and national groups, for instance, colored and white Baptist and Methodist churches, etc. Welsh Presbyterian Church. German Lutheran Church, etc., that the Pentecostal people would teach to these a wonderful lesson by example in showing that the true people of God are one regardless of what nationality or race they may belong; by abiding together in the bonds of fellowship, love, and organization, thus bringing upon them the blessings recorded in the 133rd Psalm,

> Behold how good and pleasant it is for brethren to dwell together in unity! It is like the precious ointment upon the head, that ran down upon the beard, even Aaron's beard: that went down to the skirts of his garments; as the dew on Herman, and as the dew that descended upon

the mountains of Zion: for there the Lord commanded the blessing, even life for evermore.

The terrible scourge of race prejudice, like a disease, has afflicted the nations, like a mighty monster, holds them in captivity. It is the cause of war, famine; in fact, every other ill that afflicts humanity, come out of this evil in the heart and nothing but the love of God through his people and the preaching; of the Word of love, can deliver and cleanse their hearts and minds. We trusted that the Pentecostal people would rise to redeem man by example and precept. It is alright to sing and shout and pray and preach loud, but what this poor world is longing for is the real love of God lived. For, after all, the greatest badge of discipleship of the Master, is love. "For by this shall all men know," (said Jesus), "that ye are my disciples, if you have love one to another." The thing that engages my earnest effort in proving that Jesus had Negro blood in Him, is even more vital than the fore going. The fact that Christ had Negro blood in him is vitally connected with our redemption through Calvary.

In the book of Ruth, that wonderful gospel romance, is illustrated the principle of redemption. You will recall how that a man, by the name of Elimelech, and his wife, Naomi, who with their two sons, left Bethlehem-Judea, because there was a famine in Palestine. They went to the plains or Moab and remained there for ten years, during which time Elimelech died and his two sons, who had married Moabite wives. Their names were Orpah and Ruth.

Naomi being deprived of her two sons and husband, consequently, arose with her daughters-in-law and left the plains of Moab, for she heard that the Ever-living God had visited his people and given them Bread. She entreated her daughters-in-law to return to their people and not to follow her back to Bethlehem, but Ruth would not leave her, but declared her faith in the God of Israel, which promised so little for them or her. As Dr. Simpson wrote:

> Orpah, the more demonstrative of the two, expressed great affection, and went home; but Ruth clung to Naomi with those ever memorable and noble word s which have been inscribed with the point of a diamond as the loftiest expression of loyal affection and devotion: "Entreat me not to leave thee, or return from following after thee, for whither thou goest, I will go, and where thou lodgest, I will lodge; thy people shall be my people, and thy God my God; where thou diest will I die, and there will I be buried; the Lord to do so to me, and more also, if aught but death part thee and me."

And so, two lone widows came back to Bethlehem and began to seek a livelihood in the humblest way. Ruth took upon herself, as a loving daughter, the support of the home, and went out like Jewish maidens to glean in the wheat and bar ley fields. It was there that she met Boaz, the rich farmer, who had heard d her kindness to her mother and her maidenly modesty and who became attracted to her and showed her special kindness without sacrificing in any way her own womanly independence. Naomi, meanwhile, kept watching with motherly intuition the whole situation, looking constantly to God, in whose wings they had come to trust.

At length, Naomi found that Boaz sustained to her and Ruth the peculiar relation of the Goel, or nearest of kin, whose duty it was to redeem her husband's inheritance and take his widow to be his wife. Naomi advised Ruth to take the bold, yet modest step by which she could claim her rights, Boas was a relative of the family of Elimelech and was wealthy. He entreated her kindly by letting her glean among the sheaves, and by giving her of the food and water to drink like those of his other servants.

She was mindful of her mother-in-law and saved some of her food for Naomi and told Naomi, when she returned home of Boaz kindness to her. Naomi informs her that Boaz was a near relative and that he could redeem their mortgaged property; for so it was a custom in Israel (Deuteronomy 25) when brothers resided together and one of them died and left not a son, that the wife of the dead man should not be a wife to a stranger. Her brother-in-law or the next kin should many her and the first son that she bears, he should bring up with his brother's name so that his name might not be wiped out from Israel.

But, if the man refused or is unable, he should pull off his shoes from his feet, thus signifying his inability, giving it to the next in kin who is able to redeem the property, and marry his relative's wife. So, it was that Ruth was instructed by Naomi about this ancient custom. During the winnowing of the harvest after Boaz had ate and drank and rejoiced the ill heart, and had lain down to sleep, Ruth came quietly and uncovered his feet and laid down. It happened at midnight that the man was startled and turned over and round a woman lying at his feet. He inquired, "who are You?"

She replied, "I am Ruth, your servant. Therefore, spread your cloak over your servant, for you are a restorer." Then Boaz replied to her, "The Lord bless you, my girl. You have given more kindness at the last than at the first, for you have not gone after the young men whether poor or rich, therefore, my people know that you are a virtuous woman, and I am a near relative, yet there is a nearer redeemer than I. Stay here tonight and when morning comes, if he redeems for you, good, but if he is not pleased to redeem your property, then I will. Boaz that next day went up to the gates and sat. When the near relative of whom he had spoken of passed, he exclaimed, "Come here, sit down," so he turned and sat down. Then he summoned ten of the Elders of the village.

When they had come, he addressed him in the presence of the Elders, saying, "Where is that part of our estate, which belonging to Elimelech, Naomi, who has resided in the plains of Moab wishes to sell it, so I have spoken it open to your ears to advise you to buy, in the presence of these men, the Elders of my people. If you wish to redeem it, redeem it, but if you will not redeem it, inform me, for there is no one to redeem it except yourself, and I am after you. And he replied, "I will redeem it," but Boaz answered; "On the day that you purchase the estate from the hands of Naomi, you must buy it also from Ruth, the Moabitess, the wife of the dead man, to raise up a name for the dead on the property." Then the next of kin said, "I am not able to purchase it of myself less I should injure my own property. You can purchase my right for yourself for I am unable to redeem it."

Now this was a custom in Israel, that a man took off his shoes and gave it to his next of kin; this was an attestation that he was unable to redeem the lost inheritance of his next kin. When the next of kin said to Boaz, "buy it for yourself," he slipped off his shoe. Boaz said to the Elders and all the people, "You are witnesses today, that I have redeemed all in Elimelech, also Ruth, the Moabitess, the wife of Mahlon, from the hands of Naomi, I have bought for myself to raise up a name for the dead so that his name might not be cut off from the gates of Israel." The Elders and people said, "We are witnesses, may the Ever-living bless you, and may your wife be like Rachel and Leah who built up the house of Israel." Thus, did Boaz the next of kin redeem the lost inheritance. Above all is the piety of Ruth. It was not merely the love of her mother that made her true; but it was the love of her mother's God. Very finely Boaz alludes to it when he speaks "of the wings of the Almighty under which she had come to trust."

In this wonderful romance and in the laws of Moses are imbedded and interwoven a wonderful mystery of the principal of our redemption through Christ, Hallelujah I God created Adam, the progenitor of the human race, and gave him lordship over this world. He shared with God innocency and purity. God delighted in the fellowship of man, coming down often on the wind of the day, he instructed man in the way he should go, giving him the laws of faith and obedience;

saying, "Thou shalt eat of all the trees of the garden, save the tree of knowledge of good and evil, and the day therein thou eatest of it thou shalt surely die." It is implied in the scripture that this world was formerly inhabited by angelical beings who, through disobedience, were cast down from their holy state, disembodied, they became wicked spirits under the leadership of Lucifer, the son of the morning, a former covering cherub, who essayed to become God. They sought the downfall of man through the subtility of the serpent. This was brought about through unbelief and disobedience of Eve who told her transgression to Adam, the Lord of this earth, who willingly, willfully, sold his inheritance. The Lord in anguish, aware of the transaction, came down on the wind of the day broken-hearted. He sought man in the garden of Eden, crying "Adam where art thou."

Adam, having sold himself for naught, was a slave to Satan. He feared God and hid himself in the under-bush when he heard the voice of God. With a broken heart Jehovah—Saviour continued to seek him until he found him trembling in the inter-recess of the garden. He elicited out of him his confession of guilt, the horrible transaction, that lost for him the lordship of the world, fellowship of God, and purity of heart. The Lord in mercy, knowing that the adversary, Satan was back of all this miserable deed, purposed in his heart to redeem man, saying unto the serpent, "because thou hast done this, thou art cursed above all cattle, and above every beast of the field; upon thy belly shalt thou go, and dust shalt thou eat all the days of thy life; And I will put enmity between thy seed and her seed; it shall bruise thy head, and thou shalt bruise his heel."

Note, the promise of the seed of the woman was not simply the seed of Eve, but the Woman here, is to be understood in a larger sense, that is, the Seed of the Human race. Therefore, the mixing of the blood of the three branches of the human race had a deeper significance than it is commonly thought. The very phrase, "the seed of the woman" has no basis in the" biological philosophy of man. Woman hath not seed; man is the progenitor; therefore, we must look to a higher law than Nature for the production of this seed of woman. This is a revelation. In the hoary ages of time, God, foreseeing that, to redeem man justly, according to his own principles of righteousness, it was necessary that he should become man's kinsman. Being higher than man, it was not possible to be begotten of man. He, therefore, conceived the mystery of the miraculous conception and virgin birth, saying, "The seed of the woman shall bruise the serpent's head."

After the separation of the races at the tower of Babel, the Lord began to build up the medium through which this seed should come, having purposed to become our near kinsman because of our inability to redeem ourselves, even though there would be born unto us wise men, scribes and prophets. The hope was kindled in the breast of the human race at the birth of her first child. And, that he would be the promised seed and of every man child thereafter that was born, this hope increased as a fire. It blazed brighter and brighter and at times, after a great man arose, the question would be asked, "Is this he?" And sometimes the great men like Moses would be imbued with patriarchic zeal that they indeed were the deliverer. But as they began their career of deliverance, there came a n inner revelation or a divine apparition that they were unable to redeem. Sometimes, as in the days of Moses, the divine voice would speak upon the threshold of their career, "Take off thy shoe, for the place whereon thou standest is holy ground, or in so many words, saying unto them, "Thou art unable to redeem, though thou art next in kin." Like Joshua, on entering the land of Canaan near Jericho, encountered a strange personage who had a drawn sword. Approaching in the audacity of self-confidence in his own ability to accomplish the task of destruction of the people of Canaan, and dividing the land to the people of Israel, he was quickly informed that this strange personage, and not he, was the captain of the Lord's host, and he only could redeem the land and accomplish the task. He said unto Joshua, as an acknowledgement of his inability to redeem, "Take off thy, shoe, the place whereon thou standest is holy ground."

So on through the ages though there arose David, he could only sing of redemption, but could not redeem, saying, "Over Edom have I kicked my shoe." And Solomon the wise, wrote, "I have put off my coat, and how shall I put it on? I have washed my feet, how shalt I defile them?" But with all of his wisdom he could not redeem. Not until was heard the voice of one crying ill the wilderness, the man whose meat was locust and wild honey, openly declared, upon being questioned, was he the Messiah. He answered, "No, I am the voice of one crying in the wilderness, make straight the way of the Lord. I baptize with water, but there stand one among you whom you know not, He it is who is coming after me, is preferred before me whose shoe latchet I am not worthy to unloose." John realized that Jesus was indeed the seed of the woman and that he was fully able to redeem and had not need to take off his shoes, not even to have them unloosed.

The sum total of what has been written is this, that Christ, in order to be a redeemer of man from sin, became a near kinsman when he looked and saw that there was none to help and that no eye pitied, and there was no arm to save. God disrobed himself of his glory, overshadowed the Virgin Mary a prepared vessel, a woman in whose veins flowed the blood of Japheth and of Shem, and of Ham, for so had been the purpose and work of God in mixing the bloods of all three branches of the human race, that upon the basis of kinship, He might have the right—so to speak—to redeem all men. Therefore when this miscegenation had been thoroughly fulfilled in the woman. Mary was found the fit vessel and medium through which the seed of the Woman, that is, of the human race, would come into the world to bruise the head of the serpent. So spake the prophet of him, "Lo I come in the volume of the book to do thy will, O God, a body hast thou prepared me."

Through the phenomena of the overshadowing by the Spirit, the Virgin Mary was found with child of the Holy Ghost the only begotten of the Father our near kinsman Bless God. Job, looking down the highway of the age, saw and cried in faith,

> I know that my redeemer lives and that he shall stand upon the earth in the latter day and mine eyes shall behold him and not another. Though

after my skin worms destroy this body, yet in my flesh I shall see God."

When Christ was born in Bethlehem, the Angels standing in the cloisters of invisibility stepped forth and sang over the fields of Boaz, "Glory to God in the Highest and Peace on Earth, Good will to all men." Then there was suddenly with the shepherds the Angel of the Lord which said, "Behold I bring you good news of great joy, for there is born, this day, in the city of David, a Saviour, which is Christ, the Redeemer." At last, the seed of the woman, our kinsman to us all had come. Straightway, the devil, the seed of the serpent began to bruise his heel. Our blessed Redeemer was born in such poverty that he had not means to procure a place for his birth. As there was no room, in the inn, his mother resorted to a stable. There under the golden glow of his own star, that shone through the window, he was born.

He who became poor that through his redemption he might make many rich. The seed of the serpent bruised his heel by forcing his mother to flee from the face of Herod who had designed upon his life, sought to accomplish it by having all the children under two years of age put to death. But deep in the unfathomable mind of never-failing skill, he treasures up his bright designs and works his sovereign will. It was determined that the land of Ham should be the Asylum for the refugee, as it had been prophesied, "Out of Egypt, have I called forth my son." After Herod's death (the Angel of the Lord directed Mary to return to Bethlehem. Later in the city of Nazareth, was the seed of the woman nurtured.

All of this was done that it might be fulfilled that which was spoken by the prophet Esias concerning our Lord, "Behold a virgin shall with child and shall call his name Emmanuel which interpreted is, God with us. For as much as the brethren were partakers of flesh and blood, he also himself likewise took part of the same ; that through death he might destroy him that had power over death, that is, the devil and deliver them who through fear of death were all their life time subject to bondage, for verily he took not on him the nature of angels; but he wok on the seed of Abraham that in all things he might be like his brethren, and be to them, a merciful and faithful High Priest in things pertaining to God and to make reconciliation for the sins or the people." Three things were necessary in redeeming: First, he must be a kinsman; Second, the redeemer must be able to redeem. (Ru 4:6, Jer 5:34, Jn 10:11-18) Third the Redemption is affected by the redeemer, paying the just demands in full. (I Pet 1:18, 19, Gal 3:13)

This completed truth is set forth in three words which are translated, Redemption. First, A-Zo-Ra-Zo which means to purchase our hum slave market. Man, the subject of redemption, was sold to sin. Rom (7:14) Moreover, he was under sentence of death. (Ezek 18:4) "The soul that sinneth shall die." Christ came, our blessed Redeemer, to purchase our eternal salvation, the price demanded was life, His blood. He refused not to die but gave his back to them that pluck off the hair, and hid not his face from, spitting.

> He was despised and rejected of men, a man of sorrow and acquainted with grief and we hid, as it

were, our faces from him, yet we did esteem him stricken, smitten of God and afflicted but he was wounded for our transgressions, he was bruised for our iniquities, the chastisement of our peace was upon him and with his stripes, we are healed. All we, like sheep, have gone astray, we have turned everyone to his own way, and the Lore has laid on him the iniquity of us all. He was oppressed, and he was afflicted, yet he opened not his mouth. He was led as a lamb to the slaughter and as a sheep before her shearer is dumb, so he openeth not his mouth. Surely, he has born our griefs and carried our sorrows.

He bore the cross, the counter upon which he laid the price of our redemption, for as much as we know that we were not redeemed with corruptible things, as silver and gold from the vain behavior and sins received by traditions from our fathers, but with the precious blood of Christ as a lamb without blemish and spot. He was lifted as He said, "And if I be lifted up from the earth, will draw all men unto me."

Because he is the kinsman to all men by virtue of the fact that the streams of blood of Ham, Shem, and Japheth crossed in Him, Jesus Christ, so that no man on the face of the earth could say we have nothing in him but being a kinsman to all men. When lifted up, he draws them to the cross to behold in Him their kinsman and through virtue of the fact of kinship, redemption would be realized and accepted. Praise His name. Amid darkened sky and rending veil and tottering earth, Christ was lifted before the eyes of Ham, Simon, the Cyrenean, who bore his cross, who would tell the news to his people, also before his disciples representing Shem would preach the gospel unto the Jews. While the Centurion who represented Japheth was forced by the dying hero's magnanimity to his enemies to cry: "Truly, this is the Son of God."

While the serpent was doing the last of his bruising of the seed of the woman, Christ's bosom heaved in agony as he prayed, "Father forgive them for they know not what they do." He further cried, "It is finished."

The second word of redemption in the Greek is, Ex-A-Go-Ra-Zo, which means, the purchase out of slave market never to be sold again, so our Christ wrought eternal redemption for us from the bondage of sin. The third word in this triplet of Greek words which express redemption is Lu-troo, meaning to loose (to set free). Christ gave up the Ghost when he cried, "It is finished," but he was quickened by the spirit and descended into Hades, into the prison house of departed spirits.

He stopped, as it were, in his wardrobe, the grave. and there laid his body, but by the Spirit with majestic strides, he descended unto the throne room of death, who beholding him, dropped his laden scepter and fell over, swallowed up and overcome by life. Christ, with the keys of death and the power of the world that were man's lost inheritance, opened the prison of captive spirits and led on high a host of captives. Passing through the gateway of death, the grave, He lifted his Body, his robe of humanity, glorified it, and as the bounding stone from the sepulcher went crashing, and as soldiers fell as if were dead, cried, "All power in Heaven and in earth is in my hands." Thank God, that then was our redemption consummated. Christ had paid the price, and all there remained for us was to enter in. Thank God. The Holy Spirit has made this redemption actual in our lives. May God grant that every son of Adam, wretched though he may be with the body of death tied to him may look up to the bleeding form of the Son of God and exclaim with Paul, "I thank God through Jesus Christ our Lord that I have freedom and deliverance, for the law of the Spirit (of Life in Christ has made me free from the law of sin and death, and sing with the poet:

>Alas and did my Saviour bleed?
>And did my Sovereign die?
>Would He devote that sacred head
>For such a worm as I?
>
>Was it for crimes that I have done,
>He groaned upon the tree,
>Amazing pity! grace unknown!
>And love beyond degree!
>Well might the sun in darkness hide,
>And shut His glories in,
>When Christ, the mighty Maker died,
>For man, the creature sin.
>
>Bur drops of grief can ne'er repay,
>The debt of love I owe;
>Here, Lord, I give myself away,
>'Tis all that I can do.

All this, as stated before, involved the forfeiture of the kinsman's own family name, and marred his inheritance; but it was recognized as a patriotic and social duty, overriding personal considerations. Now, this is just what Boaz did for Ruth, and w h at the nearer kinsman refuted to do. Boaz merged hill own personality and family in Ruth's family, making a real sacrifice, and thus he became her kinsman redeemer, and then, also, her husband, This is the beautiful type of Our Lord Jesus Christ, our kinsman Redeemer. For us he has sacrificed His own divine rights. This is what the apostle meant when he said, "That being in the form of God, He thought it not a thing to be eagerly grasped and retained that He should be equal with God; but made himself of no reputation, and took upon Him the form of a servant, and was made in the likeness of men; and being found in fashion as a man, He humbled Himself and became obedient unto death, even the death of the cross." Christ gave up forever a place of dignity and right on yonder throne, where he was known as God and God alone. Henceforth, He is forever known as man, still divine, but not exclusively divine, but united to the person, flesh and form of a created being, and His whole inheritance merged in ours.

He lay down His rights and His honours, and took up our wrongs and reproaches, our liabilities and responsibilities, and henceforth He has nothing but his people. He is the merchant man seeking goodly pearls, who, having found one pearl of great price, sold all that he had and bought that pearl. The Church, His Bride, is all He owns; He has invested everything in us. The Lord's portion is His people; therefore, let us make up to Him what he has laid down; let us understand His sacrifice and love, and let Him find in us His sufficient and everlasting recompense. But the redeemer not only sacrificed his own inheritance, but also brought back the forfeited inheritance of the dead husband; and so our precious Goel has brought back for us all that we lost in Adam, and added to it infinitely more—all the fulness of His grace, all the riches of His glory, all that the ages to come are yet to unfold in his mighty plan, victory over death, the restoration of the divine image, sonship with God, triumph over Satan, a world restored to more than Eden blessedness and beauty, the crowns and thrones of the coming kingdom, and all the exceeding riches of His grace and kindness toward us which in the ages to come He is to show. All this, and more, is the purchase of his Redemption, says Dr. Simpson.

> In whom the tribes of Adam boast
> More blessings than their father lost.

But the best of all the blessings brought by the kinsman Redeemer is Himself. Not only does he redeem the inheritance, but he purchases the bride and He becomes the Bridegroom. When Boaz bought the inheritance of Elimelech he took Ruth also in and she became his bride. And so, our blessed Kinsman Redeemer is also our Husband. Not only does He come down into our nature in the incarnation, but He takes us up into his person in the wondrous betrothal which is to reach its consummation in the marriage of the Lamb.

Once more ye see in Ruth's example the pattern of a faith that dares ·to claim and enter into ail the possibilities of its inheritance. It needed on the part of Ruth a very bold and decided act to claim her rights under the Levirate law. They would not have come to her as the snowflakes fall, but they had to be recognized and definitely claimed. And so, her mother told her all about it and showed her that she was doing no unwomanly or immodest thing to put herself at the feet of Boaz and in the place of which she was entitled and leave upon him the responsibility of accepting or refusing her. Still, it cost her many a struggle and many a tear before she robed herself in her wedding garments and, stealing through the eventide, lay down at the threshing floor of Boaz, putting herself and all that was dear to a woman's honour at his mercy. It was the abandonment of faith, but faith must always abandon itself before it can claim its blessing.

It was thus that Mary, in later days, consented to risk her very reputation at the angel's message and believed for the mighty blessing that was to bring the world its Redeemer at the cost, for a time, of even Mary's reputation. "Behold the handmaid of the Lord," she cried, "be it unto me according to Thy word," and the answer came, "Blessed is she that believed, for there shall be an accomplishment of the things that were told her from the Lord?"

And so, faith must ever claim its promised rights. Every victory costs a venture, and the blessing is in proportion to the cost. Faith must still see its inheritance under the promise and then step boldly forward and take what God has Given. Salvation is not now bestowed as mercy to a pauper, but it is claimed in Jesus name through baptism in water in

Jesus' name, and the reception of the Holy Ghost by all who inherits his Brother's will. So, we take His forgiveness and so we must take every blessing and answer to our prayer all along our way. God has given us the right to take this place of boldness. We are not presuming, but we are honoring His word. We are not entering beyond our rights, but we are showing our confidence in our Father's truth and love by daring to take all He has dared to give. So, let us have boldness to enter into the holiest by the blood of Jesus.

> And to its utmost fulness prove
> The power of Jesus name.

Finally, the fruit of the union was the dynasty of David and the birth of Jesus Christ, the Son of man, the King of Kings, and the Lord of Lords. Ruth's faith brought her into a family of princes and a kingdom of glory. And so, for us, too, redemption means a crown and a throne at the Master's glorious coming. But back of the throne and the crown lies the love story of redemption and the bold appropriation of faith. We must learn to know the Bridegroom now if we would sit with Him upon His throne then and share the glory of his millennial reign. Oh! shall we take Him as our Redeemer, our Husband, and our coming Lord, and have Him say to us, "Thy Maker is thy Husband and thy Redeemer the Holy one of Israel, the God of the whole earth shall He be called."

The Lord through uniting our human natures by the process of miscegenation—the mixing of the blood of Ham,

Shem and Japheth—forever abolished the basis and principle of race prejudice, because if he is a kinsman to all having their blood in his veins then whosoever hateth his brother, hateth his Lord, because whatever race that one whom he hateth maybe of, our Lord is of that race, whether Semitic, Hamitic, or Japhethic, although he is not wholly of any, he is not a Jew, not a Negro, not a white man, that is, an Anglo-Saxon, but a relative of all. Praise the Lord. He is our Saviour, not a Jewish Saviour, nor a negro Saviour, nor an Anglo-Saxon Saviour, but a human, universal Saviour, (our kinsman) by virtue of the fact, that the blood of Shem, Ham, and Japheth, representatives of the entire human race, flows through his veins, therefore, all have the same interest and right in Him and none can say to another, "You have no part in Him."

He is our Saviour" for He became our kinsman, bone of our bones, and flesh of all flesh, that as we became one flesh in Him. He might by one spirit in us, make us one in Him. For He is our peace, who hath made both one, and hath broken down the middle wall of partition between us. Having abolished in his flesh the enmity, even the Jaw of commandments contained in ordinances; for to make in himself of twain one new man, so making peace. And came and preached peace to you which were afar off, and to them that were high. And that he might reconcile both unto God in one body by the cross having slain the enmity thereby. For through him we both have access by one spirit unto the Father; the church, a temple for habitation of God through the Spirit.

Now, therefore, ye are no more strangers and foreigners, but fellow citizens with the saints, and of the household of God. And are built upon the foundation of the apostles and prophets, Jesus Christ himself being the chief corner stone. In whom, all the building fitly framed together groweth unto an holy temple in the Lord. In whom, ye also are builded together for an habitation of God through the Spirit. We cannot make a difference between flesh, for we be brethren, 1st John 4:12. If any man says, "I love God," and hateth his brother, he is a liar; tor he that loveth not his brother whom he hath seen, how can he love God whom he hath not seen? And this commandment have we from him, that he who loveth God love his brother also. No man hath seen God at any time. If we love one another, God dwelleth in us, and his love is perfected in us.

Prejudice

August, 1947

President Truman's remarkable address on Civil Rights, declared, "There is much that state and local government can do in providing positive safeguards for civil rights. That the nation cannot any longer await the growth of a will to action in the lowest state, or the most backward community. Our national government must show the way. Federal laws and administrative machinery must be improved and expanded."

The Church of Our Lord Jesus Christ is derelict in its duty of preaching the Gospel in its fullness.

"America owes most of its social prejudices," said someone, "to the exaggerated religious opinions of the different sects which were so instrumental in establishing the colonies." Hence, the Church of today stands guilty with the Church of yesterday in not preaching against prejudice, but in perpetuating it in following the customs and tradition of their Fathers and not the Bible.

Prejudice may be considered as a continual false medium of viewing things, for prejudiced persons not only never speak well, but also never think well of those whom they dislike, and the whole character and conduct is considered with an eye to that particular thing which offends them.

Prejudice is the conjuror of imaginary wrongs, strangling truth, overpowering reason, making strong men weak and weak men weaker. God give us the large-hearted charity with "beareth all things, believeth all things, hopeth all things, endureth all things, which thinketh no evil."

The present hour is a critical and decisive hour in our Nation's life, and in that of the world. The need of this hour is for real men of God to cry aloud and spare not, and show the Nation its sins and transgressions.

As President Truman says, "the Nation cannot any longer await growth of a will to action in the slowest state or most backward community."

The ministry must awake to a sense of their responsibility and fight the hydra-headed monster of prejudice, and all its attendant evils—economic exploitation, lynching, Jim Crow cars and Jim-crow churches, slum housing, etc.

H. G. Wells states succinctly the case when he states: "I am convinced myself that there is no more evil thing in this present world than race prejudice. None at all. I write deliberately—that it is the worst single thing in life now. It justifies and holds together more baseness, cruelty, and abomination, than any other sort of error in the world."

The Church should outlaw prejudice in every form—not by precept only, but by practice, and Pentecostal Churches should show the way, and as the President has said:

> Many of our people still suffer the indignity of insult, the harrowing fear of intimidation, and I regret to say, the threat of physical injury and mob violence. The prejudice and intolerance in which these evils are rooted still exist. The conscience of our nation, and the legal machinery which enforces it, have not yet secured to each citizen full freedom from fear.

He said, the support of desperate populations in battle—ravaged countries "must be won to the free way of life," since they are essential "in our continuing struggle for the peaceful solution of the world's problems." "Freedom," he asserted, is not an easy lesson to teach, nor an easy cause to sell to peoples beset by every kind of privation. They may surrender to the false security offered so temptingly by totalitarian regimes unless we can prove the superiority of democracy. Our case for democracy should be as strong as we can make it. It should rest on practical evidence that we have been able to put our own house in order."

By teaching our children the wickedness of prejudice and the power of love, we will eliminate most prejudice along racial lines in one generation. We cannot maintain our moral leadership of the world when our sins and prejudices give a lie to all our high idealism and religious profession.

The Greatest Evil In This World Is Race Prejudice

June 1957

Methodist Bishop G. Bromley Oxnam of Washington, D. C., describing segregation, "To segregate is sin. We do not segregate those we love. A man is a brother or he is not. If he is a brother, he is entitled to that status in religion, education, business, law, politics and society."[60]

It justifies and holds together more baseness and cruelty and abominations than any other sort of error in the world. It is the church's job not to foster, aid, or abet white supremacy through segregation, but to eliminate it as God said to Jeremiah, to root out, pull down, to build and to plan in the human heart through the new birth, the doctrine of the brotherhood of man by human blood, for God out of one blood has made all nations that dwell upon the face of the earth, and through divine spiritual birth (I Cor 12:13), for by one Spirit are we all baptized into one body, whether we be Jew or Gentile, whether we be bond or free, we have all been made to drink of one Spirit.

I wrote in a book, The Anthropology of Jesus Christ" many years ago, that I had hoped and trusted that the Pentecostal movement would have been the church which should redeem Christendom from the virus and plague of race prejudice and segregation as an established order of society. The true followers of Christ will be fortunately in conflict with the established order whether of society,

---

[60] Journal of the 1960 General of the Methodist Church, April 27-May 7, 1960.

government, or the church itself. A Christian moral judgement should never represent the prejudice of the community. The duty of the Christian is to use his mind is the love of God with the mind as well as with the soul and strength. As Romans 12:2 states, "Be not conformed to this world; but be ye transformed by the renewing of your mind that ye may prove what is good and acceptable, and perfect will of God."

The glory of the New Testament Church was its nonconformity to the established social pattern of the world and its setting up of the Christian standard of equality and brotherhood. But alas, the Pentecostal white brethren have conformed to the world and have fallen in line with the sect churches before they emerged out of the darkness of Catholicism through Luther, who initiated the reformation.

We have white Pentecostal churches and colored Pentecostal churches. White Bishops and Colored Bishops over respective works. We have Jim-crowed the Lord's table which is an effrontery to God, whose democratic appeal is this wise, Whosoever will let him come," And again in Matthew 11:28. "Come unto me all ye that labor and are heavy laden and I will give you rest." The net results of this attitude have caused the Pentecostal churches to degenerate like the sectarian churches. To aid and abet race prejudice is as thoroughly a denial of u Christian God as atheism is, and it is a much more common form of apostacy. Race prejudice denies the universal fatherhood of God; it denies the New Testament insistence of equality of all souls before God, it denies the central affirmation of the Gospel that God so loved the world that He gave His Son. As for Jesus of Nazareth who took for His hero the man of Samaria from a despised race, anyone who harbors race prejudice parts company with God." says Dr. H. E. Fosdick.

This, the Pentecostal people ought to have seen long ago and lifted their voices against the iniquity as Isaiah states, "Cry aloud and spare not, lift up your voices like a trumpet in Zion; show my people their sins and the house of Jacob their transgressions. But as a whole, nothing has been said or done but all the status quo of society has been accepted or supinely submitted to and a pattern followed. Up until this day, even after the Supreme Court of the United States declared unconstitutional, unlawful and unrighteous the entire system of race segregation, no white Pentecostal movement has declared its stand and support and advocacy of this revolutionary edict and begun to put into practice desegregation. No Pentecostal convention has gone on record like the Jewish Rabbinical Assembly of America. Rabbi Halpern told 100 conservative Rabbis, "We hail our Negro brethren for the restraint they have exercised in the face of provocation and commend them for the dignity and truly religious spirit in which they have met the attempt upon freedom guaranteed to them in the Constitution and reinforced by a Supreme Court decision.

Their determination to carry on the struggle against allegedly pious people deserves our praise." He calls upon the Jewish religious leaders to give aid to Negroes in the South. The great Methodist Episcopalian and the Catholic Churches have gone on record and endorsed the decision of the Supreme Court and have promised to abide by the same and they are advocating the desegregation of their churches and the abolishment of segregation in every branch of our government and nation.

But not a word from the Pentecostal brethren. No outstanding minister of the Assembly of God or the United Pentecostal Church has raised his voice in approval of the Supreme Court decision and in disapproval of the traditional concept of segregation. However, the noted Dr. Casper C. Warren of Charlotte, North Carolina, President of the Southern Baptist Convention, the leader of 8,474,741 members of 30,777 churches in the South, declared that, we must do a better job of living what we proclaim and cautioned his listeners to safeguard the church from the tendencies that would cause its disintegration and decay. "The totalitarian challenge from without is perhaps the most vicious thing we are faced with today," says Dr. Warren. "Powers that have enslaved nearly half the people of this world blot out the very existence of this church and churches like it forever. Apart from these insidious forces, there are sins galore that would tear us asunder.

Jews—these terms, if they have any meaning at all, are only as language groups; precisely as Latin. Anglo-Saxon, Arabian. It is as nonsensical to talk of the Jewish race, as it is to talk of a Christian one.

What ethnologists have to say on the alleged inferiority of certain people, remind one of a Haitian proverb, "[w]hen the rooster and the cockroach come to court, you don't have to guess which one will win." What ethnologists need most is emancipation from exploiting capitalism and complete divorce from the slave master's legend of the Negro all being abnormal and inferior to the white race.

This is definitely discounted and proven to be a false premise. History records illustrious names of great men of color: for instance, Imhotep, Father of medicine; Thotmas III, conqueror of the then known world. Akhneatom first Messiah; Lockman, first great fabulist of the world; Aesop, whose proverbs influenced the world's greatest thinkers; Cletus, comrade of Alexander the Great and also his chief cavalry leader. Hannibal of Carthage, had the reputation of being the greatest military leader and strategist of all times. Napoleon, after selecting the seven supreme military geniuses of the world, ranked him as the lint in daring... and this Hannibal," said he, "is the most audacious of all, the most astonishing; so bold, so sure, so great in everything, who, at twenty-six conceived what is highly inconceivable what one may truly call the impossible."

Cleopatra, the seventh Queen of Egypt has come down to us through twenty centuries as the perfect example of the seductive art in women. She was unique excelling in licentiousness, a woman of great charm and force and education.

It is reputed that she spoke Greek, Egyptian, Latin, Hebrew, and Arabic. Dion Cassius wrote of her: "She was splendid to see and was capable of conquering the heart that resisted most obstinately against the influence of love, and those which had been frozen by age. Her charms of speech were such that she won all who listened to her."

Among the many who fell in love with her the first and most notable is Julius Caesar, who was debonair and one of the world's greatest orators and a beloved ruler.

The second was Mark Anthony, the Magnificent, the Don Juan of his time, and a great orator. To these two men, she gave birth to several children. She became within an inch of becoming the mistress of the world but for a misunderstanding of the outcome of the Battle of Actium; mistaking the battle to be lost, she left the scene ill her ship of war, followed by Mark Anthony who died in her arms in her own mausoleum. Afterwards, she followed in death from the bite of an asp smuggled to her by slaves, conveyed to her in a basket of figs!

In Asia, following her was the noted Zenobia, Queen of the East. So much for warriors—now for scholars. Antar, poet and chivalrous figure of the East and the literature of the East. He is known as AbduI Fauras, and there is also a famous writer of the Ninth Century, Al Atheism, the destroyer of faith; materialism. the destroyer of spirituality, racialism, the destroyer of brotherhood; fear, the destroyer of peace; lawlessness, the destroyer of civil order; and pagan ideals that would destroy all the rest that is near and dear to us."

Stressing action, the Wake Forest college graduate said he preferred to approach the matter from a positive standpoint. "We as individuals," he said, must positively determine to do something about it ourselves. We must remain anchored to the fundamental pattern of the Bible if we are to build a better church tomorrow. We ought to quit making apologies for repeating truth. Let us ever continue to preach and teach by precept an example and blessed truths. We must be better than we proclaim. Christianity stands or falls upon fact."

Thank God the light is breaking for better understanding and the honest facing of facts. To save our civilization we must break down all barriers of segregation and discrimination if we aspire to moral leadership of the world. In the New York Herald Tribune, one young leader of tomorrow, Mr. Summerfield came out with the following. The problem which seems to be claiming the first consideration of more people every day is that the United States is engaged in a death struggle for the moral leadership of the world. And I would say, also, that more people every day are coming to realize as I am that there are some areas in which we may be doing things to Jeopardize our chances for that position of leadership."

Citing the case of Herman Marion Sweatt, an applicant to the Texas University Law School International News Service. January, February, 1948) and that of Mrs. Ada Lois Sipuel Fisher, still seeking admission through the courts to the University of Oklahoma's all white law school, young Summerfield (young white progressive) scored those Texans who... still find ways to rationalize their prejudices and whose misinformation had led them to think that some great disaster would result the moment segregation was broken down at any point.

It is this group, I think, which is responsible for the testimony of many school officials and politicians in behalf of segregation. I am certain that many of these leaders know the facts of the situation better than they seem to, and I don't see how anybody can believe one thing and profess another, without eventually injuring his integrity. I believe any American who considers himself educated and still denies equality of opportunity to anyone, is either making an excuse for some exclusive privilege, or he isn't educated to the democratic facts of life."

The so-called superiority of the white race, or any other race for that matter, above any other group is purely hypothetical and has no basis in fact. The leading anthropologists of the world have agreed as recently as last year, 1,956, at least as 85 percent of them, that there is no such thing as a pure race upon earth—that is distinct, separate, and different from any other of the human species.

Such terms as Hametic for the Ethiopians, and Semetic for the Jahiz, the most genial writer of the age (A.D. 778-868) if not in Arab literature, and the founder of Arab prose. He was the grandson of a Negro slave.

According to Christopher Dawson, Al Jahiz was the greatest scholar and stylist of the Ninth Century. Ykub AI Mansur, greatest of Spanish caliphs, Amou Hassan AU, the black Sultan of Morocco, Chaka Zulu conqueror and despot, and Tippoo Tib, African trail blazer are among the other great warriors.

In religion, Samuel D. Crawford Bishop of Niger, Menelik II, was the Lion of Judah, who defeated the Italians with overwhelming slaughter; Alfred A. Doggs, French General and empire builder, Isaac Wallace Johnson, African an indomitable labor leader, and Emperor Haile Selassie, the Dauntless of Ethiopia. Tune would fall me to make mention, of course, of the great Saints, like St. Augustine of Carthage, an African, and St. Benedict, the Moor, the Saint of the Catholic Church, born in Sicily; Abraham Hannibal, Russian General and chief, and Jean Louis, the world's greatest swordsman and duelist. George H. Bridgetower, prodigy of the violin; Alexander Dumas fils, the world's greatest romancer, and Alexander Dumas, the French novelist; Ira Aldridge, the greatest of the Othellos, and Samuel Coleridge Taylor, world's musical sensation; Touisaant L'Overture, Negro of whom Napoleon was jealous; Desselenes, liberator of Haiti and its first emperor.

Time would fall me to make mention of medieval and modem men of color. The great poet Robert Browning had Negro ancestry. Beethoven, the great musical genius, had definite strains of Negro blood in him. There all, until the rise of the doctrine of white superiority was generally pictured as Colored, especially Cleopatra. Shakespeare in the opening lines of his Anthony and Cleopatra, calls her tawny. In his day, mulattoes were called tawny. Captain John Smith, the Governor of Virginia and a contemporary· of Shakespeare used tawny as synonymous with mulattoes. Writing of a chief of Morocco, it was "King Mully Hamet was not black as many supposed but mulatto or in Act I, Scene 5, Cleopatra calls herself black, made by the sun, Phoebus. The above is sufficient to explode the myth of the so-called inferiority of the black or mixed people.

"In the last analysis, we see only what we hope to see, what we have been taught to see; we eliminate and ignore everything that is not a part of our prejudice," says J. M. Charcot. This is true, and perhaps, Reverend sir, your whole outlook on the race problem is the result of your Southern antecedents and background which warps your judgment and colors your vision to such an extent that you read even into the Scripture the postulates of white supremacy and the inferiority of the Negro race. You seek to certify these false assumptions or prejudices by the sanction of Scripture to make them to say these things are of divine origin and are the Will of the Creator, not thinking that this would make God the author of inequality, and the author of partiality and injustice. For God to create men unequal and demand the same responsibility and standards of them, would be a rank injustice. God forbid! This cannot be true, for it is incompatible to His divine nature.

No, beloved of God, God is not the author of inequalities or injustices. There is but one human race. Though there may be many nations, there is but one race. There are different languages and customs, but there is no basis for differences between men, for God hath made of one blood all nations of men for to dwell on all the face of the earth. It is bad enough to preach prejudice and uphold the iniquitous custom of segregation, but to make God a party to it is a monumental sin. Is God the minister of sin? To the contrary, the Scripture states that God has through the Cross of Jesus, broken down the middle wall between Jew and Gentile, and all other nations, for that matter, and has purposed that through the new birth a Holy nation should be brought into existence, where there is neither Jew nor Greek, bond nor free, black nor white; a classless nation where all distinction and differences are obliterated. (Acts 17:26; Eph: 2:11-22; I Peter 2:9) The Church is the divine agency through which this is to be brought about by the preaching and practice of the Gospel through the ministry. But, alas, through your type of minister, this will never be brought about. For you are a preacher who builds again these things which Christ destroyed. Until there are ministers who are saved through and through, baptized with the Holy Spirit, who know no difference, and who have a vision of God's one world and His new order, that will never be brought about.

Not mere separation of races is involved in segregation, but the economic exploitation, the selfishness, the pride which is the capital sin that caused Satan to fan from his holy state as a covering cherub known as Lucifer. It is in the design of segregation, the vicious and wicked psychology that fosters pride and arrogance on the part of the white man. God resists the proud, but giveth grace to the humble. It demeans the Negro, stuns the growth of his manhood, binders his development, retards his initiative, courage and cooperation, and makes it extremely difficult for him to maintain even in the Church a semblance of human dignity. At every turn he is hindered at places he cannot enter because of his color; churches, schools, restaurants, theatres, lunch counters, rest rooms, not to mention the wide-spread job barriers. Living is made like a convict serving out a sentence.

Moreover, segregation hinders fellowship and equality with other members of the family of God of other races. This is equivalent to raising a family, praising one child and berating or humiliating the other, which is unfair. This a true minister of the Gospel should not condone or practice in the Church of Christ. To these sentiments agree H. G. Wells, a noted historian. Says he, I am convinced myself that there is no more evil thing in this present world than race prejudice None at all. I write deliberately. It is the worse single thing in life now. It justifies and holds together more baseness, cruelty, and abomination than any other sort of error in the world."[61]

R. R. Moton states that; "The thinking Negro refuses to accept the idea or even the theory that race prejudice is natural and inevitable; that it is inherent in the child, either white or black." He insists that it is acquired and cultivated, and that the greatest single aid to its cultivation is segregation.

Dr. Ernest A Hooton of the Department of Harvard University has stated that "Racial prejudice is little more than the cloak to cover an apparently universal desire of selfish and morally low-grade human beings to dominate their fellow beings![62]

Allegations of racial inferiority or superiority were not based on scientific findings and had never deceived any except the ignorant and the mentally inferior, but these, unfortunately, included an enormous proportion of individuals of whatever race or nationality.

Racial difference provides the most obvious excuse for antagonism that really springs from sheer selfish desire to dominate others, and especially to justify rivalry that is political, social, or economic.

The hatreds that arise from human competition easily shift their emotional expressions from race to nationality to economic class to religious affiliations, or to any other handy pretext whereby an ugly sentiment, a sordid motive or down right viciousness may be rationalized or whitewashed.

---

[61] H. G. Wells, "Race Prejudice" *The Appeal*, October 17, 1914.

[62] The New York Times, "Dr. Hooton Assails Racial Prejudice," July 17, 1944, 9.

It is for this reason that racial prejudices will persist in spite of scientific demonstrations that there are no hierarchies of physical, mental, or cultural ability in human races, and no rank lists of virtues and vice.

We shall have to improve individual human quality before we can get an amelioration of group behavior as manifested in race discrimination, class rivalry, religious persecution, and welfare, but in my opinion, the greater part of such human betterment will have to come about by segregating and preventing the reproduction of criminalistic, mentally defective, insane and constitutionally deteriorated individual of whatever race, nationality and creed, and by studying human inheritance so that it will provide a knowledge that will enable us to breed better men.

Specifically, we shall have to have better quality of whites before Negroes will receive the justice that they deserve, and for which they clamor; and generally, before we achieve lasting peace for the world, we shall have to breed Born again. Christians, a majority of human individuals that are sufficiently intelligent to behave decently and not like packs of baboons.

Repeated mouthings of political and moral aspirations, whether the inner corner of the eves to produce what we call the slant eye. The geographical differences between men are however of small magnitude when one considers the fundamental likeness.

The population of the world was small in the days of early man, and differences, once begun, tended to persist through isolation and in breeding. Each so-called race became functionally adapted to living in the area in which it found itself. There was no question of superiority or inferiority for the white man would have suffered in the hot tropical sun as much as the Negro would have suffered in the cold North.

With the growth of civilization, man has been enabled through the use of proper clothing and scientifically prepared food and vitamins, to move into all areas of the world, no matter what his color. The, so-called, racial differences are superficial and man is essentially the same and has the same potential and wherever you find him, be he light, dark, tall, short, fat or thin, long headed or round headed.

Dr. Chisholm says, "Our danger and other people's unresolved hates and that of the world. In our own and their antagonisms; our and their indiscriminating obedience; our and their tendency to find acceptable whatever concepts may fit the emotional state of the moment." Chief Justice Charles Evans Hughes said, "Rancor and bigotry; racial animosities and intolerance are more dangerous than any external force, because they undermine the very foundations of democratic effort."[63]

---

[63] *Joplin Globe*, "Bigotry Enemy of Democracy Says Hughes," December 29, 1940, 7.

Prayer for Freedom from Race Prejudice

O God, who has made man in thine own likeness, and who doth love all whom Thou has made, suffer us not because of difference of race, color, or condition to separate ourselves from others and thereby from Thee; but teach us the unity of Thy family and universality of Thy Love.

As Thou Saviour, as a Son, was born of an Hebrew mother, who had the blood of many nations in her veins; and ministered first to Thy brethren of the Israelites, but rejoiced in the faith of a Syro-Phoenician woman and of a Roman soldier, and suffered your cross to be carried by an Ethiopian; teach us, also, while loving and serving our own, to enter into the communion of the whole family; and forbid that from pride of birth, color, achievement, and hardness of heart, we should despise any for whom Christ died, or injure or grieve any in whom He lives. We pray in Jesus precious name."

Amen

Bibliography

Alexander, Estrelda Y. Black Fire: One Hundred Years of African American Pentecostalism. Downers Grove, IL: InterVarsity Press, 2011.

——————————. Black Fire Reader A Documentary Resource on African-American Pentecostalism. Eugene, OR: Cascade Books, 2013.

Alexander, Kimberly Ervin, and R. Hollis Gause. Women In Leadership A Pentecostal Perspective. Cleveland, TN: Center For Pentecostal Leadership & Care, 2006,

Anderson, Arthur M., ed. For The Defense of The Gospel. New York, New York: Church of Our Lord Jesus Christ of the Apostolic Faith, 1972.

Barba, Lloyd. "Jesus Would Be Jim Crowed: Bishop Robert Lawson on Race and Religion in the Harlem Renaissance." Journal of Race, Ethnicity, and Religion, August 2015: 32.

Bonacci, Giulia. "The Ethiopian World Federation." Caribbean Quarterly, June 2013: 73.

Bonner, Ethel Mae. "This Is My Story." Apostolic Women's Newsletter, August 25, 1988.

Bonner, William L. My Father in The Gospel Bishop R.C. Lawson. New York, NY: Greater Refuge Temple, nod.

——————————. The Doctrinal Guide of Solomon's Temple. Detroit, MI: Solomon's Temple COOLJC, n.d.

Butler, Anthea D. Women in The Church of God in Christ Making A Sanctified World. Chapel Hill, BC: University of North Carolina Press, 2007

Casselberry, Judith. The Labor of Faith Gender and Power in Black Apostolic Pentecostalism. Durham, NC: Duke University Press, 2017.

Colon-Emeric, Edgardo A. Wesley, Aquinas & Christian Perfection. Waco, TX: Baylor University Press, 2009.

Discipline Book of The Church of Our Lord Jesus Christ of The Apostolic Faith, Inc. New York, NY: Church of Our Lord Jesus Christ, 1975.

DuPree, Sherry Sherrod. Biographical Dictionary of African-American, Holiness-Pentecostals. Washington, DC: Middle Atlantic Regional Press, 1989.

Ethiopian World Federation. The Ethiopian World Federation. n.d. https:// theethiopianworld federation.com, accessed March 30, 2018).

Ferguson, Everett. Church History: From Christ to the Reformation. Grand Rapids, MI: Zondervan, 2005

French, Talmadge L. Early Interracial Oneness Pentecostalism: G.T. Haywood and The Pentecostal Assemblies of the World (1901 - 1931). Eugene, Oregon: Pickwick Publications, 2014.

_____. Our God Is One: The Story of The Oneness Pentecostals. Indianapolis, IN: Voice & Vision Publications, 1999.

Gilkes, Cheryl Townsend. If It Wasn't For The Women. Maryknoll, NY: Orbis Books, 2003.

Gruesser, John Cullen. Black on Black Twentieth-Century African American Writing about Africa. Lexington, KY: University of Kentucky Press, 2000.

Hattersley, Roy. The Life of John Wesley A Brand From The Burning. New York, NY: Doubleday, 2003.

Hudson, Hilary T, The Methodist Armor or Popular Exposition of The Doctrine, Peculiar Usages and Ecclesiastical Machinery of The Methodist Episcopal Church, South. Nashville, TN: Publishing House Methodist Episcopal Church, South, 1912.

Jacobsen, Douglas. A Reader in Pentecostal Theology Voices From The First Generation. Bloomington, IN: Indiana University Press, 2006.

_____. Thinking in the Spirit Theologies of the Early Pentecostal Movement. Indianapolis, IN: Indiana University Press, 2003.

Johnson, Sherrod C. 21 Burning Subjects. Philadelphia, PA: Church of The Lord Jesus Christ of the Apostolic Faith, n.d.

_____. Is Jesus Christ The Son of God Now? Philadelphia, PA: Church of The Lord Jesus Christ of The Apostolic Faith, n.d.

Knepper, Cathy D. "The Crime And The Trenton Six." in In Jersey Justice: The Story of the Trenton Six, 1-22. New Brunswick, NJ: Rutgers University Press, 2011.

Lawless, Elaine J. Handmaidens of The Lord Pentecostal Women Preachers and Traditional Religion; Philadelphia, PA: University of Pennsylvania Press, 1988.

Lawson, Robert C. A Short Sketch of the Industrial Union of America, West Indies and Canada. New York: Privately Printed, 1932.

_____. *A Woman Shall Compass a Man.* s.l: s.n. s.d.

_____. *An Open Letter on the Burning Question on Marriage and Divorce.* s.l: sn. s.d.

_____. *An Open Letter to a Southern White Minister on Prejudice—The Eating Cancer of the Soul.* New York: Privately Printed, n.d.

_____. *Christ was not Crucified on Friday But on Wednesday.* s.l: s.n. s.d.

_____. *Healing through Christ: Or Divine Healing for the Body.* New York: The Church of Christ Publishing Company, s.d.

_____. *How Sin and Why the Cross,* New York, The Church of Christ Publishing Company, 1960.

_____. *Pentecostal Power.* s.l: s.n. s.d.

_____. *Prayer for Freedom from Race Prejudice.* s.l: s.n. s.d.

_____. *Prejudice* s.l: s.n. s.d.

_____. *Self-Glorification: A Disqualification for God's Work.* s.l: s.n. s.d.

_____. *Seven Reasons Why we Baptize in Jesus' Name.* s.l: s.n. s.d.

_____. *The Anthropology of Jesus Christ Our Kinsman.* New York: The Church of Christ Publishing Company, 1925.

_____. *The Design and Results of Suffering: A Sermon.* New York: The Church of Christ Publishing Company, s.d.

_____. *The Greatest Evil in the World is Race Prejudice* s.l: s.n. s.d.

_____. *The New Testament Church.* s.l: s.n. s.d.

_____. *Watch your Step!* s.l: s.n. s.d.

——————————. *What is a Biblical Marriage: or How Men and Women are Joined Together by God as One?* s.l: s.n. s.d.

Layne, Austin. "A Sketch of My Life." The Christian Outlook, May 1952: 4-5.

MacHaffe, Barbara. Her Story: Women in Christian Tradition. 2nd. Minneapolis, MN: Fortress Press, 2006.

Mason, Mary. The History And Life Work of Elder C. H. Mason. Memphis, TN: Privately Printed, 1924.

Reed, David A. In Jesus' Name The History and Beliefs of Oneness Pentecostals. Dorset, UK: Deo Publishing, 2008.

Richardson, James C. With Water And Spirit A History of Black Apostolic Denominations in The U.S. Washington, DC: Spirit Press, 1980.

Robeck, Jr., Cecil M. "Azusa Street Revival." in Dictionary of Pentecostal and Charismatic Movements, by Stanley M. Burgess, & Gary B. McGee, 31-36. Grand Rapids, MI: Zondervan Publishing House, 1988.

Rosier, Evelyn R. Outstanding Women and Their Contributions to The Church of Our Lord Jesus Christ of The Apostolic Faith Vol. I. New York, NY: Church of Our Lord Jesus Christ, 1994.

Sanders, Cheryl J. Saints in Exile The Holiness-Pentecostal Experience in African American Religion and Culture. New York, NY: Oxford University Press, 1966.

Sanders, Rufus G.W. Garfield Thomas Haywood: Father of The Modern Oneness Pentecostal Movement. Toledo, OH: H.O.T. Graphics, 2018.

Scott, Dorothy E, and Ethel Trice. Great Women of Pentecost: A Biographical Sketch of Pioneer Women of The Pentecostal

Assemblies of The World. Vol. I. Indianapolis, IN: Privately Printed, 1983.

Sims, Jane. Telling Our Story: A Brief History of Women in the Pentecostal Assemblies of the World. Indianapolis, IN: Privately Printed, 2003.

Smith, Helen. You're Going to Be Somebody. Mobile, AL: Gazalla Press, 1999.

Spellman, Robert C., Thomas Mable L. The Life, Legend and Legacy of Bishop R.C. Lawson. 2nd Edition. Scotch Plains, NJ: Robert C. Spellman Publisher, 1983.

Stewart, Alexander C. "Bishop Robert Clarence Lawson in the Pentecostal Assemblies of the World." The Contender For The Faith (Church of Our Lord Jesus Christ), Fall 2009: 16-19.

Stewart, Alexander C, and Sherry Sherrod DuPree. The Silent Spokesman Bishop Robert Clarence Lawson. Gainesville, FL: Displays For Schools, Inc., 1994.

Synan, Vinson. The Holiness-Pentecostal Tradition Charismatic Movements in the Twentieth Century. Grand Rapids, MI: William B, Eerdmans Publishing Company, 1997.

The Contender For The Faith. September - October 1951 1951: 15.

Trice, Ethel. The 70th Year Historical Souvenir Book of the Pentecostal Assemblies of the World. Indianapolis, IN: Pentecostal Assemblies of the World, Inc., 1985.

Waid, Ora. A Blessed Life in the Making The Life of Bishop R.C. Lawson. Edited by Mable L. Thomas. New York: Privately Printed, 1936.

Wentz, Richard E. American Religious Traditions The Shaping of Religion in the United States. Minneapolis, MN: Augsburg Fortress Press, 2003.

Wheeler, Henry. *History and Exposition of the Twenty-Five Articles of Religion of the Methodist Episcopal Church*. New York: The Methodist Book Concern, 1908.

Index

Abraham, 53, 66, 119, 149, 272, 278, 278, 286, 321-322, 327, 343
Adam, 15, 37, 41-42, 44, 48-49, 53-54, 56, 60, 181, 234, 265, 320, 338, 346, 348
Adultery, 183, 187-188, 192, 194, 199, 208, 210-212, 216, 219, 224-225, 229-230, 234, 241, 245, 248, 251-252, 262, 281
African Freedom Day, 265
Apostles, 14, 81-82, 84-86, 89-91, 94, 96-97, 102, 116, 142, 166, 209-210, 212, 214, 236, 248, 332, 352
Assemblies of God, v
Atonement, 54-55, 115, 260
Augustine, 286, 320, 366
Azusa Street Revival, 13, 174

Baptism of the Holy Spirit (Ghost), v, 3, 84, 100, 109-110, 166-167, 188, 215, 236
Bathsheba, 272, 278-279, 319, 328-329
Bell, Ivy, 168
Benedict, the Moor, 286, 366
Bennett, Jean, 173
Blood of Christ, 84, 97, 101-102, 166, 207, 262, 330

Boaz, 46-48, 327-328, 334-337, 342, 344, 347-349
Body of Christ, 84, 97, 101-102, 166, 207, 262, 330
Bonner, Ethel Mae, i, 167, 171
Bonner, William L., i, 170-171
Branch, Kent, 173
Brown, Elizabeth, 168
Brown, Mildred, 168

Cainhoy Miracle Revival, 173
Calvary, 11, 15, 44, 58, 64, 69, 71, 110, 115, 118, 333
Canaan, 272, 305, 317, 322, 340
Canaan, (son of Ham) 272, 317
Canaanite(s), 269, 272-274, 278, 280, 317, 319, 323-324, 327
Carter, Phyllis, 173
Carter, Ronald, 173
Church, the, (body of Christ), 175, 177, 214, 234, 263, 289, 299, 351
Church of Christ Bible Institute, 5, 169
Civil rights, 6, 265, 355
Civil Rights Congress, 266
Cox, Thomas, 6
Crucifixion, 63, 73-74, 77, 224-227

385

Cush, 272, 305-306, 310

Death (Christ), 11, 13, 16, 43-44, 52-53, 55-56, 60-63, 65-66, 68, 83-84, 98, 110, 116, 120, 122, 343, 345-346, 348
DeSilva, Mamie, 169
Devil, (see Satan) 26, 28, 38, 53, 58, 66-67, 222, 342-343
Divorce, 174, 183, 189, 191, 201, 213, 226, 228-230, 233-234, 239-244

Egypt, 20, 120-121, 236, 258, 272, 285, 300, 306-307, 309-312, 317-318, 342, 363
Egyptian(s), 30, 121, 302, 307, 311, 314, 317
Elijah, 121, 126
Emmanuel Baptist Tabernacle of the Apostolic Faith, 6
Ethiopia, 6, 20, 258-259, 272, 286, 299-300, 307, 311-313, 315, 366
Ethiopian(s) 6, 259, 272, 284, 309, 310-311, 313, 318, 331, 366, 374
Ethiopianism, 258, 262
Ethiopian World Federation, 6, 259
Eve, 37-42, 338-339

Fields, Carrie, 6
Finished Work, v, 110

Flesh (Christ), 11, 13, 15-16, 36, 52-53, 55-57, 61, 63, 66, 71, 74, 86, 206, 240, 277, 279, 326, 330, 351
Foreknowledge, 30, 31

Gentile(s), 55, 75, 86, 116, 142, 210-211, 214, 239, 279-280, 288, 315, 320, 359, 368
God the Father, 11-12, 14-16, 24, 48, 57-58, 63, 81, 83, 85-86, 90, 124, 130, 141, 148, 235, 242, 245, 248-249
Godhead, 3, 6, 11-12, 14, 57, 86
Gregory, Martin Rawleigh, 6

Ham, 272, 305, 307, 313, 315-317, 342, 344, 350-351
Hamitic, 272-273, 284, 305, 307-308, 313, 323-324, 351
Harlem, 4-5, 165-166, 258, 266
Haywood, Garfield T., 3, 13-14, 262
Healing, 115-121, 172
Hell, 63, 82, 84, 145, 234, 238, 242
Holy Ghost, 3, 12-14, 52, 54, 81, 83-86, 93, 95-96, 98, 116-117, 160, 189, 199, 204, 206-208, 214-216, 227-228, 233, 235-237, 245, 248-250, 349, 350
Holy Spirit, v, 7, 11-12, 15, 56-57, 85, 89, 91, 93, 95, 100, 107, 109-110, 130, 139

Horn, Rosa, 166

Incarnation, 15-16, 51, 55, 145, 348
Iniquity, 144-145, 160, 227, 243, 344, 361
Israel, 20, 45-47, 51, 69, 78, 116, 121, 175, 177-179, 189, 202, 206, 213-214, 220, 270, 272, 277-278, 280, 315, 317, 326, 328-329, 334-335, 337, 340, 350

Japheth(ites), 273, 305, 316-317, 324, 341, 344, 351
Japhethic, 328, 351
Jeremiah, 49, 135, 175, 177, 260, 310, 359
Jezebel, 126
Jim Crow, 3, 7, 257, 259, 356
Johnson, Margaret Giles, 168
Johnson, Sherrod C., 4, 12, 15, 169
Jonah, 74-75, 79
Judah, 48, 52, 78, 87, 177, 221, 272-278, 323-327
Judgment, God's, 31, 33, 60, 157, 160, 189, 220, 237-238, 316

King, Martin Luther, 6
Kinsman redeemer, 47-48, 51, 54-55, 274, 297, 300, 316, 339, 341-342, 346-348, 351

Law(s), 22, 36, 45-46, 50, 59, 75, 125, 181, 184-185, 189, 192-193, 200-202, 204-208, 210-213, 218-219, 223, 226-227, 233-237, 265, 270, 272, 277, 279-281, 318-319, 326, 329, 337, 339, 346, 349, 359, 365
Lawsonville, 5
Layne, Austin A., 165
Lightford, Susan, 165

Marriage, 183, 185-188, 191, 193, 195-199, 202, 205, 210, 213, 217, 224, 226-229, 232-234, 239-241, 243-244, 248, 270, 348
Mary (the mother of Jesus) 15, 52, 56, 188, 199-201, 342, 349
McCarthy, Lillian Fields, 168
Methodism, 109, 112
Missionaries, 167-169, 172
Moab(ites), 46-47, 328, 333-334, 336-337

Naomi, 46-47, 334-337
Noah, 45, 62, 241

Oneness doctrine, iv, v, vi, 3, 5-6, 11, 13, 15-17, 110, 165, 265

Parrott, James, 173
Parrott, Joan, 173
Passover, 75-77

Pentecostal Assemblies of the World, v, 3, 6, 11, 13, 101, 165
Perry, Delphia, 169
Phut, 305
Pilate, 21, 274, 324
Powell, Jr., Adam Clayton, 5, 265
Prayer Pilgrimage, 5
Prejudice, 257, 260-261, 267, 269-271, 287-290, 292, 294, 298-299, 309-310, 330, 332-333, 351, 355-357, 359-361, 367-370, 374 see racism

R. C. Lawson Institute, 5
Racism, 257, 260, 266-267
Rahab, 278-279, 327-328
Rebaptism, 3
Redemption, 12, 15, 22, 24, 45, 49, 57, 60, 65, 71, 102, 115, 333, 337, 343-346, 348, 350
Refuge Temple, 4, 108, 265
Regeneration, 12, 94
Rockefeller, Nelson, 5
Roman Catholic Church, 92, 94, 286, 361, 366
Ruth, 46-48, 308, 333-337, 347-349

Sabbath, 75, 77, 208
Sabeans, 20
Sacrifice, 15, 19, 36, 54-55, 58-60, 66, 69, 77, 97, 126, 168, 178, 315, 347-348

Salvation, 15, 51, 55, 60, 81, 83-84, 89-90, 92, 99-100, 115-116, 118, 129-130, 132, 160, 166-167, 193, 228-229, 237, 290, 343, 349
Sara, 149
Sarah, 118, 321
Sarai, 322
Satan, 28-29, 31-32, 38-39, 41, 43-45, 49, 54, 60-63, 66, 143-145, 214, 289, 338, 348, 369
Selassie, Haile, 6, 286, 366
Semitic race, 284, 307-308, 317, 323, 351
Shem, 272-273, 315-316, 321, 324, 341, 344-345, 351
Smith, Helen, 172
Sin, 15, 19, 35-36, 45, 53, 55, 58-60, 70, 98-99, 108, 112, 115, 120-121, 125, 132, 139-140, 145-146, 158-159, 180, 201, 204 206, 211, 213, 226-230, 232, 234-238, 241, 245, 251, 257, 272, 278, 288-289, 299-330, 341, 343, 345-346, 359, 368-369
Solomon, 272, 279, 313, 319, 329-330, 340
Son of God, 13, 16, 55, 58, 60, 62, 67, 94, 130, 201, 345-346
Son of Man, 56, 60, 74-75, 241-242, 252, 350
Sonship, 11, 13, 15-16, 348

Speaking in tongues, v, 93, 95-96, 109, 208-209, 215-216, 236
Stevenson, Lila, 168
Sumerians, 302, 304-307

Tamar, 273-279, 323-325, 327
Temptation, 40-41, 124, 127
Trenton Six, 266
Trinitarian, 3, 5-6, 11-13, 16, 110
True Vine Covenant Remedy Chapel Ministries, 173

United Pentecostal Church, 5, 266, 362
Uriah, 328-329

Urias, 278-279, 319
Urshan, Andrew David, 5

Water baptism, 82, 84, 100, 167, 207, 239-240
Wesley, John, 93, 107-109
Wesleyan doctrine, 107-110
Wheatley, Wilhelmena, 172
Whyte, Marie, 168
Women
    Attire, 140, 147-148, 151-155
    Preachers, 165, 169-171, 175, 177

www.ingramcontent.com/pod-product-compliance
Lightning Source LLC
Chambersburg PA
CBHW050309120526
44592CB00014B/1845